Minorities
and
Criminality

Recent Titles in
Contributions in Criminology and Penology
Series Advisor: Marvin Wolfgang

The American Response to Professional Crime, 1870–1917
Larry K. Hartsfield

The Great American Crime Myth
Kevin N. Wright

History of Criminology: A Philosophical Perspective
David A. Jones

Crime and Culture in America: A Comparative Perspective
Parvis Saney

Sex and Supervision: Guarding Male and Female Inmates
Joycelyn M. Pollock

Children and Criminality: The Child as Victim and Perpetrator
Ronald Barri Flowers

Intervention Strategies for Chronic Juvenile Offenders:
Some New Perspectives
Peter W. Greenwood, editor

Bandidos: The Varieties of Latin American Banditry
Richard W. Slatta, editor

America's Correctional Crisis: Prison Populations and Public Policy
Stephen D. Gottfredson and Sean McConville, editors

The Structure of Criminal Procedure: Laws and Practice of France, the Soviet
Union, China, and the United States
Barton L. Ingraham

Women and Criminality: The Woman as Victim, Offender, and Practitioner
Ronald Barri Flowers

Police Administration and Progressive Reform: Theodore Roosevelt as Police
Commissioner of New York
Jay Stuart Berman

Policing Multi-Ethnic Neighborhoods: The Miami Study and Findings for Law
Enforcement in the United States
Geoffrey P. Alpert and Roger G. Dunham

MINORITIES
AND
CRIMINALITY

Ronald Barri Flowers

CONTRIBUTIONS IN CRIMINOLOGY AND PENOLOGY,
NUMBER 21

Greenwood Press
NEW YORK · WESTPORT, CONNECTICUT · LONDON

Library of Congress Cataloging-in-Publication Data

Flowers, Ronald B.
  Minorities and criminality / Ronald Barri Flowers.
    p.   cm.—(Contributions in criminology and penology, ISSN
0732-4464 : no. 21)
  Bibliography: p.
  Includes index.
  ISBN 0-313-25366-8 (lib. bdg. : alk. paper)
  1. Minorities—United States—Crimes against.   2. Crime and
criminals—United States.   3. Minorities—United States.
4. Discrimination in criminal justice administration—United States.
I. Title.   II. Series.
HV6250.4.E75F55 1988
364.3'4'0973—dc19   88-5707

British Library Cataloguing in Publication Data is available.

Library of Congress Catalog Card number: 88-5707
ISBN: 0-313-25366-8
ISSN: 0732-4464

First published in 1988

Greenwood Press, Inc.
88 Post Road West, Westport, Connecticut 06881

Printed in the United States of America

∞™

The paper used in this book complies with the
Permanent Paper Standard issued by the National
Information Standards Organization (Z39.48-1984).

10 9 8 7 6 5 4 3 2 1

To you, my wife extraordinaire, I offer my deepest gratitude for your multifaceted role in bringing this work to life and bringing life to me. Thank you most graciously, Sleeping Beautiful.

This dedication is also extended most appropriately to the best sister on the planet Earth: Jacquelyn Verhonda White. "Jack," I thank you for being in my corner all the way from inception. The years passing by have a way of reminding us.

Contents

Figure and Tables   ix

Preface   xi

Introduction   xiii

I. THE VICTIMIZATION OF MINORITIES

1. The Minority Victim of Crime and Injustice Historically   3
2. Criminal Victimization of Minorities Today   21

II. THE CRIMINALITY OF MINORITIES

3. The Scope and Character of Ethnic Minority Crime   39
4. Explanatory Approaches to the Criminality of Minorities   57

III. CONTEMPORARY ISSUES IN CRIMINALITY AMONG MINORITY GROUPS

5. The Dynamics of Black Crime   83
6. Hispanics and Crime   95
7. Native American Criminality   105
8. Minorities and Organized Crime   119
9. The Delinquency of Racial and Ethnic Minorities   131

IV. RACE AND THE SYSTEM OF CRIMINAL JUSTICE

10. Differential Enforcement of the Law   149

11. Incarceration of Minorities   163

V. THE FUTURE OF CRIME, CRIMINAL JUSTICE, AND MINORITY GROUPS

12. Looking Ahead in Addressing Minorities, Crime, and Criminal Justice   179

Selected Bibliography   193

Supplementary References   199

Index   203

Figure and Tables

FIGURE

2.1 Percentage of Households Touched by Selected Crimes, by Race of Head of Household   32

TABLES

2.1 Victimization Rates, by Type of Crime and Race of Victims   23

2.2 Victimization Rates, by Type of Personal Crime and Ethnicity of Victims   24

2.3 Victimization Rates, by Race and Type of Personal Crime   25

2.4 Victimization Rates, by Type of Household Crime and Race of Head of Household   26

2.5 Victimization Rates on the Basis of Motor Vehicle Thefts, by Selected Household Characteristics   28

2.6 Victimization Rates, by Type of Household Crime and Ethnicity of Head of Household   29

2.7 Victimization Rates, by Type of Crime and Race/ Ethnicity of Head of Household   30

2.8 Percentage of U.S. Minority Population Victimized by Violent Crime   31

3.1 Total Arrests, Distribution by Race and Ethnic Origin   42

3.2   Percentage Distribution of Total Arrests, by Age and
      Race/Ethnicity   44

3.3   Rates of Arrest per 100,000 Population, by Race/Ethnicity   45

3.4   Ratio of Arrest per 100,000 Population, by Race/Ethnicity   47

3.5   Most Frequent Arrests, by Offense and Race/Ethnicity   48

3.6   Least Frequent Arrests, by Offense and Race/Ethnicity   49

3.7   Percentage Distribution of Single-Offender Victimizations   52

3.8   Percentage Distribution of Multiple-Offender Victimizations   53

7.1   Rates of Arrest per 100,000 Population, by Race/Ethnicity   107

7.2   Rates of Arrest for Substance Abuse–Related Offenses
      per 100,000 Population, by Race/Ethnicity   109

7.3   Ratio of Native American to Other Racial Groups' Arrests,
      per 100,000 Population   110

7.4   Rates of Incarceration in Federal and State Institutions,
      per 100,000 Population, by Race/Ethnicity   112

9.1   Total Arrests of Juveniles, by Race/Ethnicity   132

9.2   Most Frequent Arrests of Juveniles, by Offense
      and Race/Ethnicity   135

11.1 Minority Male Prisoners in Federal and State Institutions,
      by Race/Ethnicity   164

11.2 Percentage Distribution of Minority Female Prisoners,
      by Race/Ethnicity   171

Preface

This book, the third in a four-volume set, explores key issues in criminality as they relate to minority members of our society. The entire set reflects an increasing need for greater knowledge and understanding of the dynamics that embody crime, criminals, victims, criminal justice, and injustice. To this end, the examination in this series addresses crime and its relationship to children, women, minorities, and demography.

Although many books have been written in the fields of criminology, criminal justice, sociology, and victimology, none has provided in one set such a diverse and comprehensive study of those particular elements most influenced by these disciplines. This study is long overdue and collectively very much neglected by other researchers. Hence the aim of this multivolume exploration is to bridge the gap that exists in research on these topics and provide a lead for others to follow for further study.

The four-volume set has been designed for professional audiences, scholars, and students pursuing studies in criminology, criminal justice, law, psychology, racial and ethnic studies, victimology, and related disciplines. The volumes were written also with a general readership of concerned citizens in mind who, in a world fraught with complexities, seek to become more informed on issues that affect all of us.

Volume 3, *Minorities and Criminality*, examines the relationship between being a minority member of American society and involvement in crime and victim-related issues. It explores the historical mistreatment of minority groups, current trends in victimization, patterns in criminal behavior, arrest and imprisonment among minority members, theoretical models in criminality, differential enforcement of the law, and future implications in addressing minorities and criminality.

Volume 1, *Children and Criminality*, explores children and their relationship to crime. It stands apart from other studies of children and criminality by focusing on children as both victims and offenders. This treatise examines the dual phenomenon in historical and contemporary terms, the literature, and various approaches to understanding its dynamics such as its scope and nature, epidemiological and etiological features, the relationship to family violence, implications for theory and social action, and the outlook for the future.

Volume 2, *Women and Criminality*, is an in-depth analysis of the tripartite role of women in the areas of criminology, victimology, and criminal justice. This unique and thorough examination of women as victims and offenders of crime and professionals within the system of criminal justice covers these roles as separate entities and how they relate to each other, as well as to the larger picture of the male role in these areas of study. Explored within this investigation is the significance of historical treatment of women, the women's movement, the "new" female criminal controversy, prominent theoretical and etiological models, and future legal and social responses to the problems women face as victims, perpetrators, and criminal justice practitioners.

Volume 4, *Demographics and Criminality*, evaluates the relationship of demographic variables to crime in America. The volume probes how various demographic features—such as ecology, age, gender, race and ethnicity, education, marital status, socioeconomic status, and substance use and abuse—influence the incidence, distribution, and pattern of criminality and victimization. Also examined are theoretical approaches to the demographical correlates of crime, present trends, and future implications in theory, criminal justice, and social action.

ACKNOWLEDGMENTS

Much appreciation is given to James T. Sabin, executive vice-president of Greenwood Press, who had the foresight to recognize the importance of this project in criminological research. Gratitude is extended to the editorial staff and their various roles in bringing about the publication of this work.

My acknowledgments would be incomplete without once more thanking my partner, fellow researcher, and executive secretary, my wife—Helen Loraine Flowers—without whose support, dedication, and understanding this project would most certainly not have reached its present level.

Introduction

One of the most neglected areas of study in criminological research has been the relationship of crime and minorities or minority groups within society. There are a number of reasons for this omission. The most common is the relatively low numbers involved to make such research practical. Other explanations include fears of discriminatory policies against such groups, a history already fraught with difficulties encountered by minorities, and disinterest by researchers who prefer to focus on the larger establishment and their role in criminal involvement by minorities.

This book goes against the grain in traditional criminology by examining criminality as it relates to those minority communities that are most conspicuous in American society. The objective of this examination is to explore pertinent dimensions of criminal involvement of minorities and to create greater interest and promote future research in this understudied area of criminology.

Because *minority* is a term that is at once associated with a variety of groups and subgroups, it is necessary to clarify some terminology and definitions that apply throughout this book. The dictionary defines *minority* as (1) a number forming less than half the total and (2) a group differing in race, ethnic, or religious background from the majority of the population. These definitions are far too broad for our purposes. A more appropriate definition of minorities was given by Robin Williams, Jr.:

Minorities . . . are any culturally or physically distinctive and self-conscious social aggregates, with hereditary membership and a high degree of endogamy, which are subject to political, or economic, or social discrimination by a dominant segment of an environing political society.[1]

Yet even this comprehensive definition fails to capture the full essence of the minority groups to which our focus shall be directed. Joseph Gittler's concise definition of minority groups comes closer:

Minority groups are those whose members experience a wide range of discriminatory treatment and frequently are relegated to positions low in the status structure of society.[2]

Essentially there are four primary minority groups in the United States whose distinctive physical appearance and/or migration here has been marred by subordination, subjugation, exploitation, racism, discrimination, and socioeconomic disadvantage and, as a result, has placed an enormous burden on their propensity and vulnerability to become victims and/or offenders of crime: Blacks, Hispanics, Native Americans, and Asians. It is these minority groups that we will base our exploration on and to which we will apply the following definition: "minority group or its members who are either racially distinctive or who have been victimized by discrimination, oppression, exploitation, segregation, or persecution by the dominant or white group in the society to the point that it has hindered their ability to achieve the full freedoms and benefits of American society and to which exists a direct relationship to their involvement in crime."

Two other important terms often come up applicable to minorities: *ethnicity* and *race*. Since the definitions of these words are subject to various interpretations, we will limit their meaning to how they might fit the minority groups under examination here.

Ethnic derives from the Greek word *ethnos*, meaning "people" or "nation." An ethnic group is socially defined based on its cultural characteristics as a group "possessing a common tradition and strong feelings of belonging, living as a minority in a larger host society of a different culture."[3] *Ethnicity*, then, relates to "a sense of belonging to a particular ethnic group" and can be defined as "the existence of a distinct culture or subculture in which group members feel themselves bound together by a common history, values, attitudes, and behaviors . . . and are so regarded by other members of the society."[4]

Race generally refers to a group of persons characterized by common physical and/or biological traits that are transmitted in descent. *Racial*, then, relates to characteristics typical of a particular race.

The terms *minority, ethnic minorities, racial minorities*, and related terms will be used interchangeably to refer to those members of minority status noted, although the definitions may differentiate occasionally when in conflict with other data source definitions.

Part I of this book explores the victimization of minorities. Chapter 1 discusses the historical mistreatment of minorities and its current implications. In Chapter 2, present trends in minority member victimization are addressed.

Part II examines the criminality of minorities. Chapter 3 analyzes the scope and character of ethnic minority crime and weaknesses of statistical data. In Chapter 4, explanations for crime causation are explored from a variety of perspectives: biological, psychological, sociological, and socioeconomic, with particular emphasis on minority crime, as well as critical examinations of such theories. Also addressed is the lack of etiological study on minority groups.

Part III explores various issues in ethnic criminality. Chapter 5 discusses the dynamics and implications of black crime. In Chapter 6, the relationship between Hispanics and criminality is focused on. Chapter 7 looks at the high rate of crime among Native Americans and reasons for it. The role of minorities in organized crime is addressed in Chapter 8. Chapter 9 examines juvenile delinquency and gang membership among minority group members.

Part IV surveys the effect of race-ethnicity on criminal justice system involvement of minorities. Chapter 10 examines differential treatment issues within law enforcement and the courts. Chapter 11 explores institutionalization of minority members in jails and prisons, addressing statistical trends, race relations, racial discrimination, and capital punishment.

Part V looks to the future in the criminality of minorities. Chapter 12 explores implications for criminal justice and criminological, community, social, and research action in effecting change in current dilemmas in the involvement of members of minority status in crime.

NOTES

1. Robin M. Williams, Jr., *Strangers Next Door* (Englewood Cliffs, N.J.: Prentice-Hall, 1964), p. 304.

2. Joseph P. Gittler, *Understanding Minority Groups* (New York: Wiley, 1956), p. vii.

3. Terry G. Jordan and Lester Rowntree, *The Human Mosaic: A Thematic Introduction to Cultural Geography*, 2d ed. (New York: Harper & Row, 1985), p. 327.

4. Norman R. Yetman, *Majority and Minority: The Dynamics of Race and Ethnicity in American Life* (Boston: Allyn and Bacon, 1985), p. 6.

I

THE VICTIMIZATION OF MINORITIES

1

The Minority Victim of Crime and Injustice Historically

Any study that hopes to accurately explore the impact of crime on American minority groups must consider the associative significance of historical mistreatment of minorities and their criminality and victimization today. Sadly, the United States is largely what it is today at the cruel and unjust expense of its minorities. Yet all too often researchers and professionals fail to incorporate this perspective in addressing minorities and crime. It may well be that they prefer to erase the less than admirable aspects of our country's history from their consciousness. Perhaps now it is time to accept some responsibility for these faults and their consequences.

NATIVE AMERICANS: SUBJUGATED AND VIOLATED

Of the many racial and ethnic minorities in the United States, Native Americans arguably have been the most victimized, for they have the distinction of being the original Americans and therefore, at one time, the majority group in America. Perhaps as many as 80 million to 100 million Native Americans once lived in North and South America. In the almost 500 years since the first Europeans arrived, Native Americans have shrunk in population to become one of the smallest American minority groups. Demographic data estimate their pre-Columbian U.S. population at 900,000 to 4 million. In 1980, the Bureau of the Census reported that there were 1,418,195 American Indians, Eskimos, and Aleuts in the United States. This differential, which has included the extinction of more than fifty tribes (there are more than 500 in existence today), is the result of massacres by the whites, economic base destruction, disease, war, famine, and interracial mixing.

Genocide and Indian Removal

After the American Revolution, the "new" American government turned its attention to "negotiating" a series of land cession treaties with Indians. These negotiations were in fact forced upon the natives, who were grossly underpaid (when at all) for their land and taken advantage of in every conceivable way by the colonists. When coercion and intimidation failed, the Native Americans were confronted militarily. In some instances, they met this encroachment upon their land with resistance. Ultimately, though, the Indians were broken and displaced but not before they had relinquished claim to over 300 million acres of land.

With the Indian Removal Act of 1830, which provided for the exchanging of U.S. titled lands west of the Mississippi for those lands occupied by tribes east of the Mississippi, thousands of Native Americans were removed from the southeastern states:[1]

Cherokees, Choctaws, Chicasaws, Creeks, and Seminoles were rounded up and herded like animals over the "Trail of Tears" to Oklahoma. More than 100 people died every day at the hands of the U.S. Army as well as American citizens. . . . Vigilante groups killed and raped, and burned Indian farms and property, arresting and driving out sympathetic whites. . . . Even before Indians were out of eyesight of their property, it was being auctioned off to whites. Of the [70,000] Indians . . . that were forced to leave their homes, approximately half of them died.[2]

The only successful resistance of the removal was by the Seminole tribe. The Seminole War (1835–1842), which cost the U.S. Army $50 million, resulted in the deaths of 1,500 men. When the Seminoles finally conceded defeat, truce flags were ignored, and many of their leaders were murdered.

The victimization of Native Americans did not end here. West of the Mississippi, this subjugation, exploitation, and violence repeated itself. When gold was discovered in California, gold seekers and emigrants made their way across the Plains. The lands of Native Americans were expropriated and granted to mining corporations, the railroads, ranchers, speculators, and others seeking profit. The U.S. military was dispatched westward to protect and cultivate commerce through outposts. As compensation for their lost land and hunting opportunities, Indian tribes were relocated on reservations and given rations.

Periodically there were those who rebelled, such as the Cheyenne and the Apache. Always they were defeated. The frontiersmen, in the same manner as those in the East, resorted to untold violence and genocide to rid themselves of the problem of Native Americans. Two examples of this brutality can be seen below:

At Sand Creek in Colorado in 1864 militiamen descended upon an encampment of Cheyenne who had been guaranteed safe conduct and slaughtered most of them. And in the frigid Plains winter of 1890, U.S. forces armed with Hotchkiss machine guns mowed down nearly 300 Sioux at Wounded Knee, South Dakota.[3]

Assimilation

When extermination of Native Americans proved to be futile, the federal government looked for new ways to "control" them. Prior to 1871, the federal government regarded tribes as sovereign yet dependent nations with whom treaties could be negotiated. This practice and perception ended with the Act of March 3, 1871.[4] Native Americans were now considered government wards in a policy aimed at forced assimilation. Intense efforts were made to eliminate the cultures of Native Americans by teaching Anglo-American ways and English, making Christian church services mandatory, forcibly indoctrinating Native American children at boarding schools far from their home lands, and replacing traditional Indian leaders by paper chiefs.

With the Dawes Act of 1887, tribal lands were fragmented and dispersed among individual Native Americans, the idea being to make them small freehold farmers.[5] Remaining tribal land was declared surplus and made available to non-Indian settlement. Government officials believed that such a plan would foster practices and life-styles among Indians similar to those of the white settlers and at the same time eliminate the tribal organization economic base. Instead the result of this attempt at assimilation was that within sixty years, Native Americans had lost 86 million acres of their best land through purchase or fraudulent deals with crooked whites. More than 90,000 Native Americans were left without land, creating massive poverty and poor health. Nevertheless, the federal bureaucracy—the Bureau of Indian Affairs—did manage to, if not eliminate Native American cultures altogether, acclimate Indian people to many of the ways of whites.

Although at first glance it appeared that the government's Bureau of Indian Affairs was successful in replacing Native American ways with those of whites, a closer look reveals that fewer than a dozen Native American languages had vanished, many religious and ceremonial practices had survived and flourished, and the overwhelming majority of Native Americans remained faithful to traditional values.[6]

Inconsistent Government Policies

The fragility of the Native Americans' standing in society and their continued victimization can be seen in the shifting government policies from the 1920s to the 1970s.

In 1929 the government reversed its policy of assimilation and en-couraged Native Americans to retain their tribal customs and cultures. But after World War II, the policy reversed again as many white Amer-icans began to compare reservations with concentration camps. Presi-dent Eisenhower's desire to get the federal government "out of the Indian business" created a situation where Native Americans essen-tially were stripped of their dual citizenship as Americans and tribes-men, as well as certain benefits, such as the tax-exempt status of their land.

The Eisenhower administration sought to solve high unemployment on reservations by moving Native Americans into jobs in urban areas. But when jobs were found for them, in many instances they were given little training and left to fend for themselves in an urban society they were unaccustomed to. In a policy known as *termination*, certain tribes were "freed" from federal supervision; the result was that they lost federal funds, causing the undermining of the Native American com-munities.

During the mid-1970s, the government once more altered its national policy toward Native Americans. The Indian Self-Determination Act of 1975 encouraged Indians to assume supervision of most reservation public services as a means to strengthen Native American control over Indian concerns.[7] Self-determination programs have had only limited success; they camouflage the fact that reservation communities com-monly lack an economic base and are dependent upon federal money. With limited management skills, competition with local and state inter-est groups, and federal priorities in the use of land, economic devel-opment has been slow.

Native Americans Today

As a result of their long-time subjugation at the hands of the federal government and the American people, Native Americans as a group are perhaps worse off today than ever. Although they live throughout the United States, most are concentrated west of the Mississippi River in Oklahoma, Arizona, and California. Nearly 40 percent of all Native Americans (and almost 50 percent of those on reservations) have in-comes below the poverty line. Fifty-five percent of reservation housing is less than adequate, with unemployment on reservations exceeding 40 percent and nearly 60 percent of its youth failing to reach the eighth grade.

Native Americans have a life expectancy ten years shorter than whites and high rates of tuberculosis, dysentery, pneumonia, and other dis-eases. Most of their health problems are attributed to an inadequate diet, sanitation, and shelter. In states that have a large Indian population, as many as one-third of all Indian children are taken from their families and institutionalized or placed in adoptive or foster homes.[8]

Discrimination and prejudice against Native Americans continue to run high, particularly in areas near reservations. It is not uncommon for Indians to be the victims of Jim Crow behavior and/or police abuse. Reservations have long been the dumping grounds for garbage and toxic wastes of cities and corporations. Further Native American victimization can be seen in the continual leasing of Indian land by white farmers and corporate groups.

The most pressing problem Native Americans face today is alcohol use and abuse. Liquor is listed as one of the primary causes of death of American Indians. Robert Sundance, a Sioux who is director of the Los Angeles Indian Alcoholism Commission, explains the allure of alcohol to Native Americans and its potential consequences: "When you face racism, poverty and powerlessness, you drink to forget. . . . We will be annihilated as a race within the next century if we don't solve the alcoholism problem. Then the Indian problem is settled—genocide without firing a single bullet."[9]

Despite the plight of Native Americans, they remain virtually invisible to most of us, perhaps the saddest form of victimization of all.

BLACK AMERICANS: ENSLAVED AND OPPRESSED

If Native Americans are the least noticed minority group in this nation, black Americans are on the opposite end of the spectrum. Blacks are the largest minority in the United States, numbering 28.9 million, or approximately 12 percent of the population as of 1987. Like the original Americans, blacks have a unique, sorrowful history in America, beginning with their involuntary servitude.

Blacks in Bondage

It is uncertain exactly when the first black person arrived in North America. Some suggest it may have been with Columbus. The servitude of blacks in the United States dates back to 1619.[10] Because there was no precedent in English law concerning slaves, it is believed that these blacks were indentured servants. Not until the 1660s did legal enslavement of blacks for a lifetime come into effect; however, this was preceded by the differential treatment of blacks by whites from their arrival in this country because of their distinct physical characteristics.

The growth of slavery was closely related to the development of the agricultural plantation system of the South. To meet the considerable demand for a source of labor, slaves were imported from Africa. Often termed the Middle Passage, the trip from Africa to America was a nightmare of overcrowding, disease, and death. After 1720, native-born blacks exceeded importation as the major source of black population growth.[11]

Aside from the obvious cruelties of being enslaved and viewed as property, such as forced servitude, beatings, rape, murder, and other brutalities, blacks as humans and slaves were perhaps most victimized by their oppressors through the doctrine of black inferiority. This firmly entrenched idea that black people were different or beneath whites was to be a prominent ideology in justifying slavery and racism by its supporters.

Notes sociology professor James Vander Zanden of Ohio State University: "Slavery so completely disrupted black institutions, culture, and communication that it was virtually impossible for blacks to mount a serious challenge to their subjugation."[12] There were, of course, sporadic slave rebellions; in virtually every instance, they were suppressed and dealt with severely.

Emancipation and Jim Crow

After the abolishment of slavery, black Americans figured to have a better path in life. But this was often far from the reality of their existence for decades to come, particularly in the South. Jim Crowism—the system of legal segregation—made life especially harsh for many blacks. Racial ostracism was present in virtually every facet of life—housing, employment, public transportation, sports, and institutions. In many ways, blacks' status in many parts of the United States was lowered during the Jim Crow era. No longer did they have certain freedoms (implied or otherwise) that they had as slaves, such as relatively equal treatment on common carriers or in restaurants and voting rights.[13] Blacks as free people found themselves denied basic civil rights and freely and legally discriminated against.

Changes in the segregation policies of the South began to take place during World War II as reformers fought to improve conditions for blacks. A key step forward was the Supreme Court school desegregation ruling on May 17, 1954, in which the Court ruled that the doctrine of "separate but equal" used to keep black children out of white public schools was unconstitutional.[14] It was not until the 1964 Civil Rights Act, however, which prohibited racial discrimination in most areas, that the most significant strides were made toward eliminating formal segregation.[15] Yet even today, segregation can still be found in many parts of the South and elsewhere in the United States.

Blacks as the Victims of Racial Violence

The victimization of black people in the postslavery years did not end with segregation and discrimination. Many whites, resistant to any change that suggested blacks were their equals, engaged in violence, harassment, and intimidation against blacks. Mobs of whites were formed to prevent blacks from voting, to threaten them, to "get a point across," to teach them "their place," and so on. Often white mobs brutally attacked blacks, particularly when they were purported to have committed a crime against a white person (even if they had not). Sometimes the "crime" was insulting someone white or looking at the person too long. Lynchings of blacks frequently occurred beginning with the Reconstruction era and lasting into the 1940s as white supremacists and racists decided to dispense their own brand of justice against blacks—whether for crimes or at random because of hatred. The greatest number of black lynchings—1,111—occurred during the 1890s. In 1892 alone, 162 blacks were lynched.[16]

In many instances, the lynchings were accompanied by other violent acts, such as torture, mutilation, or immolation. The following example, cited by the Southern Commission on the Study of Lynchings, illustrates the cruelties racist white mobs were capable of:

The sheriff along with the accused Negro was seized by the mob, and the two were carried to the scene of the crime. Here quickly assembled a thousand or more men, women, and children. The accused Negro was hung up in a sweetgum tree by his arms, just enough to keep his feet off the ground. Members of the mob tortured him for more than an hour. A pole was jabbed in his mouth. His toes were cut off joint by joint. His fingers were similarly removed, and members of the mob extracted his teeth with wire pliers. After further unmentionable mutilations, the Negro's still living body was saturated with gasoline and a lighted match was applied. As the flames leaped up, hundreds of shots were fired into the dying victim. During the day, thousands of people from miles around rode out to see the sight. Not till nightfall did the officers remove the body and bury it.[17]

White racial violence against blacks also took place in the form of riots. As opposed to the individuality of lynchings, white riots were more in response to blacks as a group and the threat perceived in their changing the status quo. The result, however, was just as menacing and included destruction of property, violence, and murder.

Victimized Black Americans Today

Blacks continue to be victimized in the United States in many ways, each of which is at least indirectly associated with their past mistreatment. Discrimination and racism against black people exist in virtually every area of society. Blacks typically have lower-paying, less-prestigious jobs than whites; are considerably poorer as a group; have higher rates of unemployment, crime, and imprisonment; are the victims of overt residential segregation; are in poorer health; and are often denied their basic civil rights to an equal opportunity of a better life. In short, black people are still victimized by the dominant group, primarily because of the color of their skin.

EXPLOITATION AND DEGRADATION OF HISPANICS

Like Native and black Americans, the history of Hispanic Americans in this country is one of frustration, deprivation, subjugation, and discrimination. Unlike the other two minority groups, today's Hispanic population can attribute part of their woes to their own ancestry's failure to retain lands they had colonized.

Hispanic people are the second largest minority group in the United States. Yet the term *Hispanic* does not adequately describe what actually is a heterogeneous population of Spanish-speaking people. Of the 18.8 million people of Spanish heritage in this country (7.9 percent of the total population), as listed by the March 1987 Current Population Survey, they are classified in four distinct groups: Mexican-Americans, Puerto Ricans, Cubans, and "other Spanish," which is the second largest group and includes Latin Americans and Spaniards. Mexican-Americans, also referred to as *Chicanos* and *Hispanos*, are the largest Hispanic group, accounting for approximately two-thirds of the Spanish-speaking Americans, and have been the most victimized. Hence I shall focus on this group—their ancestry and subsequent migration into this country.

Colonial Period of Frustration

The original Spanish colonists were the ancestors of Mexican-Americans (as were American Indians and black slaves to a lesser degree) and the first Europeans to settle the borderlands of the southwestern United States. The competition between English- and Spanish-speaking colonists for conquest of the New World proved to be the prominent feature of the early colonial period.

As the Spanish migrated northeast from the Caribbean and what is now Mexico, the English migrated to the southwest from the eastern seaboard of what is now the United States. Ultimately they confronted one another and engaged in violent conflict for the land and its resources. This struggle for conquest of the Southwest led to an extended period of subjugation of the Spanish-speaking people.[18]

Following the United States–Mexico war, much of the Southwest became U.S. territory, including an area that encompassed what is now California, New Mexico, Utah, and Nevada. With the signing of the Treaty of Guadalupe-Hidalgo in 1848, many of the Mexicans of these borderlands became U.S. citizens.[19] Arizona became U.S. territory in

1854 after the Gadsden Purchase.[20] Hence these Spanish-speaking people, unable to hold on to what they had, much like the Native Americans, lost it to the stronger, dominant group of American imperialists.

Wave of Immigration and Exploitation

Mexican migration into the United States in the twentieth century is the result of the labor demand in this country and the surplus of underemployed or unemployed labor in Mexico. This immigration has occurred in two distinct phases. The first was between around 1900 to 1930 and was halted by the Great Depression. The second phase was in response to the 1940s war economy and continues in strong force today. Considerable numbers of Mexicans enter the country illegally. (It is virtually impossible to place a number on this group, although recent estimates range anywhere from 3 million to 5 million illegal aliens in the United States at any given time.) Because of the struggling Mexican economy and the greater opportunities and better life in the United States, Mexicans will continue to make their way here (or try) at all costs, despite recent reform in immigration laws.

The costs of Mexican migration are many including hard work, low wages, seasonal employment, separation from family, poor housing, and exploitation. The following account gives some indication of these hardships:

Generations of workers from Jaripo, Mexico, have made the 1,500 mile trek to the fields around Stockton [California] to pick grapes, cherries and asparagus. . . . Some of them go as (legal) residents, some of them go as illegals. But almost everyone goes. [Many make their] way into California by paying a "coyote," a person who guides workers across the border, [about] $500.

A growing number of Jaripenos have moved into Sierra Vista, a low-income, federally funded housing project within the city of Stockton. . . . At dawn, most of Sierra Vista's Hispanic residents go off to work wearing straw hats and heavy work boots, needed to labor in the fields.[21]

Testimony to the difficulty of traditional migratory work is offered by the mayor of Jaripo, Jesus Mendoza, himself a former farm worker. "I went to the United States for 27 years—as an illegal and a bracero. In all my years in the fields, I never once saw a single white or a black person working there."[22]

Illegal Hispanic immigrant workers are especially prone to a number of abuses. Many are victimized by bandits who roam the Mexican-American border and beat them up while taking their money and possessions. Some crooked employers of aliens turn them in to immigration authorities just before they are due to be paid for services performed, and the aliens discover upon deportation that stop payments have been issued on their checks.[23] When they are paid, often they receive less than the federal minimum wage. Some illegal aliens are forced into involuntary servitude by threats, intimidation, beatings, and even holding their families hostage.[24] As aliens, they are vulnerable to exploitation and victimization; the alternative for them is to be fired or apprehended by law enforcement and deported.

Illegal Mexican immigrants are often alleged to be responsible for low wages and increased unemployment among U.S. citizens, as well as being "freeloaders" of community services. The truth is that illegal Mexicans (and Mexican-Americans) often perform low or unskilled labor that most American workers shun, and because such employment is readily accessible, it would seem to negate the displacement of labor theory. Furthermore, the evidence suggests that not only do most illegal Mexican workers pay taxes and social security but that they make little use of social services.[25]

Under the 1986 Immigration Reform and Control Act, purportedly designed to make it easier for illegal aliens to obtain residency and work in the United States, immigrants who can prove they have lived continuously in this country since January 1, 1982, would qualify for amnesty and legal residency application.[26] Hispanic leaders, however, charge that Hispanic workers will be discriminated against in employment practices even more because of mass confusion and ignorance of the law and because of the second major tenet of the new law: the imposition of harsh penalties on employers who knowingly hire illegal aliens. Many believe employers will be scared into not hiring immigrants as a result or simply using the law as a means to discriminate against all Hispanics. The long-term implications of the new immigration law for legal and illegal Hispanics are uncertain. It is clear, however, that their residence will continue to be beset with problems.

Other Hispanic Groups

Although Mexican-Americans are by far the largest and of longest duration Hispanic representation in the United States, some mention should be made of the rocky history of two other emerging Hispanic groups: Puerto Ricans and Cubans.

Puerto Ricans. Similar to other ethnic immigrants, Puerto Ricans were drawn to the United States by the prospect of improving their socioeconomic status. A product of the twentieth-century immigration into this country, the Puerto Rican exodus from their West Indies homeland and its high unemployment and population began to occur in the early 1900s. (Originally a Spanish settlement, Puerto Rico became a U.S. possession in 1898.)

Most of the Puerto Rican immigrants settled in New York City and midwestern urban centers where cheap, unskilled labor was needed and readily exploited. In addition to their being handicapped by a limited grasp of the English language, many of these immigrants were of dark color and thus were forced to endure many of the same indignities and the racism common to black people in America.

Upward mobility for most Puerto Rican Americans continues to be slow; impoverishment, low income, low education, large families, and language barriers have proved to be major stumbling blocks. Furthermore, many Puerto Ricans who have succeeded in moving up the financial ladder continue to live in Puerto Rican ghettos because of business ties.

Despite facing many of the same economic hardships in the United States as in their homeland and certainly more social and cultural disadvantages, the number of Puerto Ricans migrating to the United States continues to grow.

Cubans. Cubans first began to migrate to the United States en masse following the fall of the Batista government in 1958. As much victimized by their opposition to and fear of the new government in power as they were in becoming refugees, most of these Cubans were more or less forced to leave their homeland in seeking asylum in the United States. This circumstance differs from that of most other immigrants to the United States, who were motivated principally by the chance for a better standard of living.

An estimated 266,000 Cuban refugees had entered the U.S. by the end of 1966. Like the Puerto Rican immigrants, many were dark skinned, impoverished (most lost what they had upon leaving Cuba), and limited by language and adjustment difficulties, as well as discrimination. Most settled in lower-class housing in the Miami area and were slow to assimilate. Some refugees, however, were wealthy in Cuba and have found financial success in the United States.

The second wave of Cuban refugees to the United States, totaling some 125,000 people, occurred during the 1980 Mariel boatlift. Similar to their predecessors, many of the *Marielitos* have encountered serious problems socially, economically, and culturally. For many, this branched out into criminal behavior and criminal victimization at a rate of much greater concern than the early Cuban refugees.[27]

Hispanics Today

Hispanics can be found throughout the United States, although they live predominantly in California (one of every three Spanish-origin residents resides there), Texas, and New York. With the growing number of Hispanics in this country (it is estimated that at their present growth rate they will surpass blacks as the nation's largest minority by the year 2020) comes a grim picture about the quality of Hispanic life. A 1987 report released by the National Council of La Raza, among the country's largest Hispanic groups, revealed that only about half of all Hispanics complete high school (well below the national average of 74 percent), Hispanic women have high birthrates in proportion to other ethnic groups, women head 23 percent of the Hispanic families, and a large percentage of Hispanic families are in poverty.[28] Hispanics are disproportionately the victims of low income, discrimination, prejudice, racism, injustice, and inconsistent government policies.

PERSECUTION OF ASIANS IN THE UNITED STATES

The pattern of ethnic minority group victimization in the United States has also had a prominent effect on Asians historically and can be associated with their present circumstances. Like Native Americans, blacks, and Hispanics, Asians, most notably Chinese and Japanese, have faced white hostilities, bigotry, hatred, and violence.

Chinese

The Chinese became the first free nonwhite group to emigrate to the United States. It was during California's gold rush era that the first large-scale Chinese immigration occurred. At the time, Chinese were looked upon as cheap labor, particularly in the West. In *The Unwelcome Immigrant*, a survey of the national press between 1850 and 1882, the author revealed that "the general consensus . . . was that while the Chinese were not biologically suitable for the American melting pot, it would be foolish not to exploit their cheap labor."[29] This relationship was quick to sour, however; the high visibility of the Chinese and the economic competition they posed prompted the outcry: "The Chinese must go!"

In California beginning in the mid-1800s, a series of new and revised anti-Chinese laws were aimed at taking away Chinese rights and freedom such as testifying in court, attending white schools, mining, running laundries, and gaining employment.[30] In 1882 with the Chinese Exclusion Act, the Chinese became the first group to be restricted in legal entry into the United States.[31] Subsequent exclusionary laws further reduced Chinese migration. Although the Chinese Exclusion Act was relaxed somewhat in 1943, it was not until 1965 that a normal quota of Chinese immigration was permitted.[32]

Violent Treatment of Chinese. The anti-Chinese sentiments prominent in the 1860s and decades after were manifested in brutal, violent attacks and harsh treatment of Chinese people as they became convenient scapegoats for crime, poverty, disease, and other social ills. Mayhem, murder, pillage, bloodshed, humiliation and incendiarism top the cruelties Chinese were subjected to. In one year alone, 1862, eighty-eight Chinese in California died at the hands of their oppressors.

Similar to the white violence perpetrated against blacks, white mobs were formed at the slightest pretext, and rioting was frequent. One of the worst anti-Chinese outbreaks occurred in 1865 at Rock Springs, Wyoming, where twenty-eight Chinese were murdered.[33] The white perpetrators did not have much to fear from a supportive system of justice in their persecution of Chinese. During 1872, following a violent exchange between some Chinese and the police that left a white bystander dead, a white gun-wielding mob was formed. Their wrath left eighteen Chinese murdered and many Chinese homes and stores looted and burned. Although eight of the rioters were tried and found guilty, with jail sentences ranging from two to eight years, within a year all had been freed.

Chinatowns. Arising partly in response to Chinese persecution and partly as a means of retaining their traditional culture, many Chinese banded together in Chinatowns across America as they became urbanized. Known as a Chinese ghetto, a Chinatown is "a community within a non-Chinese community, having no independent economic structure but attached symbiotically to the larger economic, political, and social base."[34] Chinatowns became almost inevitable as Chinese found themselves barred from entry into white neighborhoods and discriminated against in virtually every other way. These ethnic ghettos allowed them security and enabled them to maintain Chinese traditions and customs. Chinatowns are responsible in large part for the American perception of Chinese as thrifty and hard-working people yet also as "clannish and alien, and not particularly good subjects for acculturation into the American crucible."[35]

With the exception of those in existence in several large cities, Chinatowns have become mostly defunct in American society since World War II. The Chinese, now the largest Asian minority group in the United States, have made their way into the mainstream of society, are better treated, and as a group higher educated, employed, and enjoy higher incomes than other minority groups; nevertheless, they continue to be the victims of racism, prejudice, and misconceptions.

Japanese

The Japanese are the only American ethnic group to have been chosen for exclusion and placed in concentration camps known as relocation centers. Anti-Japanese feelings in this country emerged on the heels and as a result of the prior decades of Chinese hatred. With the passage of the Chinese Exclusion Act of 1882 and the decline of Chinese immigration, Japan was looked upon as a source of cheap labor, particularly in California and Hawaii, bringing thousands of Japanese into this country to work on plantations.

During the early 1900s, the anti-Japanese movement began to gain momentum as pressure from labor and patriotic parties was applied to create legislation to exclude Japanese in the same manner as earlier exclusionary policies against the Chinese. Japanese were discriminated against legally and illegally on a number of fronts—citizenship, marriage to whites, and access to public facilities. The 1907 Gentleman's Agreement restricting Japanese immigration succeeded in curtailing considerably their migration to the United States. This agreement, however, did not apply to relatives of those already living in this country; the result was an influx of women, designated "picture brides," who came over to wed men who had settled before them.[36]

In 1924, with the Oriental Exclusion Act, virtually all Japanese immigration was halted.[37] It was not until the Walter-McCarran Act of 1952 eliminating the consideration of race in immigration that Japanese migration began to increase substantially.[38] The Immigration Act of 1965 abolished the national origins quota system.[39]

Japanese Containment. The strong anti-Japanese sentiments became even more intense, particularly on the West Coast, following the Japanese attack on Pearl Harbor on December 7, 1941. Panic, hysteria, and irresponsibility resulted in the military authorities' ordering the swift and forcible evacuation of the Japanese beginning in early 1942 from the military zone designated number one (predominantly the Pacific coastal region). They were relocated to internment camps and concentration centers and eventually resettled in areas outside the Pacific military zone. Nearly two-thirds of those contained were U.S. citizens. Ironically, the Hawaiian Japanese population—one-third of its total population—was generally exempt from this roundup, despite Hawaii's being 3,000 miles closer to Japan.

This government action against the Japanese was clearly racist, not political; no other U.S. "enemies-in-residence" (such as the Italians and Germans) were victimized by relocation. The Japanese suffered untold deprivation and hardship as a result. Given in some instances as little as forty-eight hours' notification, many Japanese people were unable to dissolve their property and interests adequately and fairly. Buyers, quick to exploit a situation they were fully apprised of, were unwilling to deal honorably with the evacuees. Japanese farmers were especially hard hit; evacuation came before they could harvest what had already been planted and fertilized, forcing them to get whatever they could for their property.

The losses the Japanese suffered in real and personal property were

considerable. Furthermore, they were victimized by the abrupt departure of life-styles and educational, occupational, and social pursuits.
Upon the revocation of the Exclusion Order in December 1944, many
Japanese people resettled on the West Coast. Some were never able to
reestablish themselves, and none would be able to regain their lost
freedom and violated rights.[40]

Contemporary Japanese. Today the Japanese are concentrated primarily
in California and Hawaii. They were once the largest Asian group in
this country; they now rank third behind the Chinese and Filipinos.
The Japanese are one of the better educated, economically sound, as-
similated minorities in this country. Like the Chinese, they have managed to retain much of their heritage. As with other minorities whose
distinct physical characteristics set them apart from the dominant group,
Japanese are still oppressed through prejudice, discrimination, and ignorance.

This chapter examines briefly the historical implications of the most
deprived, disadvantaged, and subjugated ethnic minority groups in the
United States. Clearly this historical victimization is a direct product of
the Anglo-Saxon dominant group's belief of superiority over other groups
that emerged during the period of colonialism and imperialism. It continues today. As we examine the involvement in crime of minority group
members, we must remember the framework of their respective sta-
tuses in the shaping of American society over the years.

NOTES

1. Act of May 28, 1830, Ch. 148, 4 Stat. 411.
2. Ronald B. Flowers, *Criminal Jurisdiction Allocation in Indian Country* (Port
Washington, N.Y.: Associated Faculty Press, 1983), pp. 39–41.
3. James W. Vander Zanden, *American Minority Relations*, 4th ed. (New York:
Alfred A. Knopf, 1983), pp. 203–4.
4. Act of March 3, 1871, Sec. 3, 16, Stat. 544, 570.
5. Flowers, *Criminal Jurisdiction Allocation*, p. 8; see also Elk v. Wilkins, 112
U.S. 94 (1884).
6. E. H. Spicer, "Federal Policy toward American Indians," in *Harvard Encyclopedia of American Ethnic Groups* (Cambridge: Harvard University Press, 1980).
7. J. Guillemin, "The Politics of National Integration: A Comparison of United
States and Canadian Indian Administrations," *Social Problems* 25 (1978): 319–32.
8. A. L. Sorkin, *The Urban American Indian* (Lexington, Mass.: D. C. Heath,
1978).
9. Steve Hunley and Joseph L. Galloway, "American Indians: 'Beggars in
Our Land,' " *U.S. News & World Report* (May 23, 1983): 72.
10. Lerone Bennett, *Before the Mayflower* (Chicago: Johnson Publishing Company, 1967).

11. Robert W. Fogel and Stanley L. Engerman, *Time on the Cross* (Boston: Little, Brown, 1974).

12. Vander Zanden, *American Minority Relations,* p. 150.

13. Ibid., pp. 212–17.

14. Brown v. Board of Education, 347 U.S. 483 (1954).

15. 1964 Civil Rights Act.

16. Edgar A. Toppin, *A Biographical History of Blacks in America since 1528* (New York: David McKay Co., 1971), pp. 143–47.

17. Southern Commission on the Study of Lynchings, *Lynchings and What They Mean* (Atlanta: Southern Commission on the Study of Lynchings, 1931), p. 40.

18. Leo F. Estrada, F. Chris Garcia, Reynaldo F. Macias, and Lionel Maldonado, "Chicanos in the United States: A History of Exploitation and Resistance," *Daedalus* 110 (1981): 103–31; S. Dale McLemore, "The Origins of Mexican-American Subordination in Texas," *Social Science Quarterly* 53 (1973): 656–70.

19. Daniel D. Arreola, "Mexican Americans," in Jesse O. McKee, ed., *Ethnicity in Contemporary America: A Geographical Appraisal* (Dubuque, Iowa: Kendall/Hunt, 1985), p. 80.

20. Ibid.

21. Maria Newman and Edgar Sanchez, "Immigration Law Threatens Mexican Town's Link," *Sacramento Bee* (May 3, 1987): A1, A30.

22. Quoted in ibid.

23. J. P. Sterba, "Where They Come, What Awaits Them," *New York Times* (May 1, 1977): E3.

24. J. M. Crewdson, "Thousands of Aliens Held in Virtual Slavery in U.S.," *New York Times,* (October 19, 1980): 1, 58.

25. Arreola, "Mexican Americans," pp. 81–82.

26. Ricardo Pimentel, "Immigration Reform Looms, Ready or Not," *Sacramento Bee* (May 1, 1987): A1.

27. Institute for Cuba and the Caribbean, *The Cuban Immigration of 1959–1966 and Its Impact on Dade County, Florida* (Coral Gables, Fla.: Center for Advanced Studies, University of Miami, 1967), p. xix; "Cuban Refugee Crime Troubles Police across U.S.," *New York Times* (March 31, 1985): L30.

28. Ricardo Pimentel, "Report Offers Grim View of Hispanics' Job Future," *Sacramento Bee* (April 29, 1987): A16.

29. Stuart C. Miller, *The Unwelcome Immigrant: The American Image of the Chinese, 1785–1882* (Berkeley: University of California Press, 1969), p. 43.

30. Milton Meltzer, *The Chinese Americans* (New York: Thomas Y. Crowell, 1980), pp. 107–10.

31. Rose Hum Lee, *The Chinese in the United States of America* (Hong Kong: Hong Kong University Press, 1960).

32. Betty Lee Sung, "Polarity in the Makeup of Chinese Immigrants," in *Sourcebook on the New Immigration* (New Brunswick: Transaction Books, 1980).

33. Meltzer, *The Chinese Americans,* p. 118.

34. Rose Hum Lee, "The Decline of Chinatowns in the United States," *American Journal of Sociology* 54 (1949): 148.

35. Catherine L. Brown and Clifton W. Pannell, "The Chinese in America,"

in Jesse O. McKee, ed., *Ethnicity in Contemporary America* (Dubuque, Iowa: Kendall/Hunt, 1985), p. 195.

36. F. E. La Violette, *Americans of Japanese Ancestry* (Toronto: Canadian Institute of International Affairs, 1946).

37. Midori Nishi, "Japanese Americans," in Jesse O. McKee, ed., *Ethnicity in Contemporary America* (Dubuque, Iowa: Kendall/Hunt, 1985), p. 180.

38. Ibid.

39. Ibid.

40. Executive Order 9066 was not formally terminated until February 19, 1976.

2

Criminal Victimization of Minorities Today

Measuring the criminal victimization of minority group members in the modern era has proved to be simultaneously enlightening and frustrating. Although some profiles of the minority victim have been established through victimization surveys, the limitations of such data have hindered their reliability and given us an incomplete picture of victimized minority members.

BIRTH OF THE VICTIMIZATION SURVEY

The first survey of victims of crime is believed to have been undertaken in 1720 in Denmark when household members were interviewed.[1] It was not until 1966 in the United States, however, that the first full-scale methodological victimization survey was conducted by the National Opinion Research Center (NORC).[2] The survey emerged in large part because of the deficiencies of the Federal Bureau of Investigation's Uniform Crime Reports (UCR) in adequately assessing crime and victimization in the United States. In focusing on the crime victim, victim surveys sought to:

- Uncover hidden crime.
- Profile crime victims and the likelihood of victimization.
- Make violent crime statistics easier to understand.
- Determine crime fluctuations.
- Make possible comparative analyses of geographical areas with other studies.

The NORC used 10,000 randomly selected American households in its study, which concentrated primarily on serious crimes (such as forcible rape and aggravated assault) but also measured other crimes (such as fraud and counterfeiting). The respondents—aged 18 and over or younger married people—were asked if they or anyone else living in the household had been a crime victim within the past year, and if so, of what offense; and if the crime had been reported, and if not, why. The following findings were discovered:

- Personal and property crimes numbered twice as many as reported to law enforcement agencies.
- Violent crime was five times as prevalent in metropolitan areas as in suburbs and rural areas.
- Twice as much property crime occurred in metropolitan cities as in the suburbs and rural areas.
- Blacks had higher rates of victimization for personal crimes of violence than whites.
- Victimization was predominantly intraracial.

In spite of the considerable difference in crime rates between the NORC and official statistics, there was reason to believe NORC data still underestimated the actual degree of crime and victims. This assumption was due partly to the vast amount of unreported crime. The survey nevertheless proved clearly superior to official data in uncovering hidden crime and establishing victim characteristics, both of which previously had had little documentation.

NATIONAL CRIME SURVEY AND MINORITY VICTIMS

The most comprehensive victimization survey to date is the National Crime Survey program (NCS), sponsored by the U.S. Bureau of the Census for the Department of Justice's Bureau of Justice Statistics. Begun in 1972, this annual report, *Criminal Victimization in the United States,* measures the personal crimes of rape, robbery, assault, and larceny and the household crimes of burglary, larceny, and motor vehicle theft based on individual respondents aged 12 and over. In 1984 the survey comprised approximately 54,000 households in which about 114,000 individuals resided.

Personal Crime Victimization

Blacks are disproportionately represented overall in personal crime victimization compared to other minority groups (Table 2.1). In 1984 blacks were victims of violent crimes at a rate higher than whites and members of other minority groups (included in this category are Native

Table 2.1
Victimization Rates for Persons Age 12 and Over, by Type of Crime and Race of Victims, 1984
(Rate per 1,000 population age 12 and over)

Type of Crime	White (165,546,210)	Black (21,738,750)	Other (4,677,250)
Crimes of Violence	29.8	41.5	25.3
Completed violent crimes	10.5	18.7	10.7
Attempted violent crimes	19.3	22.8	14.6
Rape	0.8	2.1	1.7[a]
Robbery	5.0	11.8	5.9[a]
Completed robbery	3.3	9.0	2.6[a]
With injury	1.4	3.2	1.2[a]
From serious assault	0.7	1.7	0.4[a]
From minor assault	0.7	1.5	0.8[a]
Without injury	1.8	5.8	1.4[a]
Attempted robbery	1.8	2.9	3.3[a]
With injury	0.5	1.0	0.8[a]
From serious assault	0.2	0.6[a]	0.4[a]
From minor assault	0.3	0.4[a]	0.5[a]
Without injury	1.3	1.9	2.4[a]
Assault	24.0	27.6	17.7
Aggravated assault	8.2	12.8	8.6[a]
Completed with injury	2.9	4.6	2.9[a]
Attempted assault with weapon	5.3	8.2	5.6
Simple assault	15.8	14.9	9.2
Completed with injury	4.1	4.4	4.1
Attempted assault without weapon	11.8	10.4	5.0
Crimes of Theft	72.4	67.9	70.4
Completed crimes of theft	68.2	63.1	67.4[a]
Attempted crimes of theft	4.2	4.8	2.9[a]
Personal larceny with contact	2.4	5.5	4.3[a]
Purse snatching	0.5	1.5	1.2[a]
Pocket picking	1.8	4.0	3.1[a]
Personal larceny without contact	70.0	62.4	66.1
Completed larceny without contact	66.0	57.8	63.2
Less than $50	33.0	25.6	27.1
$50 or more	30.4	28.1	33.9
Amount not available	2.6	4.2	2.1[a]
Attempted larceny without contact	4.1	4.6	2.9[a]

Note: Detail may not add to total shown because of rounding. Numbers in parentheses refer to population in the group.
[a] Estimate, based on zero or on about ten or fewer sample cases, is statistically unreliable.

Source: U.S. Department of Justice, *Criminal Victimization in the United States, 1984: A National Crime Survey Report* (Washington, D.C.: Government Printing Office, 1986), p. 16.

Americans, Asians, and Pacific Islanders). This differential was greatest for robbery victimization. For crimes of theft, both other minorities and whites were victimized at a slightly higher rate than blacks.

Table 2.2 examines victimization rates among Hispanics and non-Hispanics in 1984. We can see that Hispanics have a higher rate of violent crime victimization than non-Hispanics but are victims of theft at a lower rate.

Table 2.2
Victimization Rates for Persons Age 12 and Over, by Type of Personal Crime and Ethnicity of Victims, 1984
(Rate per 1,000 population age 12 and over)

Type of Crime	Total[a] (191,962,210)	Hispanic (11,970,690)	Non-Hispanic (179,527,370)
Crimes of Violence	31.0	35.0	30.7
Completed violent crimes	11.4	15.2	11.2
Attempted violent crimes	19.6	19.8	19.6
Rape	0.9	0.6[b]	1.0
Robbery	5.8	9.2	5.6
Completed robbery	3.9	7.1	3.7
with injury	1.6	3.5	1.5
From serious assault	0.8	2.2	0.7
From minor assault	0.8	1.3	0.8
Without injury	2.3	3.5	2.2
Attempted robbery	1.9	2.1	1.9
with injury	0.6	0.5[b]	0.6
From serious assault	0.3	0.3[b]	0.3
From minor assault	0.3	0.2[b]	0.3
Without injury	1.4	1.7	1.3
Assault	24.3	25.2	24.2
Aggravated assault	8.7	10.9	8.6
Completed with injury	3.1	3.8	3.1
Attempted assault with weapon	5.6	7.1	5.5
Simple assault	15.5	14.3	15.6
Completed with injury	4.1	4.0	4.1
Attempted assault without weapon	11.4	10.3	11.5
Crimes of Theft	71.8	64.1	72.3
Completed crimes of theft	67.6	60.4	68.0
Attempted crimes of theft	4.3	3.7	4.3
Personal larceny with contact	2.8	4.0	2.7
Purse snatching	0.7	1.0[b]	0.6
Pocket picking	2.1	2.9	2.0
Personal larceny without contact	69.1	60.2	69.6
Completed larceny without contact	65.0	56.7	65.5
Less than $50	32.0	24.6	32.4
$50 or more	30.2	29.7	30.2
Amount not available	2.8	2.4	2.8
Attempted larceny without contact	4.1	3.5	4.1

Note: Detail may not add to total shown because of rounding. Numbers in parentheses refer to population in the group.

[a] Total includes persons whose ethnicity was not ascertained.

[b] Estimate, based on zero or on about ten or fewer sample cases, is statistically unreliable.

Source: U.S. Department of Justice, *Criminal Victimization in the United States, 1984: A National Crime Survey Report* (Washington, D.C.: Government Printing Office, 1986), p. 18.

Table 2.3
Victimization Rates for Persons Age 12 and Over, by Race and Type of
Personal Crime, 1984
(Rate per 1,000 population age 12 and over)

Type of Crime	Black	Hispanic	Other
Crimes of Violence	4.15	35.0	25.3
Rape	2.1	0.6[a]	1.7[a]
Robbery	11.8	9.2	5.9
Assault	27.6	25.2	17.7
Crimes of Theft	67.9	64.1	70.4
Personal larceny with contact	5.5	4.0	4.3
Personal larceny without contact	62.4	60.2	66.1

[a] Estimate, based on zero or on approximately ten or fewer sample cases, is statistically unreliable.

Source: Drawn from U.S. Department of Justice, *Criminal Victimization in the United States, 1984: A National Crime Survey* (Washington, D.C.: Government Printing Office, 1986), pp. 16, 18.

Because NCS data do not classify Hispanics as a racial minority group, it is difficult to compare Hispanic victimization data with those of blacks and other minority groups. This difficulty is compounded by the fact that the category "other minority groups" combines victimization rates for Native Americans and Asians. Nevertheless, if we were to group the data given, some general comparisons could be drawn, as shown in Table 2.3. For violent crimes, blacks are victimized at a rate higher than Hispanics and other ethnic minority groups, with Hispanics the second most victimized group. Blacks and Hispanics have similar victimization rates for assault, whereas other minorities are closer to blacks for rape victimization.

Other minorities have higher victimization rates than blacks and Hispanics for theft crimes, with the differential greatest for personal larceny victimization without contact.

Such comparisons, although statistically unreliable due to inconsistent data, will become essential in the future in studying crime and victimization patterns of minority groups.

Household Crime Victimization

Households headed by blacks had higher victimization rates in 1984 for the three major household crimes of burglary, larceny, and motor vehicle theft than did households headed by other minorities and whites (Table 2.4). Black heads of household also had the highest victimization

Table 2.4

Victimization Rates, by Type of Household Crime and Race of Head of Household, 1984
(Rate per 1,000 households)

Type of Crime	All Races (88,039,320)	White (76,577,500)	Black (9,670,340)	Other (1,791,480)
Household Crimes	178.7	171.9	232.2	181.1
Completed household crimes	151.3	146.3	190.4	157.2
Attempted household crimes	27.4	25.6	41.8	23.9
Burglary	64.1	60.6	91.7	63.5
Completed burglary	49.1	47.0	65.2	53.4
Forcible entry	20.9	18.7	37.7	27.2
Unlawful entry without force	28.1	28.3	27.5	26.2
Attempted forcible entry	15.0	13.7	26.5	10.2
Household larceny	99.4	97.4	114.7	102.6
Completed household larceny	92.8	90.8	107.2	98.2
Less than $50	45.2	44.9	47.1	49.1
$50 or more	43.1	41.8	52.8	45.0 [a]
Amount not available	4.5	4.1	7.3	4.1 [a]
Attempted household larceny	6.6	6.6	7.5	4.4 [a]
Motor vehicle theft	15.2	13.9	25.7	15.0
Completed theft	9.5	8.5	17.9	5.7 [a]
Attempted theft	5.7	5.4	7.8	9.3

Note: Detail may not add to total shown because of rounding. Numbers in parentheses refer to households in the group.

[a] Estimate, based on zero or on about ten or fewer sample cases, is statistically unreliable.

Source: U.S. Department of Justice, *Criminal Victimization in the United States, 1984: A National Crime Survey Report* (Washington, D.C.: Government Printing Office, 1986). p. 36.

rate for motor vehicle theft on the basis of number of vehicles owned than members of other minority groups or whites (Table 2.5). Other minority group–headed households were victimized at a higher rate overall than whites for overall household crimes and motor vehicle theft based on the number of vehicles owned.

The total rate of victimization for Hispanic-headed households was higher in 1984 than non-Hispanic-headed households (Table 2.6), as well as for the individual household crime rates of burglary, larceny, and motor vehicle theft.

Table 2.7 reflects a comparison of minority group victimization rates by the type of crime and race/ethnicity of the head of the household. The data, which combine race and ethnicity NCS data, allow us to examine to some extent victimization rates of households headed by minorities as defined by this book. Hispanic-headed households are shown to have higher overall victimization rates for total household crime than households headed by blacks or members of other minority groups. Of the three major household crimes, households headed by Hispanics have the highest victimization rates only for larceny, with black-headed households having slightly higher rates for burglary and motor vehicle theft. Other minority group member–headed households reveal the lowest total victimization rates, although their larceny victimization, when less than $50, was slightly higher than black- or Hispanic-headed households.

This comparison does not take into account definitional and methodological inconsistencies (for instance, some Hispanics may also be included in black victimization data); it is meant only to give some indication of likely patterns of victimization within minority group households.

Trends in Violent Crime Victimization

In long-term studies, blacks have consistently been shown to be victimized by violent crime more than other ethnic minorities. As part of its Crime Risk Index, the Bureau of Justice Statistics established a breakdown of NCS violent crime victimization data over a recent five-year period (Table 2.8). In 1982, 4 percent of the country's black population (approximately one in twenty-five blacks) were victimized by a violent crime, compared to 2.7 percent of members of other minority groups. Blacks and other minorities were most often the victims of assault, simple assault, and robbery. The lack of a breakdown of "other" minorities and the omission of Hispanics as a race make the comparisons less substantive.

Table 2.5
Victimization Rates on the Basis of Motor Vehicle Thefts per 1,000 Households and of Thefts per 1,000 Vehicles Owned, by Selected Household Characteristics, 1984

Characteristic	Based On Households			Based On Vehicles Owned		
	Number Of Households	Number Of Thefts	Rate Per 1,000	Number Of Vehicles Owned	Number Of Thefts	Rate Per 1,000
Race of Head of Household						
All Races	88,039,320	1,340,310	15.2	151,805,700	1,446,780	9.5
White	76,577,500	1,064,550	13.9	138,195,070	1,154,840	8.4
Black	9,670,340	248,840	25.7	10,791,340	263,760	24.4
Other	1,791,480	26,920	15.0	2,819,290	28,180	10.0

Note: The number of thefts based on vehicles owned is higher than the corresponding figure based on households because the former includes all completed or attempted vehicle thefts, regardless of the final classification of the event. Personal crimes of contact and burglary occurring in conjunction with motor vehicle thefts take precedence in determining the final classification based on the number of households.

Source: U.S. Department of Justice, Criminal Victimization in the United States, 1984: A National Crime Survey Report (Washington, D.C.: Government Printing Office, 1986), p. 38.

Table 2.6
Victimization Rates, by Type of Household Crime and Ethnicity of Head of Household, 1984
(Rate per 1,000 households)

Type of Crime	Total[a] (88,039,320)	Hispanic (4,758,910)	Non-Hispanic (82,997,570)
Household Crimes	178.7	254.9	174.2
Completed household crimes	151.3	206.4	148.0
Attempted household crimes	27.4	48.5	26.2
Burglary	64.1	89.4	62.7
Completed burglary	49.1	64.4	48.2
Forcible entry	20.9	36.8	20.1
Unlawful entry without force	28.1	27.5	28.1
Attempted forcible entry	15.0	25.0	14.5
Household larceny	99.4	140.2	97.0
Completed household larceny	92.8	127.7	90.6
Less than $50	45.2	48.0	45.0
$50 or more	43.1	75.2	41.2
Amount not available	4.5	4.4	4.4
Attempted household larcency	6.6	12.5	6.3
Motor vehicle theft	15.2	25.3	14.6
Completed theft	9.5	14.3	9.2
Attempted theft	5.7	11.0	5.4

Note: Detail may not add to total shown because of rounding. Numbers in parentheses refer to households in the group.

[a]Total includes household heads whose ethnicity was not ascertained.

Source: U.S. Department of Justice, *Criminal Victimization in the United States, 1984: A National Crime Survey Report* (Washington, D.C.: Government Printing Office, 1986), p. 37.

Table 2.7
Victimization Rates, by Type of Crime and Race/Ethnicity of Head of Household, 1984
(Rate per 1,000 households)

Type of Crime	All Races[a] (88,039,320)	Black (9,670,340)	Hispanic (4,758,910)	Other (1,791,480)
Household Crimes	178.7	232.2	254.9	181.1
Completed household crimes	151.3	190.4	206.4	157.2
Attempted household crimes	27.4	41.8	48.5	23.9
Burglary	64.1	91.7	89.4	63.5
Completed burglary	49.1	65.2	64.4	53.4
Forcible entry	20.9	37.7	36.8	27.2
Unlawful entry without force	28.1	27.5	27.5	26.2
Attempted forcible entry	15.0	26.5	25.0	10.2
Household Larceny	99.4	114.7	140.2	102.6
Completed household larceny	92.8	107.2	127.7	98.2
Less than $50	45.2	47.1	48.0	49.1
$50 or more	43.1	52.8	75.2	45.0
Amount not available	4.5	7.3	4.4	4.1[b]
Attempted household larceny	6.6	7.5	12.5	4.4[b]
Motor Vehicle theft	15.2	25.7	25.3	15.0
Completed theft	9.5	17.9	14.3	5.7[b]
Attempted theft	5.7	7.8	11.0	9.3

Note: Detail may not add to total because of rounding. Numbers in parentheses relate to households in the group.
[a] Includes rates for households headed by whites.
[b] Estimate, based on zero or on around ten or fewer sample cases, is statistically unreliable.

Source: Drawn from U.S. Department of Justice, *Criminal Victimization in the United States, 1984: A National Crime Survey Report* (Washington, D.C.: Government Printing Office, 1986), pp. 36–37.

Trends in Household Crime Victimization

Households headed by blacks tend to be most often victimized by serious crime (Figure 2.1). Between 1975 and 1984, blacks had overall higher rates of victimization for any NCS crime than other minority-headed households and whites. This differential was most conspicuous for burglary victimization. Other minority group–headed households were generally victimized at a percentage below blacks and above whites over the ten-year period. The 1984 figures show that violent crime victimization among each household group declined somewhat during the ten years, although victimization of other minority groups appeared to surge up at the end of 1984 for each individual crime.

Table 2.8
Percentage of U.S. Minority Population Victimized by Violent Crime, 1978–1982[a]

Offense and Characteristic	Year				
	1978	1979	1980	1981	1982
All Violent	2.94%	3.23%	3.00%	3.21%	3.15%
Race					
Black	3.51	4.06	3.39	4.55	4.04
Other	2.17	3.11	2.62	3.80	2.78
Rape	.09	.11	.09	.09	.07
Race					
Black	.17	.19	.11	.14	.10
Other	.16[a]	.04[b]	.03[b]	.17[b]	.03[b]
Robbery	.53	.62	.60	.70	.72
Race					
Black	1.15	1.18	1.15	1.60	1.45
Other	.30[a]	.55	.24[b]	.86	1.12
Assault	2.39	2.59	2.40	2.53	2.46
Race					
Black	2.29	2.82	2.22	3.00	2.67
Other	1.70	2.65	2.43	2.80	1.72
Aggravated Assault	.89	1.01	.91	.96	.89
Race					
Black	1.13	1.39	1.14	1.49	1.31
Other	.45	1.29	1.25	.93	.50
Simple Assault	1.61	1.72	1.60	1.68	1.69
Race					
Black	1.28	1.55	1.15	1.65	1.49
Other	1.24	15.0	1.31	2.06	1.25

[a]"Other" minority races generally refers primarily to Asians, Pacific Islanders, and Native Americans.
[b]Estimate, based on about ten or fewer sample cases, is statistically unreliable.

Source: Bureau of Justice Statistics, Special Report, *The Risk of Violent Crime* (Washington, D.C.: Government Printing Office, 1985), p. 4.

Other Useful NCS Data

Victimization surveys also reveal that violent crime is predominantly intraracial and that black men and women and Hispanic women are disproportionately more likely to be crime victims.

Victimized minority group members tend to report only about one-third of personal crimes and about half of violent crimes to the police.

There appears to be a direct relationship among minority group status, socioeconomic status, income, and violent crime victimization. That is, minorities, who seem to be overrepresented among lower economic groups, appear to be disproportionately victimized by crimes of violence.

Figure 2.1
Percentage of Households Touched by Selected Crimes, by Race of Head of Household, 1975–1984

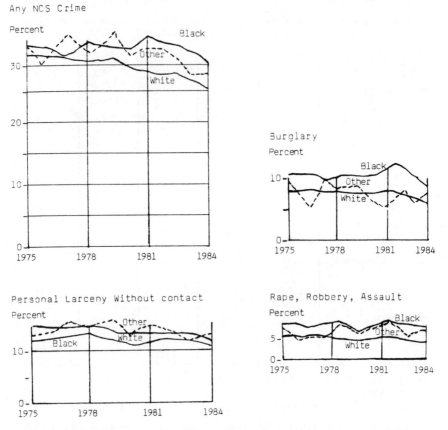

Source: Bureau of Justice Statistics Bulletin, *Households Touched by Crime, 1984* (Washington, D.C.: Government Printing Office, 1985), p. 3.

LIMITATIONS OF NATIONAL CRIME SURVEYS

A number of serious problems are present in both the methodology and the results of victimization surveys. For our purposes, the most glaring deficiency is the separate status given to Hispanics as a minority group. Because of the different NCS definitions of race and ethnicity, Hispanics are not presented in comparative terms with blacks and other minority groups, and thus their data cannot be reliably assessed in relation to other ethnic minority groups.

A second prominent shortcoming of NCS is the use of "other" as a conglomeration of various minority groups, excluding blacks, whites, and Hispanics. This grouping makes it nearly impossible to gain any reasonable understanding of the degree and characteristics of victimization among these minority groups, including Native Americans and Asians, individually. Furthermore, in many instances, other minority groups are ignored altogether in the data.

Another weakness is the absence of "victimless" crimes, such as substance abuse and prostitution, from the surveys. This is disturbing considering the disproportionate minority involvement in these crimes. Other omitted crimes that affect the true measure of crime and victimization in survey results are those the victim may not be aware of (for example, buying stolen property) and crimes in which the victims may have something to hide, possibly incriminating themselves.

NCS data are subject to underreporting and overreporting due to memory failure, untruthfulness, misrepresentation, miscoding, misinterpretation, fear of reprisal, and reluctance of victims to get involved, among other reasons.

Other problems that flaw victimization studies include ignoring the substantial number of victims under 12 years old, lack of compatibility with official data, and the limited ability to make use of such data in the study of crime and its victims.

The final problem that deserves note is the exclusion of murder victims. Obviously they cannot speak for themselves; however, given the heinous nature of homicide and the higher victimization rate for minorities, particularly blacks, it is clear that some sort of secondary victimization data need to be developed in this area.

MINORITY VICTIMIZATION AND RACISM

Because the criminal victimization of minorities appears to be predominantly intraracial, racism is generally not believed to be a prominent factor in crime perpetrated against minority group members. However, the very foundation of violent and cruel mistreatment of minorities in this country was fueled by hatred and racism by the white dominant group. Although overt white racism today generally has replaced the lynch mob with housing and employment discrimination, antiminority sentiments in the form of violence and criminal acts continue to be a factor in our society. If recent incidents are any indication, such sentiments appear to be on the upswing. The following examples give rise to this fear:

• In late 1986 in Howard Beach, a predominantly white neighborhood in New York City, three black men were attacked unprovoked by eleven white youths. One of the black men was killed by a car as he sought to escape.

• Several marchers were injured during a January 1987 civil rights march in the all-white town of Cumming, Georgia, thirty miles from Atlanta, as they were greeted by counterdemonstrators, some in Klansmen sheets or military fatigues, who pelted them with bottles, rocks, mud and chants of "Go home, niggers!"

• A black family living in Chicago became prisoners in their own home for six hours while white youths brandishing guns tossed bottles and bricks through the windows.

• In Michigan recently, a Chinese-American was beaten to death by autoworkers, and a Vietnamese family's house was broken into by four white youths wielding knives.

• In early 1988 in Contra Costa County, California, following an Asian-American woman's complaint to school officials about an attack on her son, racist graffiti showed up on their house: "Gooks live here" and "Drop charges or die."

The resurgence of hate groups and antiminority violence can be seen in official data. According to the Justice Department, the number of racist attacks in the United States rose from 99 in 1980 to 276 in 1986. Other studies that define such racist-perpetrated violence more broadly indicate that the numbers of these incidents may actually be much higher.

Blacks, Asians, and Hispanics are disproportionately targeted by racially motivated violence among the country's minority communities.[3] Although organized hate groups such as the Ku Klux Klan and the White Patriot party draw much of the attention, most race-related violence is perpetrated by individual racists. In either case, the motivations are a reflection of those that inspired racial attacks of earlier generations: white supremacy, fear, prejudice, economics, competition, scapegoating, and ignorance.

Why there has been an apparent recent increase in antiminority groups' violence is only speculative. Some believe that the Reagan administration's weak record regarding minorities invited such violence. Others contend that racist attacks have been constant through much of the 1970s and 1980s but have not been well publicized.

Whether the problem is getting worse or has simply been overshadowed by other forms of minority group member victimization, law enforcement and legislators have stepped up their assaults on the problem. Recent years have seen more arrests and prosecution of persons for racial violence. In the 1980s, twenty-nine states have passed laws specifically targeted at racial attacks, vandalism and persecution.[4] Nevertheless, members of ethnic minority communities continue to feel the heat of racially motivated victimization, a clear reminder that racial hatred is still a way of life for many.

The difficulty in measuring criminal victimization among minority group members has been illustrated in this chapter. NCS are inadequate insofar as establishing sufficiently representative data on the various racial and ethnic groups most prominent in the country. Nor are these data particularly helpful in the study of minority group victimization and criminality perpetrated against minorities. Such surveys, however, remain crucial for gaining some perspective on the victimization patterns of American minority groups. Among the most useful information derived through victimization surveys is that:

- Blacks have higher rates of victimization for personal crimes and certain household crimes (burglary and motor vehicle theft) than other minority groups or whites.
- Hispanic-headed households have higher victimization rates for total household crime than non-Hispanic households.
- Other minorities, such as Asians and Native Americans, have higher rates of theft victimization than blacks and Hispanics.
- Long-term trends reflect blacks as being the most at risk to overall criminal victimization.
- Victimization of minorities is largely intraracial.
- Violent crime victimization among minorities has declined.

Minority members appear to be facing a new and dangerous wave of racial attacks. The patterns suggest racism is spreading across the country in a way reminiscent of past generations and could be more of a threat to the minority community than more recognizable forms of victimization, such as intraracial violence.

NOTES

1. Marshall B. Clinard, *Cities with Little Crime: The Case of Switzerland* (Cambridge: Cambridge University Press, 1978), p. 222.

2. Phillip H. Ennis, *Criminal Victimization in the United States: A Report of a National Survey* (Washington, D.C.: Government Printing Office, 1967).

3. Other ethnic minorities such as Jews and Arabs are also disproportionately represented as victims of hate group violence.

4. Ted Gest, "Sudden Rise of Hate Groups Spurs Federal Crackdown," *Time* 98 (May 6, 1985): 68.

II

THE CRIMINALITY OF MINORITIES

3

The Scope and Character of Ethnic Minority Crime

The extent and nature of crime committed by American ethnic minority groups reflects wide variation. For instance, blacks, Hispanics, and Native Americans have disproportionately high rates of arrest and conviction, particularly for serious crimes, whereas Chinese-Americans and Japanese-Americans have disproportionately low rates.[1] In Chapter 4 we will focus on some theoretical propositions that seek to explain criminal involvement of minorities. But first we need to analyze statistically the dimensions of the criminality of minorities.

MEASURING CRIME WITHIN MINORITY GROUPS

There are three primary data sources in which the bulk of what we know about the incidence of criminality among minorities is gathered and recorded: official statistics, victimization surveys, and self-report surveys. Only the first two are applicable to adult-aged minority criminals, and they are the ones we will explore. Self-report surveys, which focus primarily on delinquents, will be reviewed in Chapter 9.

Uniform Crime Reports

The predominant source for compiling and measuring national crime data on minorities is the FBI's annual *Crime in the United States: Uniform Crime Reports* (UCR). Established in 1930, the UCR tabulates crimes reported to the police, the number of arrests, and the characteristics of crime and criminals. There are two categories of offenses. Part I presents detailed data on eight offenses believed to represent the most serious, frequent, and reported crimes. These eight offenses make up the Crime Index: violent crimes (murder/nonnegligent manslaughter, forcible rape, robbery, and aggravated assault) and property crimes (burglary, larceny-theft, motor vehicle theft, and arson). Part II consists of twenty-one other crimes, including embezzlement, prostitution and commercialized vice, liquor law violations, and fraud. The FBI has decided these crimes do not warrant the attention of those of Part I.

Victimization Surveys

Crime victimization surveys provide important although noncomparable offender data to official statistics. These surveys rely on random victim respondents to describe, based on their perceptions, the type and nature of the crime committed against them and a profile of the offender, including race, sex, and age.

OFFICIAL STATISTICS ON MINORITY CRIME

The most useful official data pertaining to minorities and criminality are the number of persons arrested for a certain crime as recorded by police agencies. It is important to note that these figures do not measure the actual number of individuals taken into custody, since a person may be arrested more than once during a year for the same or different offenses.

Official statistics for 1985 show that whites were arrested substantially more often than any other racial-ethnic group, followed by blacks, Hispanics, Native Americans, and Asians (Table 3.1). The percentage distribution needs some clarification, however. Whites, who represent approximately 80 percent of the U.S. population, accounted for only 71.7 percent of the nation's 1985 arrests. Conversely, blacks are arrested much more often in relation to their 12 percent representation in the general population. For example, they comprised 26.6 percent of all arrestees in 1985, more than double their population figures. The differential is even more glaring for violent crime arrests, where blacks accounted for 47.1 percent of the total. This disproportionate representation can also be seen in each individual offense listed ("driving under the influence" is the only exception).

Hispanics also reflect a disproportionately high percentage of arrests. They constituted 12.1 percent of all 1985 arrests while comprising of only 6.4 percent of the population. The actual percentage distribution of arrests for Native Americans and Asians is extremely low, although Native Americans have a high arrest rate relative to their population size.

Arrests of Minorities by Age

A percentage distribution of total arrests and Crime Index arrests of racial/ethnic groups by age in 1985 can be seen in Table 3.2. The breakdown of arrests of minorities under age 18 and age 18 and over shows little difference from arrest figures for all minority group members. Blacks by far are the most represented group of arrestees in each age bracket and every category of crime, followed by Hispanics. Of the total arrests for crimes of violence in each age category, blacks were arrested at percentages well above their overall arrest rate. They accounted for 52.4 percent of the total violent crime arrests for those under age 18 and 46.0 percent of the total arrests age 18 and over.

All racial and ethnic groups other than Asian or Pacific Islanders were arrested at a slightly higher percentage in the over-18 age category. Whereas black and Hispanic Crime Index arrests were greatest in each age group for violent crimes, Native Americans and Asians under and over age 18 showed a greater propensity for property crime Crime Index arrests.

Rate of Arrests, by Race/Ethnicity

A further measure of minority involvement in crime is the rate of arrest per 100,000 population. This method has an advantage over using the absolute numbers associated with arrests of particular minority groups, for it allows us to put in context the degree of arrests of minorities in respect to their general population as opposed to the nation's total population. For example, although whites make up by far the greatest number of actual arrests and people in the United States, they represent a low arrest rate for their population. Conversely, Native Americans, who account for the smallest ethnic group in this country, have a surprisingly higher arrest rate than whites.

Table 3.3 presents a breakdown of arrest rates per 100,000 population by race/ethnicity in 1985 for Crime Index offenses and selected Part II crimes. Although blacks show the highest rate of total arrests among all groups, Native Americans rank second, followed closely by Hispanics, with whites and Asians a distant fourth and fifth, respectively. Blacks have a significantly higher arrest rate than other groups for Crime Index offenses, most notably murder and nonnegligent manslaughter, forcible rape, robbery, and larceny-theft. Hispanics have the second highest Crime Index arrest rate, whereas Native Americans rank second in the rate of property crime arrests, a rate more than two times the rate of property crime arrests for whites.

These rates mean that certain groups, regardless of their total per-

Table 3.1
Total Arrests, Distribution by Race[a] and Ethnic Origin,[b] 1985

Offense Charged	Percent Distribution: By Race[c]					By Ethnic Origin		
	Total	White	Black	American Indian or Alaskan Native	Asian or Pacific Islander	Total	Hispanic	Non-Hispanic
TOTAL	100.0	71.7	26.6	1.1	.7	100.0	12.1	87.9
Murder & nonnegligent manslaughter	100.0	50.1	48.4	.7	.8	100.0	16.3	83.7
Forcible rape	100.0	52.2	46.5	.8	.5	100.0	10.9	89.1
Robbery	100.0	37.4	61.7	.4	.5	100.0	14.2	85.8
Aggravated assault	100.0	58.0	40.4	1.0	.6	100.0	13.3	86.7
Burglary	100.0	69.7	28.9	.8	.6	100.0	14.0	86.0
Larceny-theft	100.0	67.2	30.6	1.2	1.0	100.0	11.1	88.9
Motor vehicle theft	100.0	65.8	32.4	1.0	.8	100.0	15.3	84.7
Arson	100.0	75.7	22.8	1.0	.6	100.0	8.1	91.9
Violent crime[d]	100.0	51.5	47.1	.8	.6	100.0	13.5	86.5
Property crime[e]	100.0	67.7	30.3	1.1	.9	100.0	12.0	88.0
Crime Index total	100.0	64.5	33.7	1.0	.9	100.0	12.3	87.7
Other assaults	100.0	65.6	32.8	1.0	.7	100.0	8.7	91.3
Forgery & counterfeiting	100.0	67.3	31.6	.7	.5	100.0	6.5	93.5
Fraud	100.0	67.1	32.0	.5	.4	100.0	4.1	95.9
Embezzlement	100.0	70.4	28.2	.5	.9	100.0	5.5	94.5
Stolen property; buying, receiving, possessing	100.0	62.3	36.6	.6	.5	100.0	13.3	86.7
Vandalism	100.0	78.8	19.6	.9	.6	100.0	8.6	91.4
Weapons; carrying, possessing, etc.	100.0	65.1	33.6	.5	.8	100.0	15.1	84.9

	Total					Total		
Prostitution & commercialized vice........	100.0	55.5	43.0	.5	1.1	100.0	8.4	91.6
Sex offenses (except forcible rape & prostitution).........	100.0	78.3	20.2	.8	.6	100.0	10.5	89.5
Drug abuse violations............	100.0	68.9	30.0	.4	.6	100.0	19.2	80.8
Gambling........................	100.0	45.2	49.7	—	5.0	100.0	20.0	80.0
Offenses against family & children..	100.0	64.2	34.4	1.1	.3	100.0	5.7	94.3
Driving under the influence........	100.0	88.6	9.7	1.1	.6	100.0	13.2	86.8
Liquor laws......................	100.0	84.2	12.7	2.3	.8	100.0	8.0	92.0
Drunkenness......................	100.0	80.3	17.3	2.2	.2	100.0	19.1	80.9
Disorderly conduct...............	100.0	68.2	30.2	1.3	.4	100.0	9.9	90.1
Vagrancy.........................	100.0	68.2	28.4	2.9	.5	100.0	12.9	87.1
All other offenses (except traffic)..	100.0	65.5	32.9	.9	.7	100.0	10.7	89.3
Suspicion........................	100.0	52.3	46.8	.4	.6	100.0	13.0	87.0
Curfew & loitering law violations...	100.0	74.3	23.6	.9	1.2	100.0	10.3	89.7
Runaways.........................	100.0	84.7	13.1	.9	1.2	100.0	7.7	92.3

a Based on 11,231 agencies; 1985 estimated population 202,277,000.
b Based on 10,139 agencies; 1985 estimated population 181,038,000.
c Because of rounding, the percentages may not add to total.
d Violent crimes are offenses of murder, forcible rape, robbery, and aggravated assault.
e Property crimes are offenses of burglary, larceny-theft, motor vehicle theft, and arson.

Source: U.S. Federal Bureau of Investigation, Crime in the United States: Uniform Crime Reports 1985 (Washington, D.C.: Government Printing Office, 1986), pp. 182, 185.

Table 3.2
Percentage Distribution of Total Arrests,[a] by Age and Race/Ethnicity,[b] 1985

Offense	Arrests Under 18				Arrests Over 18			
	Black	American Indian or Alaskan Native	Hispanic	Asian or Pacific Islander	Black	American Indian or Alaskan Native	Hispanic	Asian or Pacific Islander
Total of all offenses	23.2	.9	11.7	1.0	27.3	1.1	12.2	.6
Violent crime	52.4	.6	14.5	.7	46.0	.8	13.3	.6
Property crime	25.7	1.1	11.0	1.2	32.7	1.1	12.6	.8
Crime Index total	28.6	1.0	11.3	1.1	35.9	1.0	12.8	.7

[a]The numbers given represent only the percentage of that particular age group as opposed to all arrests.
[b]Since Hispanic UCR data concentrate on ethnic origin rather than race, some Hispanics may also overlap into black or other races.

Source: U.S. Federal Bureau of Investigation, *Crime in the United States: Uniform Crime Reports 1985* (Washington, D.C.: Government Printing Office, 1986), pp. 183–84, 186–87.

Table 3.3
Rates of Arrest per 100,000 Population, by Race/Ethnicity, 1985

Offense Charged	Race/Ethnicity				
	Hispanic[a]	Black	Native American[b]	White	Asian[c]
TOTAL UCR OFFENSES	7604.1	10273.1	7859.2	3895.9	2018.5
Murder & nonnegligent manslaughter	15.1	28.5	7.7	4.1	3.6
Forcible rape	20.0	55.4	17.0	8.7	5.0
Robbery	97.9	279.2	36.6	23.8	18.8
Aggravated assault	200.3	399.8	178.4	80.8	46.9
Burglary	316.1	415.7	213.0	140.8	67.6
Larceny-theft	786.8	1359.5	978.0	419.9	353.7
Motor vehicle theft	105.4	140.6	79.4	40.1	28.3
Arson	8.2	14.4	11.6	6.7	2.7
Violent crime	333.3	762.9	239.7	117.5	74.3
Property crime	1216.6	1930.1	1282.0	607.5	452.4
Crime Index total	1550.0	2693.0	1521.7	725.0	526.8
Fraud	73.5	346.7	91.4	102.2	32.6
Prostitution & commercialized vice	51.2	163.5	32.6	29.7	31.7
Drug abuse violations	814.2	793.9	216.9	256.2	121.0
Driving under the influence	1237.3	543.2	1159.7	699.2	267.1
Liquor laws	237.1	223.2	739.7	208.0	114.1
Drunkenness	999.9	540.8	1309.8	353.9	45.3

[a]Because of a pecularity of the U.S. Census form of 1980, a number of Hispanics were also counted in the "white" and "black" categories.

[b]Uniform Crime Reports list Native Americans as American Indian or Alaskan native. The 1980 Bureau of the Census identifies 99 percent of the Native American population as American Indian and Eskimo and 1 percent as Aleut.

[c]Also includes Pacific Islanders.

Source: Arrest rates are computed for each race/ethnic group using the U.S. Bureau of the Census, *1980 Census of Population* data and the U.S. Federal Bureau of Investigation, *Crime in the United States: Uniform Crime Reports, 1985* (Washington, D.C.: Government Printing Office, 1986), pp. 182, 185.

centage of the nation's population, have a greater likelihood of being arrested relative to their individual population figures than other groups. This can be seen clearly in Native American arrest rates. According to the 1980 U.S. Census of Population, there were 1.4 million Native Americans counted—0.6 percent of the population. Yet Native Americans are disproportionately represented in arrest rates. Their 1.1 percentage of the 1985 total arrests was nearly twice their percentage of the American population. In fact, Native Americans show the highest arrest rate than any other race/ethnic group for liquor law and drunkenness violations.

Asians, on the other hand, an ethnic minority that collectively comprises approximately 2.0 percent of the U.S. population, constituted only 0.7 percent of the total arrests in 1985. As a result, they have an extremely low arrest rate relative to their population size and well below that of any other minority.

Among the sample Part II offenses shown, blacks were arrested considerably more often than other groups for fraud and for prostitution and commercialized vice, and Hispanics have the highest arrest rate for drug abuse violations and driving under the influence.

Table 3.4 compares the ratio of arrest rates for selected offenses of blacks, Hispanics, and Native Americans to that of whites and Asians. The results allow us to see the differential in rates of arrest among various ethnic groups and certain crimes. For instance, blacks are arrested 5 times as often as Asians and 2.6 times as often as whites for all crimes. Among Crime Index offenses, the black arrest rate is 11 times greater than the Asian arrest rate for murder and 6.4 times that of whites for forcible rape.

Other comparisons are just as noteworthy, such as the Native American rate of arrest for drunkenness being 28.9 times the Asian arrest rate and the Hispanic arrestees for drug abuse violations outnumbering whites by more than 3 to 1.

Patterns of Arrests of Minorities

The types and frequency of crimes committed by minority group members can also be ascertained by examining patterns of arrests by race/ethnicity in 1985.

Table 3.5 lists the most frequent arrests of racial and ethnic minorities. For three of the groups, the category "all other offenses" (those that are largely violations of local and state laws and ordinances) ranked as the offense for which they were most often arrested. The fourth minority group, Native Americans, were arrested most frequently for drunkenness. The top ten patterns of arrest frequency for each group show that the majority of the arrests are for Part II offenses, particu-

Table 3.4
Ratio of Arrest per 100,000 Population, by Race/Ethnicity, 1985

Offense	Black-White	Black-Asian	Native American-White	Native American-Asian	Hispanic-White	Hispanic-Asian
TOTAL UCR OFFENSES	2.6	5.0	2.0	3.9	1.9	3.8
Murder & nonnegligent manslaughter	6.9	7.9	1.9	2.1	3.7	4.2
Forcible rape	6.4	11.0	2.0	3.4	2.3	4.0
Larceny-theft	3.2	3.8	2.3	2.8	1.9	2.2
Motor vehicle theft	3.5	5.0	2.0	2.8	2.6	3.7
Violent crime	6.5	10.2	2.0	3.2	2.8	4.5
Property crime	3.2	4.3	2.1	2.8	2.0	2.7
Crime Index total	3.7	5.1	2.1	2.9	2.1	2.9
Fraud	3.4	10.6	a	2.8	a	2.2
Drug abuse violations	3.1	6.6	a	1.8	3.1	6.7
Liquor laws	1.0	1.9	3.5	6.5	1.1	2.1
Drunkenness	1.5	11.9	3.7	29.9	2.8	22.1

aFor these offenses, whites had a higher rate of arrest.

Source: Computed from the U.S. Bureau of the Census, *1980 Census of Population* data and the U.S. Federal Bureau of Investigation, *Crime in the United States: Uniform Crime Reports, 1985* (Washington, D.C.: Government Printing Office, 1986), pp. 182, 185.

Table 3.5
Most Frequent Arrests, by Offense and Race/Ethnicity, 1985

Rank	BLACK	Rank	HISPANIC
1	All other offenses (except traffic)	1	All other offenses (except traffic)
2	Larceny-theft	2	Driving under the influence
3	Drug abuse violations	3	Drunkenness
4	Other assaults	4	Drug abuse violations
5	Disorderly conduct	5	Larceny-theft
6	Driving under the influence	6	Disorderly conduct
7	Drunkenness	7	Burglary
8	Burglary	8	Other assaults
9	Aggravated assault	9	Liquor laws
10	Fraud	10	Aggravated assault

Rank	NATIVE AMERICAN	Rank	ASIAN
1	Drunkenness	1	All other offenses (except traffic)
2	All other offenses (except traffic)	2	Larceny-theft
3	Driving under the influence	3	Driving under the influence
4	Larceny-theft	4	Drug abuse violations
5	Liquor laws	5	Liquor laws
6	Disorderly conduct	6	Other assaults
7	Other assaults	7	Burglary
8	Drug abuse violations	8	Disorderly conduct
9	Burglary	9	Runaways
10	Aggravated assault	10	Drunkenness

Source: Compiled from U.S. Federal Bureau of Investigation, *Crime in the United States: Uniform Crime Reports 1985* (Washington, D.C.: Government Printing Office, 1986), pp. 182, 185.

larly relating to substance abuse violations. Interestingly, Asians, who rank low in Crime Index arrests, were arrested second most often for larceny-theft as were blacks. In general, however, the order of arrests of each minority group is dissimilar, although the specific crimes for which the most frequent arrests occurred are fairly consistent among the groups. The actual differences in the order of arrests may indicate opportunity, differential enforcement of the law, or cultural differences.

This same observation can be made in analyzing the least frequent arrests of minority members in 1985 (Table 3.6). Blacks and Hispanics were arrested least often for embezzlement, Native Americans for gambling, and Asians for suspicion. Each group was arrested fourth least for murder and nonnegligent manslaughter. Several Crime Index offenses are listed among each racial and ethnic group least arrested for offenses, which again offers insight into the essentially less serious nature of most criminality committed by minority members.

Long-Term Minority Arrest Trends

Examining minority group arrest patterns over a period of years shows that racial/ethnic variations in crime trends have generally remained

Table 3.6
Least Frequent Arrests, by Offense and Race/Ethnicity, 1985

Rank	BLACK	Rank	HISPANIC
1	Embezzlement	1	Embezzlement
2	Arson	2	Suspicion
3	Suspicion	3	Arson
4	Murder & nonnegligent manslaughter	4	Murder & nonnegligent manslaughter
5	Vagrancy	5	Forcible rape
6	Gambling	6	Vagrancy
7	Forcible rape	7	Forgery & counterfeiting
8	Offenses against family & children	8	Gambling
9	Curfew & loitering law violations	9	Curfew & loitering law violations
10	Sex offenses (except forcible rape & prostitution	10	Prostitution & commercialized vice

Rank	NATIVE AMERICAN	Rank	ASIAN
1	Gambling	1	Suspicion
2	Suspicion	2	Embezzlement
3	Embezzlement	3	Arson
4	Murder & nonnegligent manslaughter	4	Murder & nonnegligent manslaughter
5	Arson	5	Vagrancy
6	Forcible rape	6	Offenses against family & children
7	Prostitution & commercialized vice	7	Forcible rape
8	Forgery & counterfeiting	8	Forgery & counterfeiting
9	Robbery	9	Stolen property; buying, receiving, possessing
10	Offenses against family & children	10	Sex offenses (except forcible rape & prostitution)

Source: Compiled from U.S. Federal Bureau of Investigation, *Crime in the United States: Uniform Crime Reports 1985* (Washington, D.C.: Government Printing Office, 1986), pp. 182, 185.

constant throughout the 1970s up to 1986. That is, although whites dominate the volume of arrest statistics, blacks make up the largest minority group representation in arrest figures, including accounting regularly for nearly half of all violent crimes arrests and about one-third of the persons arrested for Crime Index offenses.[2]

In addition to the black overrepresentation in official statistics, long-term trends also reflect disproportionate involvement in criminal behavior by Hispanics and Native Americans and a pattern of low rates of arrest for Asian groups.[3]

Inadequacies of Official Statistics

The importance of official data as a reliable source for measuring crime in the United States cannot be overstated. Criminologists and other researchers routinely make use of the UCR for official interpretations of crime and criminals. Yet UCR data have a number of shortcomings that seriously impede their effectiveness as dependable information.

Two of the most critical criminal statistics relating to minority member involvement are the grouping of crimes determined to be problem crimes by the FBI and the severely limited attention paid to crimes in which whites dominate. The UCR attention placed on specific offenses designated to be the most serious as listed in the Crime Index implies to the public that the problem of crime is largely one of personal and property crimes committed by people of low incomes and minority group membership.

White-collar crime, which has a greater financial impact on the American population and in which whites have the highest crime rate, is reduced in significance in UCR data. Moreover, some crimes are not even measured. Of the eight Crime Index offenses, only arson qualifies (and only in certain instances) as a white-collar crime. Although such white-collar offenses as government corruption and price fixing qualify for the FBI's Part I offense criteria of frequently committed crimes, these offenses are not included in the UCR. There are a few white-collar crimes listed among Part II offenses (forgery and counterfeiting, fraud, and embezzlement), but their inclusion in that category implies that such offenses are of lesser consequence than Part I crimes. The reality is that these white-collar crimes inflict considerably more financial losses on the American people than do all the Part I offenses combined. Furthermore, the complexities and underreporting of white-collar crimes often make them oblivious to local law enforcement. Hence, the perception of serious crime in America and its participants becomes flawed because of the official statistics.

UCR data can also be criticized for the statistical breakdowns on minority group members. For instance, statistics on blacks and such other minorities as American Indians are listed by race and separated from data on Hispanics, who are compared only to non-Hispanics and distinguished by ethnic origin. Despite the interpretational differences between race and ethnicity (some Hispanics may also be listed as black or another race), this different classification makes it nearly impossible to compare data between blacks and Hispanics, the nation's largest and most visible minority groups. Additionally, UCR figures do not subdivide racial and ethnic groups by male and female; this important measure of crime distribution by race/ethnicity and sex must be derived through other means.

A further flaw in official data and their interpretation of criminal participation of minority groups is that crime and arrest rates are computed on the basis of census-enumerated general population figures that do not consider or count population changes, except for a census every ten years that consistently undercounts racial minorities, especially blacks.

Other general problems concerning official statistics have also been given much attention, including the following:

- Official statistics reflect only crime that police agencies are cognizant of.
- For a number of reasons, much crime goes unreported.[4]
- There are definitional problems in measuring crime (such as arrest, charge, and guilt).
- Official statistics vary.
- No federal crimes are included in UCR.
- Reporting is voluntary.
- The reliability and adequacy of reporting vary.
- There is differential enforcement of criminal statistics.
- Law enforcement manipulation of statistics influences public opinion.
- There is an overreliance on percentage changes in the total volume of Part I offenses.
- The estimating methodology used in total crime projections is flawed.
- Advancements in law enforcement efficiency (such as centralized reporting systems and specialized units) increase the number of potential arrests.

VICTIMIZATION SURVEYS AND THE MINORITY OFFENDER

The second most useful source of offender data is that derived from victimization surveys. These surveys establish profiles of offenders through asking respondents age 12 and over in randomly selected households if they have been the victim of crime and the nature of such crime, including estimating perpetrator characteristics such as race, age, and sex.

Consistent with UCR arrest figures, NCS data reflect a disproportionate black involvement in crime participation. For single-offender victimization in 1984, violent crime was predominantly intraracial (Table 3.7). Blacks were perceived to be the offender of crimes against blacks 80.6 percent of the time. The percentages show other minority group offenders to have been involved in 3.6 percent of the crimes of violence against black or white victims but do not give the race/ethnicity of other crime victims. Black offenders also were perceived to have committed 54 percent of the violent crimes against whites (data are not shown in Table 3.7).

When the offense involved multiple offenders, 34.4 percent were believed to be black groups, 9.9 percent of mixed race, and 4.5 percent other minority member offenders (Table 3.8). The percentages jumped significantly for each group for crimes of rape and certain robberies. As in single-offender victimization, most multiple-offender crimes were intraracial.

Table 3.7
Percentage Distribution of Single-Offender Victimizations, Based on Race of Victims, by Type of Personal Crime and Perceived Race of Offender, 1984

Type of victim and race of victim	Total	Perceived race of offender			
		White	Black	Other	Not known and not available
Crimes of Violence					
White (3,519,230)	100.0	78.5	16.4	3.6	1.5
Black (612,810)	100.0	17.0	80.6	1.4[a]	1.0[a]
Completed violent crimes					
White (1,150,330)	100.0	77.0	17.9	4.0	1.1[a]
Black (233,250)	100.0	13.2	85.3	0.6[a]	0.8[a]
Attempted violent crimes					
White (2,368,900)	100.0	79.2	15.8	3.4	1.6
Black (379,560)	100.0	19.3	77.6	1.9[a]	1.1[a]
Rape					
White (110,950)	100.0	77.0	15.2	7.8[a]	0.0[a]
Black (34,460)	100.0	12.6[a]	83.1	4.3[a]	0.0[a]
Robbery					
White (415,350)	100.0	54.8	38.5	5.9	0.8[a]
Black (108,470)	100.0	14.0[a]	82.7	0.0[a]	3.3[a]
Completed robbery					
White (252,910)	100.0	55.8	39.4	4.8[a]	0.0[a]
Black (72,430)	100.0	12.9[a]	84.4	0.0[a]	2.7[a]
With injury					
White (108,800)	100.0	51.3	40.6	8.1[a]	0.0[a]
Black (11,290)	100.0[a]	22.2[a]	77.8[a]	0.0[a]	0.0[a]
Without injury					
White (144,110)	100.0	59.2	38.6	2.2[a]	0.0[a]
Black (61,140)	100.0	11.2[a]	85.6	0.0[a]	3.2[a]
Attempted robbery					
White (162,440)	100.0	53.3	37.0	7.7[a]	2.1[a]
Black (36,040	100.0	16.4[a]	79.2	0.0[a]	4.4[a]
With injury					
White (50,920)	100.0	60.1	26.8[a]	6.5[a]	6.6[a]
Black (13,260)	100.0	15.6[a]	72.3[a]	0.0[a]	12.1[a]
Without injury					
White (111,520)	100.0	50.2	41.7	8.2[a]	0.0[a]
Black (22,780)	100.0	16.8[a]	83.2	0.0[a]	0.0[a]
Assault					
White (2,992,930)	100.0	81.8	13.4	3.1	1.6
Black (469,880)	100.0	18.0	79.9	1.5[a]	0.6[a]
Aggravated assault					
White (945,350)	100.0	79.6	14.9	3.6	1.9
Black (206,500)	100.0	15.1	83.2	1.8[a]	0.0[a]
Simple assault					
White (2,047,580)	100.0	82.9	12.8	2.9	1.4
Black (263,380)	100.0	20.3	77.3	1.4[a]	1.0[a]

Note: Detail may not add to total shown because of rounding. Number of victimizations shown in parentheses.

[a] Estimate, based on zero or on about ten or fewer sample cases, is statistically unreliable.

Source: U.S. Department of Justice, *Criminal Victimization in the United States, 1984: A National Crime Survey Report* (Washington, D.C.: Government Printing Office, 1986), p. 50.

Table 3.8
Percentage Distribution of Multiple-Offender Victimizations, by Type of Personal Crime and Perceived Race of Offenders, 1984

Type of crime	Total	Perceived race of offenders				
		All white	All black	All other	Mixed races	Not known and not available
Crimes of violence (1,637,960)	100.0	49.8	34.4	4.5	9.9	1.3
Completed violent crimes (750,010)	100.0	41.5	42.6	3.4	11.1	1.5[a]
Attempted violent crimes (887,950)	100.0	56.9	27.4	5.5	9.0	1.1[a]
Rape (26,480)	100.0	18.2[a]	55.1[a]	14.2[a]	12.5[a]	0.0[a]
Robbery (562,680)	100.0	27.2	55.1	3.6	12.5	1.6[a]
Completed robbery (409,030)	100.0	24.6	56.2	4.0	13.1	2.2[a]
With injury (183,220)	100.0	27.7	54.8	5.5[a]	9.6	2.4[a]
Without injury (225,820)	100.0	22.0	57.4	2.8[a]	15.9	1.9[a]
Attempted robbery (153,640)	100.0	34.3	52.1	2.6[a]	11.0	0.0[a]
With injury (38,220)	100.0	30.4[a]	50.1	10.4[a]	9.1[a]	0.0[a]
Without injury (115,420)	100.0	35.7	52.7	0.0[a]	11.6[a]	0.0[a]
Assault (1,048,800)	100.0	62.8	22.7	4.8	8.5	1.2[a]
Aggravated assault (452,890)	100.0	63.7	24.2	5.8	4.6	1.8[a]
Simple assault (595,910)	100.0	62.1	21.7	4.1	11.5	0.7[a]

Note: Detail may not add to total shown because of rounding. Number of victimizations shown in parentheses.

[a] Estimate, based on zero or on about ten or fewer sample cases, is statistically unreliable.

Source: U.S. Department of Justice, *Criminal Victimization in the United States, 1984: A National Crime Survey Report* (Washington, D.C.: Government Printing Office, 1986), p. 54.

Problems with Victimization Data

The obvious shortcomings of NCS data that immediately come to mind with respect to the minority member are the absence of information on other victims aside from blacks and whites, such as Hispanics and Native Americans, and the grouping of all other racial and ethnic group offenders, excluding blacks and whites, under "other." This lack of detailed study on other minority groups makes such victimization data virtually useless since it does not include all victims or enough information on minority offenders to be able to apply it to the study of criminals and victims of minority status.

A second problem is finding victims willing to discuss their victimization. Many experts believe this group is in the minority due to any number of reluctance factors.[5]

A third fault of victimization surveys is the questionable reliability of victims in their perceptions of offenders. A number of variables could make such a perception suspect, such as memory impairment (making the perception more of a guess), lying, interpretational qualities, and the circumstances of the incident (for example, lighting conditions or the stress of the moment might affect a victim's perception of what he or she saw).

Fourth, the offender has to be seen in order to approximate race and other attributes. In many instances of personal victimization, this may have been impossible due to the circumstances (such as darkness). Nevertheless, a victim may describe the person from how he or she "sounded."

Fifth, because victimization surveys are primarily concerned with the victim, too little attention is given to offender data to make them a reliable measurement of criminal offenders.

Finally, victimization data on offenders are of only limited value since the information they give can already be readily found in official data and private research.

Data reveal wide variations in the extent and patterns of criminality among minority groups. Blacks, Hispanics, and Native Americans are disproportionately represented in arrest figures, whereas Asian-Americans have a very low rate of arrest. For Crime Index offenses, blacks and Hispanics show a higher representation in violent crime arrests than property crimes. Conversely, Native American and Asian Crime Index arrestees are more likely to be arrested for property offenses. Overall, the bulk of minority group crime is of Part II offenses, much of it related to substance abuse violations.

Although official and victimization data with respect to minority status offenders continue to be the major source of information in tracking crime and arrest patterns, the serious limitations of such data severely hinder their effectiveness in presenting a complete and accurate picture of the criminality of American minority groups.

NOTES

1. To some extent, the low Chinese crime rate can be attributed to the Chinese being close knit and preferring to settle criminal and other matters outside the American courts and their white majority dominance. See also Gwynn Nettler, *Explaining Crime*, 3d ed. (New York: McGraw-Hill, 1984), pp. 136–37; Harwin L. Voss, "Ethnic Differentials in Delinquency in Honolulu," *Journal of Criminal Law, Criminology and Police Science* 54 (1963): 322–27.

2. U.S. Federal Bureau of Investigation, *Crime in the United States: Uniform Crime Reports, 1975–1985* (Washington, D.C.: Government Printing Office, 1976–1986).

3. *Uniform Crime Reports* began to record data on arrestees of Hispanic origin only in 1980. Prisoner data on Hispanics before that year, however, support the disproportionate Hispanic involvement in criminal activity.

4. Reasons for unreported crime include fear of reprisal; lack of faith in the

criminal justice system, especially police; the belief that police do not want to get involved; unnecessary hassle; and knowing the offender and not wanting to see him or her get into trouble.

    5. Ibid.

4

Explanatory Approaches to the Criminality of Minorities

As we have observed, there are basic differences among the ethnic and racial groups we are focusing on in the type and patterns of crime committed and the relative amounts of particular crimes. Because of this variation in criminality among the peoples of these different minority groups and the unique histories of each group in the United States, there have been relatively few theoretical propositions that have attempted to explain the criminality of minorities collectively. There is also a dearth of individual substantive research on criminal participation and its dynamics with respect to three of the four groups we are examining: Hispanics, Native Americans, and Asians. The fourth group, blacks, has been given by far the most attention by criminologists, no doubt due to their numbers as the nation's largest minority and therefore the most visible group of minority offenders and the interrelationship between this and their particular circumstances over the years beginning with their involuntary migration to the New World.

Is this emphasis fair to blacks who, for the most part, have been cast in an unfavorable light or to other ethnic and racial minority groups who have become "lost" in more generalized criminological research and cost-effective criminal justice policymaking—often at the expense of these groups who, because of such policies, must rely more on overtaxed human services? This is a question that cannot be adequately addressed within the confines of this chapter. Instead, our direction of discussion will be better served by examining those theories of prominence that either by implication or direct association seek to explain the criminality of the minority community in general.

BIOLOGICAL THEORIES OF CRIMINALITY

Biological theories represent one of the earliest positivist attempts to explain criminal behavior. Through the use of scientific methodology and empirical testing, these theories placed much emphasis on a "born criminal" approach, suggesting that biological determinants such as physical characteristics, heredity, and genes distinguish criminals from noncriminals. For the most part, biological theories have been disregarded as credible by modern criminologists, who rely primarily on sociological and psychological perspectives in the study of crime causation. Biological approaches also present the weakest basis for explaining the criminality of minorities. Nevertheless, because biological explanations of crime continue to be actively supported by some, we will examine some of the key research in this school of thought.

Atavistic Theories

Italian physician Cesare Lombroso (1836–1909), referred to as the Father of Criminology, is generally credited with bringing a positivistic perspective to explaining crime with his theory of atavism.[1] Lombroso studied prisoners and the cadavers of executed offenders in an attempt to determine scientifically if criminals were physically different from noncriminals.

He theorized that criminals possess atavistic qualities, or primitive genetic anomalies, in their physical makeup (for example, enormous jaws and large nasal spines). According to Lombroso, repeat offenders (such as assaultists) were in fact "born criminals" or "biologically predisposed." Not only did he believe criminals could be recognized by physical stigma but that various criminal types could be differentiated on the basis of different physiological makeup.

Although Lombroso's major premise was that criminality is a product of biological heredity, he also posited that environmental factors, such as educational deficiencies, alcoholism, and seasonal changes, could contribute to criminal behavior.

Lombroso's theories have since been dismissed because of, among other reasons, the relatively small size of his prisoner samples, his lack of control groups from the general population for comparison with his findings, and his failure to account for biological determinants that might not be the result of hereditary traits but other factors, such as poor nutrition. One notable critic, Charles Goring, disproved the theory in his 1913 book, *The English Convict*, finding no consequential physical differences between prisoners and the general population.[2]

Body-Type Theories

As recently as the 1950s, body-type theories were in vogue. The 1939 publication of Ernest Hooton's *Crime and the Man* established early prominence in this field.[3] Hooton, a Lombroso supporter, held that criminals are biologically and socially inferior to noncriminals. After comparing thousands of measurements of the physical characteristics of prisoners and noncriminals, he argued that the majority of native-born criminals are physically as well as mentally deficient and genetically inferior in body and mind. He observed that criminals tend to be physically characterized by such traits as mixed eye color, denoting racial impurity; thin, straight, or reddish hair; tattooing; and long necks. The environmental and social factors Hooton related to criminality included divorce, undereducation, and membership in the lower classes.

Another advocate of the body-build perspective, William Sheldon, wrote a series of books in the 1940s on somatotypes, or body types, and criminality. He believed that temperamental traits are dependent on body type, which was then associated with susceptibility to crime and delinquency.[4] Sheldon described three basic body types; meso-morphs—the muscular, aggressive, active type—were the most likely to engage in criminal behavior.

Following Sheldon's principles, Sheldon Glueck and Eleanor Glueck's study of delinquents and nondelinquents revealed that mesomorphs were twice as representative among delinquents.[5] A recent analysis of biological theories of criminality, however, has found little evidence of a sound correlation of certain body types, temperaments, and crime.[6]

Body-type theories have been largely invalidated in explaining criminal behavior. One criticism often raised is the methodology used by body-type theorists. For example, Hooton's use of prisoners in his sample group of "criminals" can hardly be representative of all criminals, for their imprisonment may have been more a result of selective enforcement of the law or discrimination than the actual incident for which they were committed. Furthermore, their physical characteristics can also be found in noncriminals.

Another limitation of body-type theories is their failure to explain the correlation between physical characteristics and social acts. For example, why do some people born with "aggressive temperaments" become, say, attorneys rather than criminals? Clearly this theory cannot stand up under such scrutiny.

Hereditary and Genetic Theories

The role heredity plays in criminality also has early roots in the biological school of criminal behavior. The "bad seed" theory, or the

belief that criminal or delinquent behavior is the result of genetic trans-
mission of physical or mental traits or abnormalities from one genera-
tion to another, has long been advocated. Although no solid evidence
supports this approach or explains why it does not apply to all deviants or deviant behavior, a number of recent studies have explored
the relationship between genetics and criminality.

XYY Chromosome. Much controversy has ensued over research on the
XYY chromosomal pattern in men and its relationship to criminality
and aggressive behavior. Scientific observation in the early 1960s revealed a genetic abnormality in some males: they possess an extra Y
sex chromosome. The normal human chromosome count is forty-six,
the female pairing being XX and the male XY. This rare added Y in
some men has been shown to appear more frequently in tall prisoners
and institutionalized mentally retarded persons than in the general
population.[7] Some researchers have suggested that this XYY comple-
ment is evidence that these men may be more prone to aggressive behavior, resulting in criminality that is particularly violent. This assumption is based largely on the notion that an extra Y reflects a more
aggressive man.

More recent work has failed to support these claims. Although some
criminologists have found that XYY prisoners are not significantly disproportionate to XYY men in the general public, others have argued
that XYY individuals have a lower propensity for aggressive behavior
than those with the normal chromosomal pattern. A cohort study of
tall men in Denmark by Herman Witkin and associates found that although the XYY men (12 out of 4,139) engaged in more criminal activity than the XY men of comparable height, age, and social status, there
was no evidence that they were any more violently predisposed.[8]

Twin Studies. Another approach to establishing a genetic link with
criminality has been the study of twins. Researchers have compared
the criminality of identical twins with that of fraternal twins. The assumption is that if criminal tendencies are in fact inherited traits, then
identical twins (both of a single fertilized egg) will be more resembling
in their criminal behavior than fraternal twins (who come from sepa-
rately fertilized eggs).

Early studies supported the notion that identical twins had a higher
concordance rate of criminal behavior than fraternal twins.[9] Recent more
comprehensive studies have found such differences, if any, to be minimal.[10] Moreover, even were these differences significant, it would be
virtually impossible to establish whether they were inherited or envi-
ronmentally based, or, for that matter, to what extent either factor may
have come into play.

Adoption Studies. The significance of hereditary influences on criminal
behavior has been explored by comparing the criminality of adopted

children with that of their adoptive and biological parents. This school of thought assumes that if adopted children display behavior closer to that of their biological parents than their adoptive parents, there is greater validity in a genetic association to criminality. Conversely, should the adoptees prove more like their adoptive parents, environment would seem a stronger variable for criminal behavior than heredity.

A number of studies have shown a relationship between the criminality of biological parents and the criminal behavior of their children. One notable Denmark study of male adoptees found that children whose biological fathers had engaged in criminality had a greater likelihood of themselves committing crimes and, further, that when both the biological and adoptive fathers had criminal backgrounds, the child's tendency to follow the same path increased considerably.[11] These findings were supported in a study of Danish male adoptees.[12]

Although these studies seem to give validity to a genetic basis for criminal behavior, the researchers did not ignore an environmental influence of criminality. Instead they suggested that a combination of the two likely contributed to criminal participation, corroborating to some extent recent genetic research by C. Robert Cloninger, who contends: "I don't think that there's a specific gene for criminality itself, only genetic factors that influence susceptibility."[13] Cloninger postulates that it takes environmental factors such as social class and family life to trigger these tendencies.

Brain Disorder Research

Criminality has been associated with a number of brain dysfunctions and impairments in learning capabilities. Some evidence suggests that delinquents have a higher rate of epilepsy through which seizures may impair self-control.[14] Other studies point to abnormal electroencephalogram recordings of the brain activity in criminals and delinquents, linking this to violent and aggressive behavior, limited impulse control, destructiveness, and poor social adaptation.[15]

Dysfunctions of the brain have also been blamed for some learning disabilities such as dyslexia and hyperactivity, which some researchers suggest predispose these individuals to deviant behavior, rejection, and poor educational achievement.[16] Additional research posits a relationship between violent crime and brain tumors.[17]

Brain dysfunction may explain some criminal behavior; however, research in this area is limited in that it does not explain why some criminals show no brain or neurological problems. Furthermore, much criminality associated with brain disorders also suggests the strong influence of environmental factors, which in effect negate the role of biological dysfunctions singularly in criminal behavior.

Other Biological Research and Criminality

Modern biological explanations of criminal behavior are focusing on a number of areas, including the roles of nutrition, allergies, environmental contaminants, and sex differences in criminality.[18] Much of this work is too new to evaluate.

Ineffectiveness of the Biological Approach to Crime

Biological research is inadequate to explain racial/ethnic and class variations in crime rates. There is no evidence to suggest that the high crime rate among minorities is a matter of biological differences, particularly when one considers that race and ethnicity represent socially defined groupings rather than biologically based classifications. Yet if biological theories purport to explain the cause of street crime, particularly violent crime, and minorities and the lower class are disproportionately involved in such offenses, it is implicit in the biological perspective that biologically these group members are inferior to whites and other classes of people—an absurd way of thinking.

Although many modern biological researchers acknowledge the role of environmental variables in criminal behavior, their emphasis is still foremost on biological determinants, which have not been supported through sufficient empirical testing. Other shortcomings of biological explanations include the inattention given to crime rate fluctuations over time, gender differences in crime rates, and why crime declines with age after peaking in the early twenties.

PSYCHOLOGICAL THEORIES OF CRIMINALITY

Psychological theories of criminal behavior also have early roots in criminological research. These theories, formulated by psychologists, psychiatrists, and other experts in mental health, attribute criminality to mental, emotional, and personality disorders. Psychological hypotheses in explaining crime are also problematic and, except for a few instances, generally offer explanatory treatments of minority criminality by implication only. Yet overall, the psychological approach to crime appears to offer hope in the future of criminological theory.

Psychoanalytic Theories

The work of Viennese doctor Sigmund Freud (1856–1939) is most responsible for the establishment of psychoanalytic concepts of criminality.[19] Fundamentally these theories pose that criminal behavior is a product of basic unresolved conflicts and drives existing deep within the human psyche. Freud divided the personality into three distinct parts: the id (source of biological drives), the ego (the part of the psyche that compensates for the necessities of the id by assisting people in tailoring their actions to remain within the limits of social convention), and the superego (the conscience part of the psyche; it decides whether one is right or wrong in behavior). When these personality elements are imbalanced, the theory postulates, antisocial behavior may result.

Whereas Freud focused more on the correlation between criminal behavior and an unconscious sense of guilt the person established during childhood, psychoanalyst August Aichorn's (1878–1949) work is believed to be most responsible for applying the psychoanalytic perspective to criminality.[20] After studying delinquent youths, Aichorn theorized that they were predisposed psychologically to committing crime. He referred to this as *latent delinquency*, which he described as present in youths whose personality impelled them to act on impulse, self-satisfaction, and instinctive urges without feelings of guilt.

Psychoanalytic theory does not disregard the socialization aspect of criminality. It suggests that the id-ego-superego personality could lead to a "socialized criminal."[21] That is, if the social environment condones or is supportive of criminal behavior, an individual could be socialized to commit crime. This approach contends that people exposed more to antisocial influences than law-conforming influences may reflect this in their personalities and modes of behavior.

The solution to these behavioral problems, believe the proponents of this school of thought, is psychoanalysis—an individualistic therapy program that concentrates on delving deep into the individual's past experiences to uncover unconscious conflicts.

The major drawback to psychoanalytic research is that it cannot be tested empirically. Because personality is unobservable and unmeasurable, the basis of psychoanalytic findings is essentially the "analyst's interpretation of a patient's interpretation of what is occurring in the subconscious."[22] This is not sufficient evidence to account for criminal behavior.

Personality Disorder Theories

Although personality disorder theories also rely on personality and emotional problems as being responsible for criminal behavior, unlike psychoanalytic theories, they do not necessarily attribute these problems to unconscious conflicts. Rather, these theories contend that personality flaws are contributory to criminality.[23]

In its extreme form, personality disorder theories attribute criminal behavior to psychopathic or sociopathic personalities, which means chronic antisocial behavior. Psychopaths are largely regarded as callous individuals who lack moral standards. They are seen as having troubled social relationships, limited societal ties, and no fear of retribution for crimes committed.

Social scientists generally reject the psychopath hypothesis, citing its vagueness and its woeful attempt to create a category for a personality disorder that would otherwise be unclassifiable.

Less extreme personality disorder theories associate such variables as emotional instability, paranoia, aggressiveness, and insecurity with criminal behavior. The reviews of these types of proposals have been mixed. Some studies have failed to establish a relationship between criminality and personality disorders.[24] However, some researchers believe that there is some merit in personality disorder research.[25] The consensus of most criminologists is that the correlation between crime and personality might become a stronger force in criminology when definitional and measurement problems in personality attributes are resolved.

Intelligence Quotient Theories

A theory of criminality causation containing both psychological and biological elements pertains to the controversial relationship between intelligence and criminal behavior. Many early criminologists believed that a lower-than-average intelligence quotient (IQ) among delinquents and criminals was the primary cause of their criminality.[26] Most scientific circles today discount this relationship because of a consistent cultural (and therefore racial) bias and methodological problems.

Nevertheless, many continue to pursue the correlation between IQ and crime. Much of this research has focused on racial and class variations in delinquency. Blacks and members of the lower class (delinquents and nondelinquents) are almost routinely shown to possess lower IQs than whites and upper-class members, the implication being that the former groups are more likely to be less intelligent as well as criminally predisposed.

Much of the IQ argument today focuses on heredity versus environmental-based causation. Heredity theorists such as Arthur Jensen[27] and Richard Herrnstein[28] contend that race and class, respectively, account primarily for IQ differences. However, social scientists Sandra Scarr and Richard Weinberg, who studied blacks adopted by white families, argue that the social environment is the leading factor affecting the average IQ of black children.[29]

Travis Hirschi and Michael Hindelang's review of significant IQ research led to their conclusion that IQ is a more important factor in predicting criminality than race or class.[30] They dismiss the rejection of

IQ tests as racially and class biased, noting that major differences in IQ are also observable in criminals and noncriminals of intraracial and intraclass groups. The researchers' major proposal is that low IQ affects school performance, which in turn produces failure and incompetency; they posit a strong correlation between these variables and juvenile and adult criminality.

The weaknesses of IQ tests continue to outweigh any conclusions that can be drawn from them, however. Because whites design most tests, they will likely reflect this cultural bias, intentional or not, in their results. Also there is confusion over the significance and interaction of biology, psychology, and sociology in interpreting results. Finally, until the measurement and definitional problems of IQ tests are resolved, they cannot be considered reliable.

A Perspective on Psychological Theories and Crime

Psychological theories of criminal deviance have some usefulness in exploring behavioral patterns of deeply disturbed, violent individuals, as well as some lesser forms of psychological disorders. But they are limited in explaining most types of criminal behavior because only a small segment of society's broad criminal element could be termed psychologically disturbed. The limitations of this approach to crime are further observable as they relate to the criminality of minorities. A substantive correlation between the disproportionate minority crime rate and psychological explanations has not been established.

SOCIOLOGICAL THEORIES OF CRIME

Biological and psychological theories examine criminal behavior in terms of individual abnormalities or flaws; sociological theories, in contrast, generally regard criminality as a normal response to social structure, elements of social life, and situations related to crime formation. On the whole, these theories appear to be more practical than the other two in assessing the criminality of minorities; however, they too present serious deficiencies in understanding why some people commit crimes and others do not.

Anomie and Social Structure Theory

Emile Durkheim (1858–1917), a preeminent sociologist at the turn of the century, made a substantial contribution to criminology with the concept of anomie, defined as a condition of relative normlessness in a group or society.[31] Durkheim's concept pointed to a property of the social and cultural structure rather than a property of individuals confronting that structure. He regarded an anomic condition as occurring when the existing social structure is unable to control individuals' desires. This condition generally came about as the result of social disruption caused by natural or human-induced disasters such as war, economic depression, or famine. Durkheim also referred to an anomie of prosperity, which transpired when one's concepts of behavior, norms, and rules was disrupted by unexpected good fortune.

The concept of anomie was applied to societal conditions and cultural values in the United States by Robert Merton.[32] He attempted to associate particular modes of behavior to the social position of the individuals participating in the behavior. Merton argued that two elements of every culture interact to create potentially anomic situations: culturally defined goals and the socially structured means for attaining them. Given that some people (such as minority group members and those of the lower class) have unequal access to approved means, they are unable to achieve the goals of society unless they deviate from the norm.

Merton developed five basic modes of adaptation to the goals and means in our society:

- *Conformity* to culture goals and means.
- *Innovation,* that is, accepting the culturally prescribed goals of success without using legitimate means for their attainment.
- *Ritualism,* which refers to the person who conforms to the mores defining the means but rejects the cultural goals.
- *Retreatism,* applying to individuals who reject both the culturally prescribed goals and the institutionalized means.
- *Rebellion,* the rejection of cultural goals and the social means for obtaining them.

Martin Haskell and Lewis Yablonsky outlined a further adaptation to the means-ends concept:

- *Dropping out,* or rejecting both culturally defined goals and the legitimate means by taking no action to effectuate change.[33]

Among these adaptations, innovation and retreatism are most applicable to criminal behavior—innovation particularly so when the desired goal seeker becomes emotionally involved. That is, the "success attainment" stressed throughout American society creates an "emotional investment" in striving for that goal, resulting in a willingness to resort to illegitimate means to attain it when legitimate means are blocked. This adaptation is believed to account for the high rate of crime of the lower class, where access to acceptable means is extremely limited. Innovation can also apply to other social classes when its members view as limited the legitimate means for the attainment of social success (examples are tax evaders and fraudulent stock manipulators).

Retreatism concerns the rejection of the goals and the means of the culture. Retreatists, viewed as alienated societal dropouts, include substance abusers, psychotics, neurotics, vagrants, and outcasts. In rejecting cultural goals and unwilling to use institutionalized means in reaching them, these individuals are often regarded as immoral and antisocial, even when there are no easily identifiable victims of their retreatism. In some instances, however, retreatists are implicated in secondary offenses associated with their particular need, such as theft or robbery to support drug dependency.

A number of problems exist in Merton's adaptation of Durkheim's anomie concept. One concerns his failure to establish an explanation for the various classes of criminal behavior (such as middle and lower) or the patterns within these groups. A second is that although Merton's theory may be helpful in explaining disparities in crime rates or why some may choose innovation (such as in theft) and others retreatism (for example, alcoholism), it does not account for why one person may become a criminal while another does not or, for that matter, why some retreaters may indulge in drugs and others alcohol. Also Merton's work has been attacked for its "assumption that this society displays goal, value, and normative consensus rather than the plurality of world views suggested by its class, racial, and ethnic differences."[34]

Despite the flaws in Merton's structural formulation, the theoretical sophistication of his work was responsible for further criminological research and theory into the relationship between criminality and differential economic opportunity during the 1950s and 1960s, most notably the work of Albert Cohen[35] and Richard Cloward and Lloyd Ohlin.[36]

Differential Association Theory

A prominent approach in the sociopsychological explanatory models of criminal behavior is Edwin Sutherland's differential association theory. Sutherland, long recognized as one of the foremost U.S. criminologists, introduced differential association theory in the 1939 edition of his text *Principles of Criminology*.[37] The theory was modified in 1947 and has since remained the same. Differential association theory attempts to explain the reasons for the crime rate distribution among various groups and why any particular individual does or does not engage in antisocial behavior.

The theory advances that the probability of criminal behavior varies directly with the priority, duration, frequency, and intensity of an individual's contacts with patterns of crime and criminal behavior and inversely with his or her noncriminal contacts. Contacts with criminal elements tend to take place most frequently when a person's perceptions of his or her situation are supportive of norm violations. Thus, many types of nonconformity (such as crime, mental illness, and substance abuse) are likely to be concentrated in urban areas that are characterized by cultural traits that tend to alienate persons both from one another and from middle-class norms.

Differential association theory postulates that crime, like all other behavior, is learned. It points out the general circumstances under which there is likely to be more criminal behavior instead of less to be learned and thus a greater probability that the person will acquire a set of "definitions" more favorable to criminal than noncriminal behavior. The theory argues that criminal behavior is a social rather than antisocial activity. Hence, if most of an individual's associations are with persons who frequently violate the law and who express attitudes that seek to justify their actions, the individual has a greater likelihood of becoming a criminal or delinquent than someone who associates with persons who do not violate the laws or approve of such violations.

Critics of the theory of differential association argue that its vagueness in terminology makes it virtually untestable. For instance, how can one determine the number and intensity of the influences on a given person's beliefs? How does it account for impulsive crimes (assuming the impulse nature of criminality cannot be learned)? The theory also fails to address the origin of crime.

Additionally, although differential association theory explains many criminal patterns, there are others in which it is not applicable—for example, embezzlers who appear to be without positive reinforcement in their environment and social background. Also, the assumption of rationality and systematic qualities in criminal behavior appears to make little sense regarding certain crimes such as malicious or spontaneous violence where purpose or criminal associations may be virtually nonexistent.

Even with these limitations of differential association theory, Sutherland's work in this field has stood the test of time and remains among the most influential explanations of criminal behavior.

Control Theory

Control theory assumes that all individuals have the potential to commit crimes and that society provides numerous opportunities for criminal behavior. In his 1969 book, *Causes of Delinquency*, Travis Hirschi applied this sociological theory to juvenile delinquency.[38] He advanced the theory that delinquents lack the intimate relationships, goals, and moral standards that bind other people to conform to the norms of society. As a result, they are free to violate the law.

Control theory posits that although most people have the inclination for deviant behavior occasionally, it is their fear and their attachment to others that will dictate whether they in fact commit deviant acts. Delinquents, according to this theory, do not actually have their own norms of deviance; rather, they are without sufficient norms that strictly oppose delinquency. This inadequate conformity to social convention and values is associated with the absence of attachment to important social institutions, creating a freedom in which criminal behavior becomes possible.

Under control theory, the high rate of minority crime can be attributed to a weaker attachment to social institutions such as school or jobs, economic opportunity (as related to their disproportionate representation in the lower classes), and family (there is some indication that minorities have higher rates of broken homes and illegitimacy than whites).

Control theorists concern themselves less with the motivation to deviate and more with the institutions that produce conditions conducive to law violations (or refraining from violating the law). On the one hand, a person can be driven to commit crime by his or her association with criminals, the desire for material success, and social approval; yet these motivations can be mitigated (or eliminated) by the social control that comes from attachment to family, friends, school, and employment.

A major shortcoming of control theory lies in its failure to point to the social-structural causes of criminal motivation. One cannot assume that the freedom to commit crime by someone living in poverty, for example, means that that person will engage in crime.

Another problem is that the theory seems to explain criminality too much in terms of socioeconomic differences between deviants and non-deviants (although the theory purports to be equally applicable to all social and economic classes). Furthermore, control theory emphasizes rationality in criminal behavior and thus does not explain impulsive or passion-related crimes.

The faults notwithstanding, many feel control theories show the greatest promise of social process theoretical approaches to explaining crime.

Labeling Theory

Labeling theory concentrates on the interactive elements of deviance, taking into consideration not only criminal behavior and the offender but also those who define the situation and the person as deviant or criminal. Two primary aspects of the labeling theory are the symbolic interactionist theory and the looking-glass self concept.

Symbolic interactionist theory postulates that all reality is grounded in the symbols we use to talk about it; as sociologist William Thomas put it, "If men define situations as real, they are real in their consequences."[39] A typical example can be seen in a member of a minority group who may be viewed and therefore labeled as a criminal by the police after being accused of robbing a store, even if he did not. The consequences may be arrest, degradation, and even conviction.

The looking-glass self, put forth by Charles Cooley, assumes that people tend to regard themselves as they are defined by others.[40] Thus an individual seen as antisocial is likely to view himself or herself in the same light. Because people tend to behave in terms of their self-identity, the definition of self is significant in determining behavior. However, it is those who interpret such behavior that establishes whether it is criminal or noncriminal. Explains Edwin Schur:

Human behavior is deviant to the extent that it comes to be viewed as involving a personally discreditable departure from a group's normative expectation, and it elicits interpersonal and collective reactions that serve to "isolate," "treat," "correct," or "punish" individuals engaged in such behavior.[41]

Thus, criminality is defined as such by social groups' response to persons, their behavior, and the results of this response as opposed to the moral weight of the offense itself. In its strictest sense, labeling theory would suggest that such crimes as murder and rape are heinous only because of the label attached to them.

Referring to the labelers as "moral entrepreneurs," Howard Becker describes the labeling process and its effect:

Social groups create deviance by making rules whose infractions constitute deviance, and by applying those rules to particular people and labeling them as outsiders. From this point of view, deviance is not a quality of the act a person commits, but rather a consequence of the application by others of rules and sanctions to an "offender." The deviant is one to whom the label has successfully been applied; deviant behavior is behavior that people so label.[42]

The correlation between labeling and social power is an important element of labeling theory. Theorists contend that this power is most commonly found in the hands of those who control the sources of legitimate authority and the instruments of force in a society, such as lawmakers and their associated interests. Persons who occupy the low end of the social and economic scales tend to be the least powerful in this regard and have no reciprocal power to affix stigmatizing labels to those who have labeled them. Such individuals are limited essentially to trying to defend themselves in this uneven distribution of power as best they can. This interpretation is supported by studies that indicate that lower-class members, particularly of minority groups, are more likely to be arrested, prosecuted, and given harsher sentences upon conviction than the more favored dominant group members whose interests the criminal justice system represents most.[43]

Although the validity of labeling theory is supported in most academic circles, it does have several shortcomings. Among the most critical are its inability to establish the circumstances that must be present before a person or an act is labeled deviant, the narrowness of its approach, its failure to explain disparities in crime rates, and the disregard for the personal decision making in deviance formation.

Perhaps the major contribution of labeling theory is that it enables us to examine the variables of social power and interpretation as they relate to crime and criminals.

Critical Theory

A prominent sociological approach to explaining racial disparities in criminality is the recent emergence of the social conflict perspective referred to as Marxist, radical, new, or critical criminology.[44] Critical theorists regard crime as an element of the capitalist mode of production whereby all classes engage in crime but are treated differently by the system of criminal justice.

According to this theory, racial differences in criminality are explicated "in terms of the historically conditioned relation of different ethnic groups to the means of production."[45] While all members of society generally have the same basic interests and values, conflict characterizes the relationship between those who own the means of production (the ruling class) and those employed in production or unemployed (the working and lower classes). Crime then becomes a reactive measure, particularly to those groups in the least favorable position in the production process.

Thus, critical theory views the high rate of street or lower-class crime as the result of underemployment, unemployment, and demoralization, as well as capitalist exploitation, victimization, and racism. Because the laws are a product of wealthy capitalists, their socially harmful "crimes" are generally not defined as such by the criminal justice system.

Critical criminologists reject crime as defined by law and focus instead on those socially harmful behaviors that are crimes against basic human rights such as the "crimes" of the ruling class where the lower class is victimized through exploitation and discrimination. They posit that the underlying reasons for conventional crime are contradictions in the economic system of capitalism and that only the overthrow of such a system and the establishment of a socialist state will solve the problem of crime.

Much criticism has been leveled at critical theory. That relevant to this book includes the failure of this approach to link discrimination and deprivation to the crime rate of minority groups, the unexplained intragroup disparities in criminality, and the inexplicable differences in crime between racial and ethnic groups that have been similarly victimized and discriminated against. Other shortcomings of critical theory are its predictability, disregard for objective reality, and its overdramatization in stating the obvious.

Radical or critical criminology nevertheless must be considered sound in its interpretation of the capitalist system and its relationship to street crime and therefore the minority and lower-class communities to which most such crime is attributable. Furthermore, this perspective encompasses a historical context to the study of criminality and the class conflict that may be responsible for it.

SOCIOECONOMIC THEORIES OF CRIME

In addition to more formal sociological theories of criminal behavior, sociologists have applied a number of other theories to crime in relation to the socioeconomic system. These propositions are perhaps the most applicable to the crime of minorities compared to general crime theories because these groups tend to be overrepresented in socioeconomic circumstances believed to be most conducive to criminality. We shall examine four of the more useful socioeconomic explanations of crime.

Social Class

The correlation between social class and criminality has been the subject of debate and study for many years. Traditionally criminologists have believed that crime is primarily a lower-class phenomenon that by implication often links crime with minority groups. This view holds that those at the bottom of the social structure ladder have the greatest incentive to commit criminal acts because they are unable conventionally to obtain the desired goods and life-styles of higher class societal members and because they are more likely to participate in violent crimes as a response to their rage and frustration against the greater society. The lower-class association with crime has been supported by official statistics that consistently indicate a disproportionately higher rate of crime in low-income, high-poverty inner-city areas than suburban or higher-class areas,[46] as well as self-report data in which researchers have generally concluded that lower-class youths are more likely than other-class youths to be labeled and processed as delinquents.[47]

The primary criticism of using official data to interpret class differences in criminal activity is that such statistics may be more of a reflection of differential treatment within the criminal justice system than actual crime rate differences. Perhaps the strongest support for this position is the work of Charles Tittle and colleagues, who concluded after a review of thirty-five studies on the relationship between social class and crime that little, if any, evidence exists supporting the lower-class theory of crime and that official statistics likely reflect a class bias in lower-class processing.[48]

Recent research has tended to be inconsistent on the class and crime controversy. One of the most widely noted arguments for the existence of a class and crime interrelation can be seen in the work of Delbert Elliot and Suzanne Ageton.[49] Using a national sample of 1,726 youngsters ages 11 to 17 and a complex self-report system, the researchers found that lower-class youths were much more likely than their middle-class counterparts to engage in serious offenses such as robbery, sexual assault, and vandalism; that lower-class youths were significantly more likely than those of the middle class to have committed many serious property and personal crimes; and that when lower- and middle-class youths are compared for serious delinquent acts, lower-class youths are considerably more delinquent. Conversely, a prominent study by Michael Hindelang, Travis Hirschi, and Joseph Weis concluded that no relationship exists between social class and crime, whether the form of measurement was official or self-report data.[50]

Social class as a measure of criminal activity is inadequate on the whole because it is both too broad to be able to account for all criminality and too narrow to explain criminal behavior that likely exists due to a wide range of societal and individual variables.

Economic Deprivation

The relationship between economic factors and crime has been well documented. Unemployment, poverty, urbanization, and relative deprivation have been shown to be causal in higher rates of crime among those living under such conditions than not. Studies by Cohen[51] and B. Lander[52] found that low-income urban residents living in rented, crowded homes and neighborhoods commit a disproportionate number of criminal acts, and Dutch criminologist Willem Bonger postulated that crime is caused by poverty.[53]

Some researchers have presented evidence linking unemployment with criminality.[54] Others have suggested that poor or unemployed people commit more crimes because they are more relatively deprived—in other words, some people violate the law because of the discrepancy between their expectations in a society of much wealth and material goods and their capabilities to achieve these things themselves.[55]

That economic deprivation in one sense or another has an influence on crime does appear to have some foundation. Violent crime and most property offenses in America are largely a product of the urban lower classes, at least statistically, with low-income blacks and other ethnic minorities particularly overrepresented.

Yet economic theories of crime are not without their drawbacks. For example, many crimes, such as white collar, are committed by higher-income individuals but often go undetected. Also most people of lower or strained economic circumstances remain law-abiding citizens, whereas many crimes, such as murder and rape, are committed regardless of the economic status of the offender. Moreover, differential enforcement of the law, even within the same class, may be more responsible for the disproportionate representation of certain segments of the population such as minorities where it concerns economic deprivation than their actual representation in the criminal population.

In short, although economic factors are likely prominent in criminal activity, current criminological research pays far too much attention to the lack of economic means in criminal behavior and far less to the variables of greed and the significance of economic gain as a motivation for criminality without regard to social class or economic status.

Breakdown in the Family Structure

An explanation of crime among juveniles and, indirectly, adults that has received much attention over the years concerns the breakdown of traditional family relations. This point of view holds that delinquency or crime is a product of changes in the stability of the family, an important subfacet of social control.

The broken home theory is the most often studied aspect of family structure in relation to criminality. A broken home is generally defined as one in which one or both parents are missing due to desertion, divorce, or death, thereby leaving the child(ren) without adequate family stability, guidance, and supervision, which is linked to their becoming involved in delinquent or criminal activity. A number of prominent researchers, such as the Gluecks[56] and F. Ivan Nye,[57] have argued that a larger proportion of delinquents than nondelinquents come from broken homes. Other studies, however, have presented strong evidence to contradict this correlation.[58]

Broken home theories are generally ineffective in explaining crime and delinquency, for they do not explain why those from stable homes and backgrounds fall into criminal patterns or why those from broken homes lead conventional lives. The broken home at best can be viewed as a factor that might account for some antisocial behavior. Even then, this usually occurs only when combined with other factors (such as peer group pressure or role models).

Another related facet of family structure breakdown associated with delinquency is parental supervision, or lack of it. This thesis assumes that when parents allow children to "get away with anything," delinquency is often the result. There is some support for the parental supervision theory. Recently W. Gove and R. Crutchfield associated boys from broken homes or homes suffering from poor marital relations with higher rates of delinquency.[59] Other studies have linked variables in parental supervision such as lack of discipline and affection with delinquent behavior.[60]

These types of theories on delinquency or criminality cannot be sufficiently tested to draw any reasonable conclusions.

Racism and Minority Crime

Fundamental to the social and economic perspective on minority crime is the underlying theme of racism. As we discovered in chapter 1, most minority groups have been the victims of racism throughout our country's history. Much of this has taken place in the form of discrimination, economic suppression, and violence aimed at racial and ethnic minorities.

That racism has led to crime and violence against minorities; it has also been instrumental in the criminality of minorities. This theory posits that from the standpoint of historical, social, and economic racism (and therefore conflict), the disadvantaged minority has not only had very good teachers in dispensing criminal and violent behavior but that because of the fabric of a society that has draped the minority in a seemingly endless blanket of subjugation, discrimination, humiliation, degradation, poverty, and denied opportunities, criminal behavior has been an inevitable consequence.[61]

There are those who would argue that racism alone cannot explain the high rate of minority crime, particularly when some minority groups, such as blacks and Hispanics, show substantially higher rates of criminality than others, such as Asians. Can it be shown conclusively that blacks, for example, have experienced racism to a proportionately greater degree than Asians to account for crime rate differentials between them?

A likely explanation is that while racism is certainly not solely responsible for minority crime, it is equally certain that as an intrinsic

part of the American heritage, its effect has been indelible in the behavior of those most victimized by it. In other words, although minority crime may be a product of many societal and personal conditions,
it is the minority's general place in society as established over centuries
that is the undercoating of his or her circumstances. Differential rates
of crime among minority groups may be less a matter of disparity in
racism or discriminatory treatment than a difference in subsequent
adjustment and reaction by racial and ethnic minority groups to its
effects. In sum, the correlation between racism and crime cannot be
dismissed for its place in causation theory.

There is a paucity of etiological studies of ethnic minority crime and
its causation. Rather, most research seeking to explain the criminality
of minorities comes from general biological, psychological, and sociological explanations of crime that are then often applied to minority
group members, most notably blacks and Hispanics, or members of the
lower classes, in which these and other minority groups are disproportionately represented. Biological theories are weakest in this respect;
sociological perspectives offer the most solid foundation. Yet overall,
most theories of crime causation fall short in sufficiently explaining minority crime or, for that matter, the crime of all people in society. Instead, these theories are successful only in explaining certain patterns
and types of crime for certain individuals or groups but not all criminal
behavior at all times and clearly not that of all participants in crime.
Much more research is needed in studying etiologically and empirically
the individual and collective criminality of America's racial and ethnic
minorities.

NOTES

1. Cesare Lombroso, *Criminal Man* (New York: Putnam, 1911).

2. Charles Goring, *The English Convict: A Statistical Study* (1913; Montclair,
N.J.: Patterson Smith, 1972).

3. Ernest A. Hooton, *Crime and the Man* (Cambridge: Harvard University
Press, 1939).

4. William H. Sheldon, *Varieties of Temperament* (New York: Harper & Row,
1942).

5. Sheldon Glueck and Eleanor T. Glueck, *Physique and Delinquency* (New
York: Harper & Row, 1956).

6. Vicki Pollock, Sarnoff A. Mednick, and William F. Gabrielli, Jr., "Crime
Causation: Biological Theories," in Sanford H. Kadish, ed., *Encyclopedia of Crime
and Justice*, vol. 1 (New York: Free Press, 1983), p. 309.

7. A. A. Sandberg, G. F. Koepf, T. Ishiara, and T. S. Hauschka, "An XYY
Human Male," *Lancet* 262 (1961): 488–89; Saleem Shah and Loren Roth, "Bio-
logical and Psychophysiological Factors in Criminality," in Daniel Glazer, ed.,
Handbook of Criminology (Chicago: Rand McNally, 1974), p. 135.

8. Herman A. Witkin et al., "XYY and XXY Men: Criminality and Aggression," in Sarnoff A. Mednick and Karl O. Christiansen, eds., *Biosocial Bases of Criminal Behavior* (New York: Gardner Press, 1977), pp. 165–87; see also L. Ellis, "Genetics and Criminal Behavior," *Criminology* 20 (1982): 43–66; R. G. Fox, "The XYY Offender: A Modern Myth?" *Journal of Criminal Law, Criminology and Political Science* 62 (1971): 59–73.

9. Pollock, Mednick, and Gabrielli, "Crime Causation: Biological Theories."

10. Ibid.

11. Barry Hutchings and Sarnoff A. Mednick, "Criminality in Adoptees and Their Adoptive and Biological Parents: A Pilot Study," in Mednick and Christiansen, *Biosocial Bases*, pp. 127–41.

12. Sarnoff Mednick, William Gabrielli, and Barry Hutchings, "Genetic Influences in Criminal Behavior: Evidence from an Adoption Cohort," in Katherine Teilman Van Dusen and Sarnoff A. Mednick, eds., *Perspective Studies of Crime and Delinquency* (Boston: Kluver-Nighoff, 1983), pp. 39–57.

13. C. Robert Cloninger, quoted in Andrea Dorfman, "The Criminal Mind: Body Chemistry and Nutrition May Lie at the Roots of Crime," *Science Digest* 92 (1984): 44.

14. Pollock, Mednick, and Gabrielli, "Crime Causation: Biological Theories."

15. Ibid.; Sarnoff A. Mednick and Jan Volavka, "Biology and Crime," in Norval Morris and Michael Tonry, eds., *Crime and Justice: An Annual Review of Research*, vol. 2 (Chicago: University of Chicago Press, 1980) pp. 85–158.

16. Harold R. Holzman, "Learning Disabilities and Juvenile Delinquency: Biological and Sociological Theories," in C. R. Jeffrey, ed., *Biology and Crime* (Beverly Hills, Calif.: Sage Publications, 1979), pp. 77–86.

17. H. D. Kletschka, "Violent Behavior Associated with Brain Tumors," *Minnesota Medicine* 49 (1966): 1853–1855.

18. See, for examples, Dorfman, "The Criminal Mind"; Mednick and Volavka, "Biology and Crime"; J. Kerschner and W. Hawke, "Megavitamins and Learning Disorders: A Controlled Double-blind Experiment," *Journal of Nutrition* 109 (1979): 819–26.

19. Sigmund Freud, *New Introductory Lectures on Psychoanalysis* (New York: W. W. Norton, 1933).

20. August Aichorn, *Wayward Youth* (New York: Viking Press, 1935).

21. Ibid.; Donald H. Russell and G. P. Harper, "Who Are Our Assaultive Juveniles? A Study of 100 Cases," *Journal of Forensic Sciences* 18 (1973): 387–93.

22. Joseph F. Sheley, *America's "Crime Problem": An Introduction to Criminology* (Belmont, Calif.: Wadsworth Publishing Co., 1985), p. 202.

23. Ibid.

24. G. P. Waldo and S. Dinitz, "Personality Attributes of the Criminal: An Analysis of Research Studies, 1950–65," *Journal of Research on Crime and Delinquency* 4 (1967): 185–201.

25. D. C. Gibbons, *Society, Crime and Criminal Careers*, 3d ed. (Englewood Cliffs, N.J.: Prentice-Hall, 1977).

26. See, for example, William Healy and Augusta Bronner, *Delinquency and Criminals: Their Making and Unmaking* (New York: Macmillan, 1926).

27. Arthur Jensen, *Bias in Mental Testing* (New York: Free Press, 1979).

28. James Q. Wilson and Richard Herrnstein, *Crime and Human Nature* (New

York: Simon & Schuster, 1985); see also Arthur Jensen, "How Much Can We Boost IQ and Scholastic Achievement?" *Harvard Educational Review* 39 (1969): 1–123.

29. Sandra Scarr and Richard Weinberg, "IQ Test Performance of Black Children Adopted by White Families," *American Psychologist* 31 (1976): 726–39.

30. Travis Hirschi and Michael J. Hindelang, "Intelligence and Delinquency: A Revisionist Review," *American Sociological Review* 42 (1977): 571–86.

31. Emile Durkheim, *The Rules of the Sociological Method,* trans. Sarah A. Solovay and John H. Mueller, ed. George E. G. Catlin (New York: Free Press, 1895, 1966).

32. Robert K. Merton, *Social Theory and Social Structure* (Glencoe, Ill.: Free Press, 1957).

33. Martin R. Haskell and Lewis Yablonsky, *Juvenile Delinquency,* 2d ed. (Chicago: Rand McNally, 1978), p. 397.

34. Sheley, *American's "Crime Problem,"* p. 220.

35. Albert Cohen, *Delinquent Boys* (New York: Free Press, 1955).

36. Richard A. Cloward and Lloyd E. Ohlin, *Delinquency and Opportunity: A Theory of Delinquent Gangs* (New York: Free Press, 1960).

37. Edwin H. Sutherland, *Principles of Criminology* (Philadelphia: Lippincott, 1939).

38. Travis Hirschi, *Causes of Delinquency* (Berkeley: University of California, 1969), p. 34.

39. William I. Thomas, *The Unadjusted Girl: With Cases and Standpoint for Behavior Analysis* (New York: Harper & Row, 1923).

40. Charles H. Cooley, *Human Nature and the Social Order* (New York: Scribner's, 1902).

41. Edwin Schur, *Labeling Deviant Behavior* (New York: Harper & Row, 1972), p. 21.

42. Howard Becker, *Outsiders, Studies in the Sociology of Deviance* (New York: Macmillan, 1963), p. 9.

43. Christy Visher, "Gender, Police Arrest Decisions, and Notions of Chivalry," *Criminology* 21 (1983): 5–28; Marjorie Zatz, "Race, Ethnicity and Determinate Sentencing," *Criminology* 22 (1984): 147–71.

44. Gresham M. Sykes, "The Rise of Critical Criminology," *Journal of Criminal Law and Criminology* 65 (1974): 206–13; Thomas Bernard, "The Distinction between Conflict and Radical Criminology," *Journal of Criminal Law and Criminology* 72 (1981): 366–70.

45. Daniel Georges-Abeyie, ed., *The Criminal Justice System and Blacks* (New York: Clark Boardman, 1984), p. 29.

46. Marvin Wolfgang, "Delinquency in Two Birth Cohorts," in Van Dusen and Mednick, *Perspective Studies,* pp. 7–17.

47. See, for example, James Short and F. Ivan Nye, "Reported Behavior as a Criterion of Deviant Behavior," *Social Problems* 5 (1958): 207–13.

48. Charles Tittle, Wayne Villemez, and Douglas Smith, "The Myth of Social Class and Criminality: An Empirical Assessment of the Empirical Evidence," *American Sociological Review* 43 (1978): 643–56.

49. Delbert Elliot and Suzanne Ageton, "Reconciling Race and Class Differences in Self-Reported and Official Estimates of Delinquency," *American Socio-*

logical Review 45 (1980): 95–110. See also Delbert Elliot and David Huizinga, "Social Class and Delinquent Behavior in a National Youth Panel," *Criminology* 21 (1983): 149–77.

50. Michael Hindelang, Travis Hirschi, and Joseph Weis, *Measuring Delinquency* (Beverly Hills: Sage Publications, 1981), p. 196.

51. Cohen, *Delinquent Boys*.

52. B. Lander, *Toward an Understanding of Juvenile Delinquency* (New York: Columbia University Press, 1954).

53. Willem A. Bonger, *Criminality and Economic Conditions*, trans. Henry P. Horton (Boston: Little, Brown, 1916).

54. Richard B. Freedman, "Crime and Unemployment," in James Q. Wilson, ed., *Crime and Public Policy* (San Francisco: ICS Press, 1983), pp. 89–106.

55. Leo Radzinowicz and Joan King, *The Growth of Crime: The International Experience* (New York: Basic Books, 1977).

56. Sheldon Glueck and Eleanor T. Glueck, *Unraveling Juvenile Delinquency* (New York: Commonwealth Fund, 1950), p. 122.

57. F. Ivan Nye, *Family Relationships and Delinquent Behavior* (New York: John Wiley & Sons, 1958), pp. 43–48.

58. Charles J. Browning, "Differential Impact of Family Organization on Male Adolescents," *Social Forces* 8 (1960): 37–44; L. Rosen, "The 'Broken Home' and Male Delinquency," in M. E. Wolfgang, L. Savitz, and N. Johnson, eds., *Sociology of Crime and Delinquency*, 2nd ed. (New York: John Wiley & Sons, 1970).

59. W. R. Gove and R. D. Crutchfield, "The Family and Juvenile Delinquency," *Sociology Quarterly* 23 (1982): 301–19.

60. Browning, "Differential Impact of Family"; William McCord, Joan McCord, and Irving Zola, *Origins of Crime* (New York: Columbia University Press, 1959).

61. For more on this position, see Robert Elias, *The Politics of Victimization* (New York: Oxford University Press, 1986), pp. 95–96.

III

CONTEMPORARY ISSUES IN CRIMINALITY AMONG MINORITY GROUPS

5

The Dynamics of Black Crime

Black crime is a problem of serious proportions. Blacks have considerably higher overall rates of arrest, conviction, and imprisonment than whites or other minority groups. Although black people make up only 12 percent of the nation's population, they account for more than 25 percent of all persons arrested. This percentage rises to blacks' comprising more than 33 percent of the Crime Index arrestees and a staggering 47 percent of those arrested for violent offenses.[1] One study estimated that blacks living in cities of more than 250,000 people stood a 51 percent chance of ever being arrested for a Crime Index offense compared to a white rate of only 14 percent.[2] Evidence suggests that these types of discrepancies have existed for decades, appearing as far back as the U.S. Census of 1910.[3] This chapter will examine some of the correlates of blacks and criminality.

INTRARACIAL NATURE OF BLACK CRIME

Not only are blacks disproportionately likely to be offenders of crime, but they also are disproportionately represented as victims of crime. Victimization data reveal that black crime is primarily intraracial. According to the NCS, in 1985 84 percent of the violent crimes perpetrated against blacks were committed by black offenders.[4] Hence black America faces the worst plight of both worlds of criminal involvement.

Black Victims

It has long been a misconception that whites are most likely to be the victims of black crime, to the point that many whites are irrationally afraid of blacks. Alvin Poussaint, a black psychiatrist, points this out when he says, somewhat irritably: "It happens to me. Whites react to blacks as if they were potential thieves and criminals."[5]

Yet the reality is that black crime against whites is relatively low. In *What the Negro Can Do About Crime,* the authors comment: "If white Americans fear crime and violence, that fear is even more overwhelming for black Americans, since most of them live in the midst of it."[6] The evidence supports this contention. In 1985, blacks were victims of crimes of violence and household crimes nationwide at a rate higher than whites or any other racial group. Black males had the highest victimization rates for violent crimes when race and sex were considered.[7]

That blacks have been most often victimized by other blacks can be seen even when black violence was in theory directed toward the white establishment, such as the black-initiated riots that occurred in many cities during the late 1960s. Most of the looting, destruction of property, and physical confrontations took place in urban areas where fellow blacks bore the brunt of the personal and economic consequences.

A recent "Victim Risk Supplement" to the NCS found that blacks were more likely to feel unsafe at home at night than whites by nearly 2 to 1.[8] Although black victims reported personal crime victimization to the police at a slightly higher rate than whites in 1985, blacks not reporting crime because they believed the police would be "inefficient, ineffective, insensitive," or not care to be bothered, was nearly twice as high as white victims not reporting crime for the same reasons.[9] This lack of faith in the response of the criminal justice system to crime in the black community is seen as an important indicator of why so much black-participant crime goes unreported and why many black victims feel they must fend for themselves, thereby escalating the intraracial violence.

Poor blacks are especially disproportionately victimized. They must contend with the crime itself and the often devastating economic impact. Santa Clara (California) County deputy district attorney Ulysses Beasley illustrates this dilemma:

If someone from an affluent upper middle class white neighborhood has their car or television stolen, at worst, the victim suffers a major inconvenience. The matter is reported to the police and the insurance company, and is often eventually "taken care of." Contrast the black woman raising a family in the ghetto who barely manages to pay her bills for absolute necessities and whose one luxury in life is a television which she is paying off on time. When that television is stolen and the payments remain, the problem is rarely "taken care of." It continues to be felt.[10]

Black Fratricide

Black-on-black violence is especially alarming in homicide statistics. In the United States, most notably in lower-class urban neighborhoods, "brother is killing brother in a kind of racial fratricide."[11] More than 40 percent of the total murder victims in the country are black, and nearly 95 percent of such homicides were perpetrated by blacks.[12] The likelihood is greater for blacks than whites to be murdered as a result of an argument with a family member or acquaintance than as a result of a robbery or street crime.

Other figures on black homicide are equally frightening. Black men face a 1 in 21 chance of being murdered during their lifetimes compared to a 1 in 131 chance for white men. A black female stands a 1 in 186 chance of becoming a murder victim; the chance is considerably less for a white woman—1 in 606.[13]

The leading cause of death among black males between ages 15 and 24 is murder by other blacks. The murder rate for this age group of black males is seven times greater than that of the greater population. More than one of every three such black deaths is attributed to homicide. Recently some health officials contended that the rate of murder among black youths is so staggering that it should be considered a public health issue.[14]

PATTERNS IN BLACK SELF-DESTRUCTIVE BEHAVIOR

Another disturbing pattern of black criminality-victimization that is drawing the attention of researchers is an apparent trend toward self-destruction by black Americans, "who are killing themselves—directly or indirectly—much more often than their white counterparts."[15] Social scientist Catherine Smallwood-Murchison points out that "alcoholism, drug addiction, suicide, homicide and avoidable accidents all show the ever-rising incidence of [self-destruction] in the black community and its disproportionate share compared to society as a whole."[16] Federal statistics support this. Twice as many blacks per capita die from cirrhosis of the liver, generally associated with alcoholism, than whites. Nearly seven times as many black men and ten times as many black women are slain annually compared to their respective white counterparts.

Although black Americans are generally less likely than whites to commit suicide, between 1980 and 1984 the number of black suicides rose 9.5 percent compared to 8.6 percent for white suicides. In 1984, 31.6 percent more black men and 17.3 percent more black women died as a result of accidents than did white men and women. Many experts believe that some of the victims hastened their death by placing themselves in danger or failing to avoid it. According to Smallwood-Murchison, "Coupled with the rising [black] suicide and homicide rates, there is also a rise in . . . [deaths where] an individual plays an indirect, covert, partial or unconscious role in [his or her] own demise."[17]

Sociologists contend that self-destructive, aberrant behavior in black communities nationwide has reached crisis proportions. This pattern of self-destruction has been linked to such traditional explanations as prejudice, discrimination, and poverty and more current ones such as a breakdown in the family structure. Some experts suggest that social and economic improvements are to blame for self-destruction by blacks. In general, this is seen as manifesting itself through the greater expectations blacks have today as better opportunities for gains they were once denied present themselves. This makes many who are unable to capitalize on these improved conditions feel inadequate, frustrated, and disenchanted with their lives and society. Conversely, some blacks who succeed are also victimized by self-destruction as a result of the pressures and change in lifestyle with social and economic gain.

BLACKS IN CORRECTIONAL FACILITIES

The overrepresentation of blacks in arrest and conviction rates for crimes is clearly reflected in their proportion of the general incarcerated population. Black adults comprise approximately 11 percent of the nation's adult population. Yet according to the Annual Survey of Jails as of June 30, 1986, 41 percent of the persons held in local jails in the United States were black compared to 58 percent white.[18]

The disproportion of blacks is equally as alarming in state and federal prisons. U.S. Department of Justice data for December 31, 1984 reveal that 47 percent of the state prisoners and 33 percent of the federal prisoners in the U.S. were black.[19] Overall, blacks comprised 46 percent of the prison population. Black males accounted for 45 percent of the nation's male prisoners, while black females represented 48 percent of the female prisoners nationwide at the end of 1984.[20]

Blacks are about 8 times more likely to be imprisoned than whites or other minorities. The likelihood of black males' being imprisoned is at least 8 times that of white males or those of other ethnic groups and 204 times that of white females. Black females are 8 times more likely to be imprisoned than white females and face at least a 6 times greater likelihood than other minority group females. During their lifetime, black male natives are 6 to 7 times more likely to serve time in prison than white males born in the United States. Similarly, black female natives are 6 to 8 times more likely to be imprisoned within their lifetimes than white females.[21]

Black juveniles held in juvenile custody facilities also exhibit a high rate in proportion to their population. Blacks under the age of 18 account for approximately 13 percent of the nation's juvenile population. On February 1, 1983, more than 30 percent of the residents of public and private juvenile custody facilities were black.[22]

These figures on black incarceration are not meant to suggest that the differences in black crime and that of whites and other groups are actually so exaggerated; some evidence indicates that racial discrimination within the criminal justice system may account for higher incarceration rates for blacks.[23] Rather, this is meant to present further evidence of the severity of the problem the black community is facing in its involvement in crime and the system of criminal justice.

THE BLACK-WHITE CRIME DIFFERENTIAL

Despite the apparent differences in crime rates between blacks and whites, the two racial groups for which most comparisons in racial disparities are made, many scholars contend that black and white crime rates are not dissimilar when the variables of sex, age, and socioeconomic conditions are constant. There is much evidence to refute this school of thought, however.

A number of studies indicate that although the differences between black and white crime rates are reduced somewhat when comparable background factors are present, blacks still maintain a higher crime rate than whites. Marvin Wolfgang's Philadelphia study of criminal homicide revealed that black men between the ages of 20 and 24 had a rate of conviction more than twenty-five times greater than white men of the same age group. Wolfgang found a similar disparity between the two racial groups upon comparing those with similar occupations.[24] In a study of forcible rape, criminologist Menachem Amir and author of *Patterns in Forcible Rape* found that when comparing black and white rapists who had similar occupations, the black rate of rape was four times that of whites.[25]

A study that compared the contact blacks and whites had as juveniles with the police revealed the black percentage to be 50 as opposed to 29 percent for whites.[26] When similar social classes of the two groups were analyzed, blacks still showed a greater likelihood of having had police contact. In fact, blacks of a higher class were shown to have had police contact at the same percentage of whites of the lower class.[27]

Charles Silberman, author of the prominent book *Criminal Violence, Criminal Justice*, applied the racial differential in crime rates to blacks and Hispanics of comparable socioeconomic status, groups that are disproportionately represented in crime figures.[28] His findings showed that blacks are more likely to be arrested and convicted than Hispanics:

- In 1973 in Arizona, the number of black prisoners was 5 times greater in relation to population size than the number of Mexican-American prisoners.

- There were 3.4 times as many first-time black prisoners in the Utah state prison in 1972 as Chicano prisoners, with more than 5 times as many blacks in prison a second time.

- In New Mexico, the number of black inmates in 1973 was almost 3 times that of Mexican-American prisoners with respect to population size.

Silberman found the pattern to be constant over time, noting that "analysis of data assembled by the 1931 Wickersham Commission suggests that there were large disparities between black and Mexican-American arrest and conviction rates for violent crimes in the 1920s as well."[29]

Thus, the differential in black crime rates in relation to whites and other racial and ethnic groups is still evident even when similar variables in background are present, although evidence exists that this disparity in black-white rates of crime is narrowed when background variables are similar.[30]

EXPLAINING THE RACIAL DISPARITY

Racial differences in the crime rate have most often been explained in terms of black-white differences; hence, it is virtually impossible to account through studies for the disparity between black rates of crime and those of other ethnic minorities, although the causes may in fact be similar to black-white differentials. Prior to the availability of victimization data, many liberal-radical researchers attacked UCR data as simply representative of differential treatment of blacks in the criminal justice system. Most criminologists today, however, dismiss such notions as solely being responsible for racial differences in the prevalence of crime.

The Black Experience in America Theory

Few can agree on the reasons for the racial disparity in crime. Some relate it to the historical roots of the black experience in this country, which certainly has done much to rob black people of their family life, identity, and culture and thus a normal life as a group. In *American Violence and Public Policy*, James Comer argues that the enslavement of black people left in them a bitter taste, made more bitter by racism and lack of opportunity. The result is a combination of anger, rage, and negative self-images. Writes Comer of black violence:

In reaction to failure, the most vibrant and reactive often become disruptive and violent in and out of schools both individually and in groups or gangs. Neighborhoods and communities of adequately functioning families are then overwhelmed by the reactive and most troubled individuals and families. Models of violence and other troublesome behavior for children abound in relatives, friends, and neighbors unsuccessful in previous generations.[31]

Comer regards the intraracial aspect of black violence as a reaction to being unable to cope with the society at large or relate to black and white leaders and institutional accomplishments.

Silberman also views black criminality in terms of their historical mistreatment in American society, which he describes as differing from any other American racial group. He contends that "black Americans have discovered that the fear runs the other way, that whites are intimidated by their very presence; it would be hard to overestimate what an extraordinary liberating force this discovery is . . . 350 years of festering hatred has come spilling out."[32]

Using the colonial model to analyze black violence, Frantz Fanon, a black psychoanalyst and author of *The Wretched of the Earth*, explained such violence as politically necessary for black people seeking their independence and personally necessary for "colored natives" striving to be "men."[33] Fanon argued that the degradation the natives endured as a result of the systematic violence of colonialism made "psychic wholeness" possible only through violent acts against the white masters and rulers whom they desired to replace.

Robert Staples's examination of black crime addresses the main features of colonialism as they apply to American society and economic exploitation of black people. He correlates the black rate of crime to the fact that

the racist fabric of white America denies blacks a basic humanity which permits the violations of their right to equal justice under the law. In America, the right to justice is an inalienable right; for blacks, it is still a privilege to be granted at the caprice and goodwill of whites who control the machinery of the legal system and the agents of social control.[34]

Conflict Theories

Conflict theories of racial disparities have typically emphasized the disproportionate rate of black arrests as the result of discriminate treatment by law enforcement. These theories advance that the laws represent the best interests of the segments of society that have the power to mold public policy; those who are affected most by the criminal justice system (blacks, Hispanics, the lower class, and others) are in the

least powerful position to shape public policies and therefore are most
likely to be overrepresented in arrest and crime figures.

Richard Quinney held that "the differences in arrest rates are not,
however, due entirely to the fact that [blacks] may be involved more
than whites in law-violating behavior, but that in similar situations
[blacks] are more likely than whites to be apprehended."[35] Conflict
theorists William Chambliss and Robert Seidman argue that there is a
highly selective system in the administration of the criminal law with
a wide amount of discretion. This results in a "systematic bias in law
enforcement."[36] The researchers contend that because of such a bias,
blacks face a greater likelihood of being scrutinized and thus are more
observed in any law violations as well as arrested should they be caught
under suspicious circumstances.

Conflict theorists rarely deny outright a relationship between race
and criminal participation; rather they prefer to address those "power-
related differentials" in law enforcement as they relate to the disproportionate involvement of the lower-class minority.

Social and Economic Theories

Racial differences in crime rates are also expressed in social and economic theoretical propositions. James Wilson and Richard Herrnstein,
coauthors of *Crime and Human Nature*, cite three prominent socioeconomic theories that seek to explain racial disparities in criminal involvement:

1. Blacks more than whites face a greater shortage in economic opportunities;
   hence they resort to crime in greater numbers.
2. Black family life does not promote sufficiently conventional norms and values.
3. The higher rate of black crime is a product of many blacks' acquiring through
   experience hostilities toward the outer world and its value system.[37]

Another major socioeconomic theory of racial differentials in crime is
Marvin Wolfgang and Franco Ferracuti's subculture of violence theory.
The authors advance that the black experience is largely responsible for
this violent subculture in inner-city black ghettos where violence is seen
as an answer for daily encounters. They further propose:

There is reason to agree . . . that whatever may be the learned responses and
social conditions contributing to criminality, persons visibly identified and socially labeled as [blacks] . . . appear to possess them in considerably higher
proportions than do persons labeled white. Our subculture of violence thesis

would, therefore, expect to find . . . [extensive] learning of, resort to, and criminal display of the violence value among minority groups such as [blacks].[38]

Further studies have supported the existence of a subculture of violence.[39]

Genetics and Black Crime

Perhaps the most controversial explanation for the high rate of black crime is genetic inferiority. The plausibility of this approach is highly questionable. To suggest genetic differences in racial groups is logical; after all, racial makeup is a matter of genetics. To link this with crime rates, however, is to imply that heredity predisposes some to criminality more than others.

Wilson and Herrnstein seem to support the genetic approach to black criminality. They refer to "constitutional" differences between blacks and whites—that is, differences "present at or soon after birth that influence the behavioral patterns during childhood development."[40] These differences, they suggest, are in body type, personality, and IQ scores. The implication is that blacks are deficient or abnormal in these areas, and these abnormalities can then be associated with their high rate of crime.

Citing research that supports this contention, the authors hold that "if blacks are more likely to have an impulsive temperament or a somewhat lower measured IQ, these traits may be the result of prenatal care as well as inheritance."[41] They further link genetic factors to the black male vulnerability to "changing circumstances, such as the greater availability of handguns, alterations in economic opportunities, or the pressures of racial animosity."[42] Although they seem to recognize the environmental factors in black criminality (such as the accessibility of weapons), they regard genes and environment as mutually exclusive. When they do interact, the implication is that genetics weigh heavier in crime causation.

This approach has major problems. For example, it does not account for the essentially equal access whites have to guns. Nor does it explain the higher crime rates of whites in white-collar crime. The genetic explanation of racial differentials in crime rates cannot be considered adequate.

CRITICISM OF THEORIES ON RACIAL DIFFERENTIALS IN CRIME

Most etiological theories on racial and ethnic disparities in rates of crime are openly suspect. They focus almost entirely on black-white differences in crime rates, generally ignoring explanations that account for other ethnic group differentials, such as the disproportionately high Native American rate of crime or the disproportionately low rate of Asian crime as compared to other groups. Given acknowledged differences in background and cultural variables from one racial group to the next, one cannot presume that black-white differentials in crime can account for the differentials in other American ethnic groups on the high and low end of crime rates.

A second criticism lies in associating black crime with the black experience in this country. Although it would be naive to suggest that slavery, racism, deprivation, and related factors American blacks have uniquely endured have not had at least some negative effect on behavior within this group, the fault of this theory is that it cannot adequately explain why blacks should be affected more by their victimization and injustice than other ethnic minorities, such as American Indians and Chinese-Americans, whose history in this country has also been one of considerable hardship.

Socioeconomic theories on the differential criminality of racial groups can be attacked on the premise that they do not account for those who do not suffer from various disadvantages in their social and economic life (such as poverty, minority status) yet still commit crimes.

Hereditary theories of criminality are insufficient in that they can be construed as racist. They also focus too little on environmental variables or the role of discriminatory policies in crime. Nor do they credibly account for criminals who show no biological deficiencies.

A more reasonable approach to racial differences in crime prevalence is that no one explanation can be sufficient; rather, a number of elements likely contribute to this differential, including racism and discrimination, social and economic hardships, subcultural system, and variables related to family life, values, and physical and biological traits. In short, further study is necessary in order to formulate a sound, comprehensive etiology of black-white differences in crime rates.

The seriousness of black involvement in crime in the United States cannot be underscored. Blacks have higher rates of arrest and conviction for criminality than all other ethnic and racial groups, as well as higher rates of victimization. Contrary to popular belief, black-on-black violence, not black violence against white or other groups, accounts for the vast majority of black crime. Two areas of most concern are the highly disproportionate involvement of blacks in violent crime and the apparent trend by blacks toward self-destructive patterns. Current explanations in the rate of criminal participation by blacks fall short of supplying the answers needed to understand this crisis and curtail it.

NOTES

1. U.S. Federal Bureau of Investigation, *Crime in the United States: Uniform Crime Reports 1985* (Washington, D.C.: Government Printing Office, 1986), p. 182.

2. Alfred Blumstein and Elizabeth Graddy, "Prevalence and Recidivism in Index Arrests: A Feedback Model," *Law and Society Review* 16 (1981–1982): 265–90.

3. Gwynn Nettler, *Explaining Crime*, 3d ed. (New York: McGraw-Hill, 1984), p. 137; Marvin E. Wolfgang, "Race and Crime," in H. J. Sklare, ed., *Changing Concepts of Crime and Its Treatment* (London: Pergamon, 1966), p. 46.

4. U.S. Department of Justice, *Criminal Victimization in the United States, 1985: A National Crime Survey Report* (Washington, D.C.: Government Printing Office, 1987), p. 5.

5. David Whitman and Jeannye Thornton, "A Nation Apart," *U.S. News & World Report* (March 17, 1986): 22.

6. J. A. Parker and Allan C. Brownfeld, *What the Negro Can Do about Crime* (New Rochelle, N.Y.: Arlington House, 1974).

7. *National Crime Survey*, pp. 3–4.

8. U.S. Department of Justice, *BJS Data Report, 1986* (Washington, D.C.: Government Printing Office, 1987), p. 27.

9. *National Crime Survey*, pp. 75, 84–85.

10. Ulysses Beasley, "Crime and Its Impact on Minorities," in George Nicholson, Thomas W. Condit, and Stuart Greenbaum, eds., *Forgotten Victims: An Advocate's Anthology* (Sacramento: California District Attorneys Association, 1977), p. 170.

11. Jack E. White, "When Brother Kills Brother," *Time* (September 16, 1985): 32.

12. Ibid.

13. Whitman and Thornton, "A Nation Apart."

14. Terri Minsky, "The Odds on Being Slain—Worse for Young Black Males," *Boston Globe* (February 23, 1984): 1, 47.

15. Gracie Bonds Staples, "Self-Inflicted Death Plagues US Blacks," *Sacramento Bee* (December 8, 1986): A14.

16. Catherine Smallwood-Murchison, quoted in ibid.

17. Ibid.

18. U.S. Department of Justice, *Bureau of Justice Statistics Bulletin: Jail Inmates 1986* (Washington, D.C.: Government Printing Office, 1987), p. 1.

19. U.S. Department of Justice, Bureau of Justice Statistics, *Prisoners in State and Federal Institutions on December 31, 1984* (Washington, D.C.: Government Printing Office, 1987), p. 3.

20. Ibid., pp. 18–19.

21. U.S. Department of Justice, Bureau of Justice Statistics, *The Prevalence of Imprisonment* (Washington, D.C.: Government Printing Office, 1985), pp. 3, 5.

22. U.S. Department of Justice, Office of Juvenile Justice and Delinquency Prevention, *Children in Custody: Advance Report on the 1982 Census of Public Juvenile Facilities* and *Children in Custody: Advance Report on the 1982 Census of Private Juvenile Facilities* (Washington, D.C.: Government Printing Office, 1984).

23. Scott Christianson, "Our Black Prisons," *Crime and Delinquency* 27 (1981): 364–75; Terrence P. Thornberry, "Race, Socioeconomic Status and Sentencing in the Juvenile Justice System," *Journal of Criminal Law and Criminology* 64 (1973): 90–98.

24. Marvin E. Wolfgang, *Patterns in Criminal Homicide* (Philadelphia: University of Pennsylvania Press, 1985), p. 39.

25. Menachem Amir, *Patterns in Forcible Rape* (Chicago: University of Chicago Press, 1971), pp. 69–72.

26. Marvin E. Wolfgang, Robert M. Figlio, and Thorsten Sellin, *Delinquency in a Birth Cohort* (Chicago: University of Chicago Press, 1972).

27. Ibid., p. 55.

28. Charles Silberman, *Criminal Violence, Criminal Justice* (New York: Random House, 1978).

29. Ibid., p. 123.

30. Edward Green, "Race, Social Status, and Criminal Arrest," *American Sociological Review* 35 (1970): 476–90.

31. James P. Comer, "Black Violence and Public Policy," in Lynn Curtis, ed., *American Violence and Public Policy* (New Haven, Conn.: Yale University Press, 1985), p. 80.

32. Silberman, *Criminal Violence,* pp. 153–65.

33. Frantz Fanon, *The Wretched of the Earth* (New York: Grove Press, 1965).

34. Robert Staples, "White Racism, Black Crime, and American Justice: An Application of the Colonial Model to Explain Crime and Race" (paper presented at the International Association of Criminology Conference, Caracas, Venezuela, November 1972).

35. Richard Quinney, *The Social Reality of Crime* (Boston: Little, Brown, 1970), pp. 129–30.

36. William Chambliss and Robert Seidman, *Law, Order, and Power* (Reading, Pa.: Addison-Wesley, 1971), pp. 322–46.

37. James Q. Wilson and Richard J. Herrnstein, *Crime and Human Nature* (New York: Simon & Schuster, 1985).

38. Marvin E. Wolfgang and Franco Ferracuti, *The Subculture of Violence: Toward an Integrated Theory in Criminology* (London: Tavistock, 1967), p. 264.

39. See Neil Alan Weiner and Marvin E. Wolfgang, "The Extent and Character of Violent Crime in America," in Lynn Curtis, ed., *American Violence and Public Policy* (New Haven, Conn.: Yale University Press, 1985), pp. 17–39.

40. Wilson and Herrnstein, *Crime and Human Nature.*

41. Ibid., p. 466.

42. Ibid., p. 472.

6

Hispanics and Crime

Hispanic-Americans are the second largest minority group in the United States, numbering some 7.9 percent of the total population. This percentage would be even larger if the estimated 3 million to 6 million illegal aliens, most of Spanish heritage, were taken into account. Yet in the area of crime and criminal justice, little information exists on this prominent segment of the population. In this chapter, we will explore this problem and what we do know about the relationship between Hispanics and crime.

PROBLEMS OF STUDYING HISPANICS AND CRIMINALITY

The limited research on Hispanic involvement in crime can be attributed to a number of factors. Foremost may be the diversity of the Hispanic community. The U.S. Census categorizes Hispanics or those of "Spanish origin" in four groups: Mexican-Americans or Chicanos, the largest group, and Puerto Ricans, Cubans, and "other," which comprises people from other Latin American Spanish-speaking countries and from Spain. Because of the uniqueness of each group as well as subgroups, it becomes impossible to study all Hispanics as representative of one ethnic or minority group.

A second major problem in research is the inconsistency in defining or categorizing Hispanics in terms of race or ethnicity from one data base to the next. In some instances, they are classified as a racial group; in others, they are an ethnic group. Sometimes Hispanics are referred to as "other" or "nonwhite." In some studies, they are tabulated as either black or white and in other studies as Hispanic and black or white. With such confusing classifications, Hispanic members often become lost in the study of other minority groups or because of comparative difficulties are not studied at all.

Hispanics have not always been recognized as a distinctive racial or ethnic minority in the criminology field, as UCR data show. Only since 1980 has the FBI collected systematic arrest data on people of Hispanic origin. Prior to that, most Hispanics were classified as white. Thus this has had a significant effect historically on scientific accuracy of Hispanic crime—its incidence and etiology.

Another prominent reason to account for the lack of research on the Hispanic community is that many criminologists and sociologists have considered Hispanic involvement in criminality as essentially a mirror image of that of blacks, who have been studied extensively, and thus do not justify individual attention.

Most of the study done on Hispanics focuses almost solely on Mexican-Americans. We know virtually nothing about Puerto Ricans, Cubans, and other Hispanic groups. These dilemmas notwithstanding, a portrait of the Hispanic in relation to criminality has begun to emerge in recent years.

CRIMINALITY OF HISPANICS

Hispanics have a disproportiontely high rate of arrests and convictions; 1,172,609 Hispanics were arrested in 1986.[1] This comprised 12.7 percent of the total arrests, or nearly twice their percentage of the population. For violent crime arrests, the rate was even higher: 14.7 percent. Although the Hispanic rate of arrest is lower than that of blacks, they are nearly twice as likely to be arrested as whites of non-Hispanic origin.

Latin Machismo and Criminality

Much has been made of the notion of machismo—the Latin quality or perception denoting masculinity—and its effect on the behavioral patterns of cultures that subscribe to this emphasis on the macho or virile man. Many theorists attribute Latin criminality in large part to this attitude of machismo, particularly with respect to the exploitation and victimization of women. Some have suggested that violence against women is more likely to be a product of machismo-oriented cultures than cultures that favor more equality of the sexes.[2] Brazil is one such culture that has traditionally condoned violent male aggression against women who insulted their "masculine honor."[3]

The idea of machismo seems to be rooted in the Latin communities' sense of cultural isolation and family. A number of studies on Latin prisoners have supported this contention. Anthropologist Theodore Davidson's study of the Latin prison gang, La Familia, revealed that it emerged as a result of racism, isolation, and the barrio culture through which machismo is intricately woven.[4] In a clinical examination of Latin prisoners, Robert Johnson found that 70 percent of the sample group's concerns related to being separated or abandoned by family or their inability to serve a constructive role within their group.[5]

The Latin perspective on the importance of extended family kinships is tied innately to Latin machismo. Through a complex interrelationship of duty and dependency, the macho male is obligated to his family. He provides for them and is greatly dependent upon them, most notably his wife, for emotional support and nurturance, perpetuating his machismo. Because of this dependency on their separated family, many Latin prisoners suffer from a loss of identity and self-esteem, which has been related to Latin prisoner self-injury and violence.[6]

Despite the association of Latin machismo and criminal behavior, there is little in the way of statistical evidence to support this relationship. It is far too simplistic to speak of machismo in terms of the Latin culture, when similar modes of behavior and attitude and reaction to it can be seen in virtually every ethnic and racial group. A valid approach to this subject in the future might be more comprehensive, longitudinal studies of machismo and its cause and effect on ethnic patterns of behavior.

Hispanics are typically arrested most often for violations of state and local laws and ordinances and substance abuse crimes such as alcohol-related crimes and drug abuse violations. For Crime Index offenses, Hispanics are most likely to be arrested for larceny-theft, burglary, and aggravated assault.

HISPANIC INCARCERATION

There are proportionately more Hispanics incarcerated in penal facilities than in the population at large. On June 30, 1986, Hispanics accounted for 14 percent of the nation's jail inmate population.[7] Of this total, 12 percent were male. Approximately 18 percent were also classified as white and 5 percent as black.

Criminality of Cuban Refugees

The problem of Cuban refugees and crime in the United States has been given considerable attention in recent years, reaching a critical juncture in late 1987 when rebellious, fearful Cuban inmates took control of two federal penitentiaries. The uprisings at the Federal Detention Center in Oakdale, Louisiana, and the U.S. Penitentiary in Atlanta were in response to a new immigration agreement that would have allowed the United States to return more than 2,500 undesirable Cuban refugees, predominantly criminals and mentally ill, to Cuba.[8] The Cuban prisoners were among the 125,000 people who fled the fishing port of Mariel en route to the United States in 1980.

The fact that most of these *Marielitos* were apparently willing to die rather than be deported underscores the need for more humane government policies and a greater understanding of the circumstances that caused them to abandon their homeland. The hard-line position by the Cuban prisoners, which left one inmate dead and considerable damage to both prisons, forced the government to take a hard look at the dilemma of the Cubans. The result was that an agreement was reached placing a moratorium on deportations of all the estimated 3,800 Cuban refugees currently being held in federal, county, and state prisons nationwide. Whether this is only a temporary concession on the part of the federal government or a move in the right direction remains to be seen.

Of equal concern is the reported criminal activity of Cuban refugees in the United States. Indications are that many of those who came in 1980 had committed major crimes in Cuba. One estimate suggests that as many as 40,000 of the refugees were convicted criminals.[9]

To law enforcement officials, this is the primary explanation for the disproportionately high incidence of crime attributed to Cubans across the country.[10] Others blame the Mariel refugee crime problem on poor handling by the Carter administration of the resettlement of Cuban immigrants, many of whose criminal backgrounds were undetected at the time. Yet there are those who blame the Castro regime and the intolerable principles of a dictatorship government for the troubles many refugees have run into.

A recent finding suggests that Cuban refugee crime is not necessarily disproportionate to that of all other racial or ethnic groups. In a study of homicide in Dade County, Florida, it was found that the murder rate of Cuban immigrants was roughly the same as that of native blacks.[11] This is still alarming, considering that in 1985, blacks were arrested for murder more than three times as often as Hispanics nationwide.

The dilemma of Cuban refugee crime and how best to deal with it can be solved only by a joint effort of law enforcement and government at the federal, state, and local levels. The answer would not seem as simple or discriminatory as deporting those allowed to come here in the first place.

Studies report that Hispanics who have strong cultural ties have disproportionately high rates of jail suicide.[12] This is often linked to feelings of depression and isolation associated with incarceration.

Data on Hispanics in prisons show that during 1984, their numbers rose by 17 percent, nearly twice the increase for the total prison population. Hispanic imprisonment was proportionately higher in federal than state institutions (24 percent to 14 percent), and more Hispanic males were imprisoned than females (15 percent to 13 percent).[13] Typically the highest proportion of Hispanic prisoners is in the West and Southwest: New Mexico (48 percent), California (26 percent), Colorado (24 percent), and Arizona (23 percent). Twenty-three percent of New York's inmate population is Hispanic. Texas, Utah, Connecticut, and New Jersey reported that Hispanics comprised between 10 and 20 percent of their prisoners.[14]

One of every sixteen prisoners in the United States is of Hispanic origin. Hispanics are more likely than any other ethnic and racial groups to be imprisoned due to a drug-related offense.

The percentage of Hispanic juveniles incarcerated in juvenile custody facilities is also high in relation to their 6 percent of the adolescent population. As of February 1, 1983, 6.7 percent of the juvenile prisoners in private juvenile custody facilities were Hispanic compared to 11.8 percent of those in public juvenile custody facilities, which housed more than double the Hispanic delinquents as private facilities.[15] One of every twelve juvenile inmates is of Hispanic origin.

EXPLAINING HISPANIC CRIME

Few studies have attempted to account for the incidence and range of Hispanic crime. Some researchers, however, believe that the socioeconomic and emotional variables of Hispanic life place Hispanics in a high-risk group for criminality and victimization.[16] Hispanic unemployment, income, educational, occupational, and median age levels are below or lower than those of the general population. For instance, the jobless rate among Hispanics is typically 40 to 50 percent greater than the national unemployment rate. Among those who are employed, most are concentrated in lower-paying, lower-skilled jobs than the general work force. In 1981, one-fourth of all Hispanic families in the nation were classified by the Census Bureau as "poor," in comparison to 8.8 percent of white families. Furthermore, the unfamiliarity of living in a foreign culture can deprive Hispanics of "familiar cues and controls."[17] Other studies suggest that the high rate of Hispanic arrests and incarceration can be attributed in part to language barriers and discriminatory treatment by the criminal justice system.[18]

An important factor often overlooked in causation or motivational approaches to Hispanic involvement in criminality is the mistreatment they and their ancestors have endured over the years, from an abusive, exploitative, prejudiced America, beginning with its early attitudes of Anglo-Saxon racial supremacy and superiority over Spanish colonists and any other ethnic or racial minorities, which manifested itself through colonialism, expansionism, and imperialism. These events no doubt left their mark on the Hispanic community through distrust, defiance, resistance, and alienation against the larger group, as well as placing them in a position of susceptibility in the social class structure (as evidenced by their social standing) and behavioral patterns.

VICTIMIZATION OF HISPANICS

The most comprehensive profile to date of the Hispanic victim of crime is a 1980 U.S. Department of Justice, Bureau of Justice Statistics report.[19] The report, based on NCS data gathered from 1973 to 1978, revealed that Hispanics generally have higher criminal victimization rates than non-Hispanics, yet their rates of reporting crime to law enforcement are lower than for non-Hispanic victims, most notably for household and personal larcenies.

The study showed no apparent changes in the estimated crime rates for the Hispanic population during the years studied. In spite of the comparatively higher Hispanic rate of victimization, the actual distribution of violent crime victimization among Hispanics is similar to that of the non-Hispanic community. According to the NCS, Hispanic-headed households had higher victimization rates than non-Hispanics for total household crime and the individual crimes of burglary, household larceny, and motor vehicle theft. Hispanics were victimized more by forcible entry burglaries and completed motor vehicle theft than their non-Hispanic counterparts.

The NCS also found that:

- Hispanic males are victimized more often than Hispanic females.
- Hispanics aged 12 to 19 constituted the greatest number of violent crime victims and offenders.
- Perpetrators of violent crime against Hispanics tend to be poor, unemployed, and from broken homes.
- Most single-offender crimes of violence against Hispanics are perpetrated by males aged 21 and over.
- Hispanics are victimized more by multiple-offender crimes than are non-Hispanics.
- Hispanics are less likely than non-Hispanics to be victimized by black offenders.
- Hispanic victims and their offenders are generally of comparable age.

NCS data for 1985 confirm these general characteristics of Hispanic victimization.[20]

HISPANIC ATTITUDES ON CRIME AND JUSTICE

Although the evidence remains scanty, some research has sought to establish Hispanic feelings about crime and related issues such as the police and civil liberties. Such data, when analyzed correctly, can yield considerable information about the variables of Hispanic involvement in crime—for example, why Hispanics are less likely than other racial and ethnic groups to report crimes to the police.

A significant study in this area was undertaken by A. Miranda.[21] It compared Mexican-American attitudes toward the police with those of white and black respondents as compiled in an earlier survey by the National Opinion Research Center (NORC). Additionally, Miranda tested the major hypothesis of Richard Block's 1971 study relating to fear of crime and of the police and support for increased police power and civil liberties in a Mexican-American neighborhood. The setting for the Miranda study was a southern California Mexican barrio of roughly 150,000 residents. A representative sample produced 170 completed interviews.

Miranda found that while the hypothesis that fear of crime is related to greater support of the police was only moderately supported by the black and white NORC respondents, the support was strong in the Mexican-American sample group. The hypothesis that people who fear the police most are more likely to support civil liberties protections showed considerable support among whites but not blacks in the NORC study. Seventy percent of the Mexican-Americans in fear of the police favored the protection of civil liberties. This fear of law enforcement in combination with perceived violations of their civil rights in general may be an important factor in Hispanic member reluctance to report victimization; in a sense, they may feel that they too are being selectively victimized through policies and discrimination by those who are supposed to protect them.

The Miranda study also found that among each of the three racial and ethnic groups, rises in the crime rate generally resulted in more support for increased police power and less for civil liberties; conversely, fear of the police had the effect of lower support for police power and more for civil liberties protections. These similarities notwithstanding, each group tended to differ in the degree in which it supported or feared the police, as well as the degree that it feared crime and advocated civil liberties.

As in other areas of Hispanic participation in crime and criminal justice, considerably more study is needed on this subject with respect to its significance in understanding the criminality and victimization of Hispanics.

ILLEGAL HISPANICS AND CRIME

An important aspect of Hispanic involvement in criminal matters often overlooked is the impact of the illegal or undocumented alien on American criminality. Illegal aliens are defined primarily as persons crossing the American border absent inspection, possessing fraudulent documents, or overextending a work or study visa stay. Although illegal aliens come from many places, including Asia and Europe, it is estimated that most are Mexican nationals, followed by other groups of Hispanic origin, such as Central and South Americans. The government estimates that of the more than 1 million illegal aliens believed to reside in New York City, more than 75 percent are primarily Colombians, Argentinians, Dominicans, Ecuadorians, and natives of various other Central American republics.[22]

Because these Hispanic members are here illegally and therefore for the most part invisible in terms of documentation, it is difficult to assess their role in crime and victimization, adding to the already difficult problem of studying legal Hispanic Americans. There are considerably more questions than answers. Should these people be labeled "criminal" merely because they are here illegally, particularly since many were more or less forced into the United States by a crippled Mexican economy and a demand for their cheap services? What is the incidence of "real" crime among illegal Hispanics? How many are counted in criminal statistics? Are they being victimized more than documented Hispanics or other American racial groups? There are no concrete answers to these questions. The Immigration Reform and Control Act of 1986 may help us gain a better profile of this subgroup in relation to their activities and life in America. Immigration reform can enable us to establish a better profile of illegal aliens by virtue of an expanded number of documents needed to establish identity. This can be most helpful, especially in longitudinal studies, in tracking demographic patterns of illegal and documented Hispanics. Greater requirements for residency and an expanded number of documents needed to establish identity will make it easier for demographers and criminologists to characterize illegal aliens.

What does appear apparent is that illegal Hispanics generally have characteristics similar to legal Hispanics regarding criminality and victimization. That is, they are mostly undereducated, underemployed, discriminated against, and living in high-crime areas—factors that put them at greater risk of being victimized or an offender. Actually, illegal Hispanics are particularly vulnerable to exploitation by landlords, employers, and others and other forms of abuse, as well as crime, as both victims and perpetrators.[23]

Hispanics are the fastest-growing racial and ethnic minority in the United States. Yet there is a paucity of research on Hispanic groups in the area of social science, most notably criminality and criminal justice. Most of the research that has been done focuses almost exclusively on Mexican-Americans, the largest of the Hispanic contingent in this country. We know very little about the crime and victimization patterns and characteristics of Puerto Ricans, Cubans, and those from Central and South America and Spain. In order for us to step forward in the field of criminology, it is not enough to know that the rate of crime and victimization among Hispanics is disproportionately high. We need to investigate the reasons why—the differences between different Hispanic groups and subgroups, and in comparison to other ethnic minorities. Related issues require further study as well, such as the role of language barriers in criminal involvement and discriminatory treatment of Hispanics within the criminal justice system.

NOTES

1. U.S. Federal Bureau of Investigation, *Crime in the United States: Uniform Crime Reports 1986* (Washington, D.C.: Government Printing Office, 1987), p. 185.

2. See Stuart L. Hills, *Demystifying Social Deviance* (New York: McGraw-Hill, 1980); Herman Schwendinger and Julia Schwendinger, *Rape and Inequality* (Beverly Hills: Sage Publications, 1983).

3. See Jim Brooke, "Feminism in Foreign Lands: Two Perspectives: Macho Killing in Brazil Spurs Protestors," *Boston Globe* (January 2, 1982): A23.

4. Theodore Davidson, *Chicano Prisoners: The Key to San Quentin* (New York: Holt, Rinehart & Winston, 1974).

5. Robert Johnson, *Culture and Crisis in Confinement* (Lexington, Mass.: D. C. Heath, 1976), pp. 71–75.

6. Ibid., pp. 81–93; J. W. Moore, *Homeboys: Gangs, Drugs and Prison in the Barrios of Los Angeles* (Philadelphia: Temple University Press, 1978), pp. 100–106.

7. U.S. Department of Justice, Bureau of Justice Statistics, *Jail Inmates 1986* (Washington, D.C.: Government Printing Office, 1987), p. 2.

8. "US, Cuba Restore Accord," *Sacramento Bee* (November 21, 1987): A1.

9. "Cuban Refugee Crime Troubles Police across U.S.," *New York Times* (March 31, 1985): L30.

10. Ibid.

11. William Wilbanks, *Murder in Miami* (Lanham, Md.: University Press of America, 1984), p. 26.

12. L. French and J. B. Porter, "Jail Crises: Causes and Control," in William Taylor and Michael Bresswell, eds., *Police and Criminal Psychology* (Washington, D.C.: University Press of America, 1978).

13. U.S. Department of Justice, Bureau of Justice, *Prisoners in State and Federal Institutions on December 31, 1984* (Washington, D.C.: Government Printing Office, 1987), p. 3.

14. Ibid., data for Hispanic prisoners on December 31, 1983.

15. U.S. Department of Justice, Office of Juvenile Justice and Delinquency Prevention, *Children in Custody: Advance Report on the 1982 Census of Public Juvenile Facilities* and *Children in Custody: Advance Report on the 1982 Census of Private Juvenile Facilities* (Washington, D.C.: Government Printing Office, 1984).

16. Bonnie J. Bondavalli and Bruno Bondavalli, "Spanish-Speaking People and the North American Criminal Justice System," in R. L. McNeely and Carl E. Pope, *Race, Crime, and Criminal Justice* (Beverly Hills: Sage Publications, 1981).

17. Ibid., p. 65.

18. Leo M. Romero and Luis G. Stelzner, "Hispanics and the Criminal Justice System," in Pastora San Juan Cafferty and William C. McCready, eds., *Hispanics in the United States: A New Social Agenda* (New Brunswick, N.J.: Transaction Books, 1985).

19. U.S. Department of Justice, Bureau of Justice Statistics, *The Hispanic Victim* (Washington, D.C.: Government Printing Office, 1981).

20. U.S. Department of Justice, *Criminal Victimization in the United States, 1985: A National Crime Survey Report* (Washington, D.C.: Government Printing Office, 1987), p. 4.

21. A. Miranda, "Fear of Crime and Fear of the Police in a Chicano Community," *Sociology and Social Research* 64 (1980); Phillip H. Ennis, *Criminal Victimization in the United States: A Report of a National Survey*, National Opinion Research Center, University of Chicago (Washington, D.C.: Government Printing Office, 1967).

22. Romero and Stelzner, "Hispanics and the Criminal Justice System," p. 228.

23. K. Wagenheim, *A Survey of Puerto Ricans on the U.S. Mainland in the 1970s* (New York: Praeger, 1975).

7

Native American Criminality

As approximately 1.4 million of the nation's estimated 226.5 million population as of 1980, Native Americans represent one of the smallest American racial groups and thus their volume of crimes committed is barely noticeable. Therefore, it is not common knowledge that the rate of Native American arrests is in fact quite high—second only to blacks among all racial and ethnic groups. That is, viewed in relation to their numbers in the population, Native American arrest figures are proportionately excessive, especially for alcohol-related offenses. This disproportion is also reflected in incarceration rates of Native Americans.

LITERATURE ON NATIVE AMERICAN CRIME

Not surprisingly, there have been very few studies on the problem of Native American criminality. Although most criminologists are presumably aware of the disproportionate reflection of Native Americans in criminal statistics, actual research on the subject has been virtually nil, particularly when compared to the considerable attention devoted to blacks and their high crime rate. We do not know enough to draw any conclusions on Native American participation in crime.

There has been some research in this area of study, however. In the 1940s Norman Hayner established in a comparison of three reservations a direct association between increased Native American crime and increased Native American contact with whites and wealth.[1] And after comparing poor and wealthy Native American tribes, Hans Von Hentig concluded that death and crime were the result of both "extreme misery and extreme luxury."[2]

Two prominent studies in the 1960s went further in analyzing Native American crime by addressing both reservation and nonreservation crime and arrest rates and those of other racial and ethnic groups. Combining UCR and U.S. Census data for 1960, Omer Stewart calculated the rate of arrests per 100,000 population for Native Americans, blacks, whites, and Asians. He found the Native American arrest rate to be approximately seven times greater than the national average, nine times the white rate, three times that of blacks, and fourteen times the Asian rate.[3] When alcohol-related offenses only were considered, the Native American rate of arrest was roughly twelve times the national average, fifteen times the white rate, six times the black rate, and forty-two times the Asian rate. Stewart also noted that the Native American rate of arrests was considerably higher than the national rate and that of other groups in urban arrests. He supported his findings with data from South Dakota, Denver, and a number of tribes.[4]

Charles Reasons's longitudinal study essentially concurred with Stewart's findings. His investigation into Native American crime, using official statistics from 1950 to 1968 and the 1950 and 1960 Census reports for persons aged 14 and older, also verified the disproportionately high rate of Native American arrests compared to whites, blacks, and Asians.[5] He found a much greater disparity between the Native American arrest rate and that of other groups for alcohol-related arrests than did Stewart.

In both studies, the results contradicted the rates cited in some criminology textbooks, most notably Edwin Sutherland and Donald Cressey's *Principles of Criminology*, where the Native American arrest rate was said to be around three times the white rate.[6] This could be due to the difference in years measured, data, or methodology used, however. A more recent study by Gary Jensen and colleagues supported the Stewart and Reason findings.[7]

CRIME AND NATIVE AMERICANS

Rate of Arrest

As of the mid-1980s, Native Americans continued to be arrested out of proportion to their representation in the population. However, my investigation into their rate of arrest per 100,000 population in respect to other ethnic and racial groups reveals a somewhat different pattern than did earlier studies. Data from the 1980 Census of Population and 1985 UCR show that blacks have the highest arrest rate, followed by Native Americans, Hispanics, whites, and Asians. But when only alcohol-related offenses (driving under the influence, liquor laws, and drunkenness) are considered, the Native American arrest rate is higher than that of all other racial/ethnic groups. In either case, the disparity is not as great as that proposed by other researchers.

Table 7.1
Rates of Arrest per 100,000 Population, by Race/Ethnicity, 1985

OFFENSE CHARGED	Total	Native American[a]	White	Black	Hispanic[b]	Asian[c]
TOTAL UCR OFFENSES	4520.7	7859.2	3895.9	10273.1	7604.1	2018.5
Murder & nonnegligent manslaughter	6.9	7.7	4.1	28.5	15.1	3.6
Forcible rape	14.0	17.0	8.7	55.4	20.0	5.0
Robbery	53.0	36.6	23.8	279.2	97.9	18.8
Aggravated assault	115.8	178.4	80.8	399.8	200.3	46.9
Burglary	168.0	213.0	140.8	415.7	316.1	67.6
Larceny-theft	519.6	978.0	419.9	1359.5	786.8	353.7
Motor vehicle theft	50.7	79.4	40.1	140.6	105.4	28.3
Arson	7.4	11.6	6.7	14.4	8.2	2.7
Violent crime	189.5	239.7	117.5	762.9	333.3	74.3
Property crime	745.8	1282.0	607.5	1930.1	1216.6	452.4
Crime Index total	935.3	1521.7	725.0	2693.0	1550.0	526.8
Other assaults	241.9	392.4	190.8	677.6	298.7	89.3
Weapons; carrying, possessing, etc.	69.1	59.9	54.1	198.3	142.4	36.0
Sex offenses (except forcible rape and prostitution)	38.3	51.0	36.0	66.1	55.1	16.1

[a]Uniform Crime Reports lists Native Americans as American Indian or Alaskan Native. The 1980 Bureau of the Census identifies 99 percent of the Native American population as American Indian and Eskimo and 1 percent as Aleut.

[b]Because of a peculiarity of the U.S. Census form of 1980, a number of Hispanics were also counted in the "white" and "black" categories.

[c]Also includes Pacific Islanders.

Source: Arrest rates are computed for each race/ethnic group using the U.S. Bureau of the Census, *1980 Census of Population,* data and the U.S. Federal Bureau of Investigation, *Crime in the United States: Uniform Crime Reports, 1985* (Washington, D.C.: Government Printing Office, 1986), pp. 182, 185.

Table 7.1 compares rates of arrest per 100,000 people by race/ethnicity in 1985 for total UCR offenses, Crime Index offenses, and selected Part II offenses. We can see that the black arrest rate is greater in every instance than the other groups and the national average. For violent crimes, blacks are more than three times as likely to be arrested as Native Americans. Native Americans show the second highest rate of arrest overall and for property crime and other assaults. However, their total arrest rate is only slightly greater than that of Hispanics, who have the second highest rate of arrest for Crime Index offenses, violent crime, and crimes such as weapons possession and sex offenses. The Native American arrest rate for all offenses is nearly twice that for the nation as a whole, two times the white rate, and nearly four times the Asian rate.

Table 7.2 expands on the theme of alcohol-related offenses with respect to arrest rates by reflecting rates of arrest by race/ethnicity for substance abuse–related offenses. These offenses include those often associated with alcohol and/or drugs, including disorderly conduct, vagrancy, loitering, and family-type offenses. A comparison between these and alcohol-only-related arrest rates is also presented. Native Americans have the highest rate of arrests for all substance abuse–related offenses. They are arrested more than twice the national rate and that of whites and over six times as often as Asians. The disparity between the Native American arrest rate and that of blacks and Hispanics is not as great. In fact, for drug abuse violations, blacks, Hispanics, and whites have a higher arrest rate than Native Americans, indicating that their representation in substance abuse–related offenses is still concentrated in offenses associated with alcohol.

Native Americans actually show a lower rate of arrest for alcohol-associated offenses than substance abuse–related crimes; however, the differential between their arrest rate for alcohol-related offenses and that of other groups is slightly greater. For example, their rate of arrest for alcohol-associated offenses is approximately two and a half times the national, white, and black rate and seven and a half times that of Asians. Hispanics have the closest alcohol-associated arrest rate to Native Americans and actually show a higher rate of arrest for driving under the influence.

The ratio of the Native American arrest rate for various types of offenses to the arrest rates of the other racial and ethnic groups presented can be seen in Table 7.3.

In summary, this analysis shows that:

• The overall rate of arrest of Native Americans today is not higher than that of all other groups, as indicated by some earlier work.

Table 7.2
Rates of Arrest for Substance Abuse–Related Offenses per 100,000 Population, by Race/Ethnicity, 1985[a]

Offense Charged	Total	Race/Ethnicity				
		Native American	Black	Hispanic	White	Asian
TOTAL	1859.1	4085.3	2920.2	3716.3	1782.6	644.3
Driving under the influence	656.2	1159.7	543.2	1237.3	699.2	267.1
Liquor laws	205.4	739.7	223.2	237.1	208.0	114.1
Drunkenness	366.4	1309.8	540.8	999.9	353.9	45.3
Drug abuse violations	309.0	216.9	793.9	814.2	256.2	121.0
Disorderly conduct	256.0	516.6	660.8	350.5	209.9	62.6
Vagrancy	13.2	61.1	31.9	24.6	10.8	4.3
Curfew and loitering law violations	31.5	44.2	63.7	35.5	28.2	25.4
Offenses against family and children	21.3	37.1	62.6	17.0	16.5	4.4
Alcohol-associated offenses[b]	1228.0	3209.3	1307.2	2474.3	1261.1	426.5

[a]Studies have shown that some offenses, such as disorderly conduct, loitering, vagrancy, and family related, are directly associated with substance abuse.

[b]Includes driving under the influence, liquor laws, and drunkenness.

Source: Arrest rates are computed for each race/ethnic group using the U.S. Bureau of the Census, *1980 Census of Population* data and the U.S. Federal Bureau of Investigation, *Crime in the United States: Uniform Crime Reports, 1985* (Washington, D.C.: Government Printing Office, 1986), pp. 182, 185.

Table 7.3
Ratio of Native American to Other Racial Groups' Arrests, per 100,000 Population, 1985

OFFENSE	Native American Total Population	Native American/ White	Native American/ Black	Native American/ Hispanic	Native American/ Asian
Violent crime	1.3	2.0	3.2[a]	1.4[a]	3.2[a]
Property crime	1.7	2.1	1.5[a]	1.0	2.8
Alcohol-related crime	2.5	2.5	2.4	1.3	7.5
Substance abuse-related crime	2.2	2.3	1.4	1.1	6.3
TOTAL, UCR OFFENSES	1.7	2.0	1.3[a]	1.0	3.9

[a]For these offenses, the black and Hispanic ratio of arrest was greater.

Source: Computed from the U.S. Bureau of the Census, *1980 Census of Population* data, and the U.S. Federal Bureau of Investigation, *Crime in the United States: Uniform Crime Reports, 1985* (Washington, D.C.: Government Printing Office, 1986), pp. 182, 185.

• Native Americans continue to show the highest arrest rate for alcohol-related offenses, as well as for substance abuse–related offenses. In neither instance, however, is the disparity between them and other groups (aside from Asians) excessive.

• When Hispanics are included in arrest rate comparisons by race/ethnicity, they show an arrest rate quite similar to Native Americans, particularly for alcohol- and substance abuse–related offenses.

• Native Americans have a strikingly high overall rate of arrest relative to their population size.

The analysis does not take into account age group differences, reservation data, urban-rural differences, or other variables. Nor can we discount the possibility that differential treatment exists within the criminal justice system that could explain racial disparities in arrest rates. Rather, the examination is intended to approximate a current analogy of the Native American rate of arrest nationwide as it compares with that of other racial and ethnic groups, using the best national data available. The evidence suggests that Native Americans are arrested proportionately more than their population calls for, most notably for alcohol-related crimes.

Native American Confinement

As would be expected by their high arrest rate, Native Americans are overrepresented in U.S. correctional institutions. Most jail, prison, and juvenile custody statistics group Native American prisoners in "other" categories; hence it is difficult to assess accurately Native American incarceration figures. For instance, data on the jail population as of June 30, 1986, estimate that 1 percent of the jail inmates are Native Americans, Aleuts, Asians, and Pacific Islanders.

The disproportionate incarceration of Native Americans can best be seen through prisoner statistics. Although Native Americans comprise 0.6 percent of the general population, on December 31, 1984, they constituted approximately 2 percent of the federal prisoners in the United States and 1 percent of the state prisoners.[8] Proportionately, slightly more Native American males than females were incarcerated in federal institutions, whereas more females than males tended to be confined in state facilities. Almost half of the 4,086 Native Americans were housed in federal prisons and prisons in three states (Alaska, North Carolina, and Oklahoma).

The overrepresentation of Native Americans in prison is greater in states in which Native Americans are more heavily concentrated. For instance, Native Americans account for about 25 percent of South Da-

Table 7.4

**Rates of Incarceration in Federal and State Institutions, per 100,000
Population, by Race/Ethnicity, 1983**

		Race/Ethnicity				
	Total	Native American	Black	White	Hispanic[a]	Asian
United States	193.0	288.1	755.9	119.9	281.4	46.0
Federal Institutions	14.1	46.2	39.4	10.9	51.2	5.7
State Institutions	178.9	241.9	716.4	109.0	230.2	40.2

[a] Prisoners of Hispanic origin are also included in figures by race. Nevertheless, the data listed are useful for comparing Hispanic minority group members to other ethnic minorities.

Source: Calculated from the U.S. Bureau of the Census, *1980 Census of Population* data and the U.S. Department of Justice, Bureau of Justice Statistics, *Prisoners in State and Federal Institutions on December 31, 1983* (Washington, D.C.: Government Printing Office, 1986), pp. 18, 21.

kota's prison population[9] and 10 percent of the prison inmates of Oklahoma.[10]

The rate of Native American incarceration in federal and state institutions is shown in Table 7.4. Native Americans have the second highest rate of incarceration for the United States, federal, and state institutions, or a total rate more than two times the white rate and six times greater than that of Asians. Interestingly, while blacks have the highest overall confinement rate, Hispanics have the highest for federal incarceration. Asians have by far the lowest rate in all categories.

These findings support the arrest data about the general makeup of the Native American rate of crime involvement as it relates to other racial and ethnic groups and its disproportion with respect to the Native American representation in the population.

CANADIAN INDIANS AND CRIME

Because of the intrinsic relationship between American Indians and their Canadian counterparts and the similar circumstances that dispossessed them of the land they once ruled, it might be useful to compare the Canadian Indians' representation in crime and incarceration data.

Native Canadians are disproportionately convicted of crimes, particularly felonies. Studies show that throughout the country, Canadian natives are overrepresented in jails and prisons and in fact are the largest racial minority in Canadian correctional facilities. This minority group comprises only around 1.3 percent of the Canadian population yet represents nearly 7 percent of the inmates in federal institutions.[11]

The following examples reflect this significant disparity:

In Canada's four western provinces, the Yukon, and the Northwest territories, [Native Canadians] constitute about 1.3 percent of the Canadian population, yet they are incarcerated in proportions ranging from a low of 10 percent of the inmates in one jail on Vancouver Island to highs of 100 percent of the inmates of jails for women at Oakalla (British Columbia) and the Pas (Manitoba). In western Canadian correctional institutions, these "natives" contribute 14 to 60 percent of the inmate population, depending on the year and jurisdiction.[12]

Canadian native women are proportionately more greatly represented in Canadian prisons than native men. Native Canadian prisoners are more likely to have a previous record, be convicted for crimes against persons, have higher recidivism rates, and have shorter sentences than nonnative offenders.[13] One study found that 13 percent of all Canadian Indian federal prisoners had been convicted of manslaughter compared to 5 percent of the non-Indian population (less than 1 percent of the Native American Indians were arrested for manslaughter in 1985).[14]

The majority of the Canadian natives imprisoned are from rural reservations, unemployed, and possess low educational and job skills.[15] One Indian is likely to be incarcerated in Canadian penitentiaries for every eight non-Indians.[16] A significant proportion of Native Canadian prisoners, similar to American Indian inmates, are convicted of alcohol-related offenses.[17]

EXPLAINING THE CRIMINALITY OF THE INDIAN

Clearly there is a reason or reasons for the high rate of Indian arrest and conviction. Conflict and labeling theorists would argue that Native Americans and Canadian Indians are being victimized by racial discrimination and visibility, which increases their vulnerability to unjust treatment within the criminal justice system compared to the dominant group. This position has some merit; studies have shown differential treatment to exist in one form or another throughout the system of criminal justice.

Discrimination, however, cannot serve as the only reason for the overrepresentation of Native Americans in crime rates, especially where it concerns substance abuse–related offenses, which comprise the bulk of Native American involvement in crime.[18] Even among minorities, the differences here are alarming. Why are Native Americans much more likely to be arrested for alcohol-related offenses than blacks, whom many believe are the most victimized American minority by discriminatory policies? Why are Native Americans arrested more than seven times as often for alcohol-related offenses as Asians, a minority that is more than three times as large as they are?

Such questions have been debated for some time. Here we shall consider several etiological explanations of Native American participation in crime.

Cultural Conflict

Many believe a clash in cultures is the main reason for the extent and patterns of Native American criminality. That is, because of the unique position of Native Americans as the original Americans and because they have had to exist under two distinct cultures, they have been unable or unwilling to adjust successfully on all levels.

In *Culture, Conflict and Crime,* Thorsten Sellin argues that criminal law is largely representative of the dominant group in society whose moral ideas differ from those to whom the law is subjected.[19] Conflict results because not all members of the society are equally accommodating to the criminal law and its norms. There are three ways in which conflicts between the norms of divergent cultural codes can occur: when codes clash on the border of contiguous cultural areas, when colonization imposes one cultural group's criminal laws upon another, and when members of one cultural group migrate to another area. All of these cultural clashes appear to be responsible for the Native American–white conflict.

The European migration to America and subsequent colonization was the beginning of the long conflict in cultures between whites and Native Americans. The conflict was aggravated with the forced westward movement of Native Americans, the near genocide of their race and culture, and a series of government "solutions" to the "Indian problem," including resettling them on reservations and inconsistent shifts between assimilation and retention of the Native American culture.

Criminal law is one primary area in which this conflict in cultures is most evident. Native Americans, particularly those living on reservations, are subject to several different sets of laws and brands of punishment depending on the jurisdiction in which an offense occurred.[20] The differences quantitatively and qualitatively between tribal law and federal and state codes can be considerable. Whereas tribal punishment for a crime may be a few months in jail, the same crime may mete a Native American a few years in prison in state court. Von Hentig[21] and Warren Cohen and Phillip Mause[22] have noted that little to no stigma is attached to tribal court conviction because it is not looked upon as a moral judgment on the convicted and because many older Native Americans believe their value system is superior to that of the white establishment.

The urban Native American is even more susceptible to cultural conflicts in criminal law. A major problem is the conflict of individual and society. A study of 100 relocated Navahos found that 30 percent believed conflict with the law was a primary concern.[23] The often perplexing set of laws, regulations, rules, and customs of urban living is tough on urban natives. Therefore it is reasonable to assume Native American emigrants may find themselves thoroughly mystified by it all in relation to their own cultural codes, manifesting in frustrated modes of behavior.

Anomie

Anomie stresses the differential opportunity structure for legitimate and illegitimate means in attaining culturally defined goals. Arthur Riffenburgh postulated that the conflict of normative standards led to an anomic state among Native Americans, with criminality often ensuing.[24]

Richard Jessor and associates applied this theory to an explanation of different rates of crime within a multiethnic community.[25] Following a five-year study of a community composed of 46 percent whites, 34 percent Hispanics, and 20 percent Native Americans, the researchers found that limited access to legitimate means for attaining culturally prescribed goals was a prominent factor in deviance but was not sufficient to produce deviance. The degrees of anomie and of access to unapproved means were found to be significant contributors to criminality.

Although economically better off than the Hispanic group, the Native Americans displayed a considerably higher rate of deviance (such as alcohol-related arrests and convictions). Both minorities, though, felt that they had unequal access to the opportunity structure compared to whites. The authors learned that the Hispanics had less anomie than the Native Americans, more normative control, and stricter views toward deviant behavior; the Native Americans exhibited greater normlessness and exposure to antisocial role models. Thus this suggests that Native American deviance is caused primarily by conflicts of cultures.

Other studies have associated anomie with high Native American rates of suicide[26] and low achievement motivation.[27]

Economic Determinism

Related to the anomie theory of Native American criminality is economic determinism. A number of researchers have pointed to economic factors as major determinants for the high rate of Native American crime. While some, such as Hayner[28] and Von Hentig,[29] have associated sudden income to increased crime among Native Americans, others, such as Stewart[30] and Mhyra Minnis,[31] have regarded poverty as significant.

Such approaches seem reasonable. Native Americans as a group are perhaps more disadvantaged economically than any other American minority group. Native Americans generally have significantly lower incomes, unemployment, education, poverty, and other socioeconomic difficulties than the U.S. population as a whole. However, neither economic deprivation nor the desire for more is sufficient to explain crime, particularly when some ethnic groups, such as Asians, who also have suffered from economic disadvantage, have a much lower crime rate than Native Americans. Economic determinism, then, can be viewed as one factor in conjunction with others that may be contributory to the rate of Native American crime.

Alcohol Usage

Although each of the explanations of Native American crime can account for some of the high incidence of alcohol-related offenses committed by Native Americans, none adequately reflects reasons for the prominence of alcohol (over other vices such as drugs or violent crime) in the Native American life-style or the disparity between alcohol-related offenses and those of other ethnic groups. There is little consensus on this topic. The hypothesis that most agree on seems to be that the Native Americans' particular and long history has, more than any other group, had the effect of establishing an appreciation for alcohol, a need for it to cope with the life and times they have been forced into, and a shorter time to have developed self-control and cultural response to the implications of alcohol use and abuse. This has led to their greater involvement in alcohol consumption and alcohol-related crimes than other groups.

Several researchers have addressed the issue of the Native American and the high rate of alcohol-related crimes. In *Indian Americans*, Murray Wax describes the early "vulnerability of Indians to distilled liquors" in relation to criminal conduct.[32] Riffenburgh associates Native American excessive use of alcohol and crime with the frustration and confusion encountered by Native Americans due to their contact with the non-Indian culture and its conflicting conduct and cultural norms.[33] Edward Dozier's article reflects the inadequacies and disillusion felt by Native Americans relating to historical, cultural, and social factors as being responsible for their excessive drinking and secondary deviance.[34]

Stewart notes that the Indian Intercourse Act of 1832, which selectively prohibited Native American use of alcohol for more than a century, did not allow Native Americans the opportunity to "learn the proper everyday, family, self-regulated use of alcoholic beverages."[35]

The answer to the problem of high rates of Native American arrests for alcohol-related offenses may lie in each of these themes. The one factor that seems clear is that the Native American plight today is tied to the policies of and treatment by the federal government and the dominant people of this country ever since their cultures clashed. It is here where we must affix blame and seek long-overdue solutions.

Although Native Americans are one of America's smallest minorities, they have one of the highest rates of arrest and conviction of any other racial and ethnic group in the country. Native Americans have a higher rate of arrest for substance abuse–related offenses, particularly those involving alcohol, than every other group. It appears as if the reasons behind the incidence and type of crime among North American Indians are related to their arduous and frustrating history as second-class citizens on a continent they once ruled and their low position in the social and economic structure. The study of Native Americans and criminality is extremely limited to date, however; thus there is still much to be learned about this group's participation in crime and explanations for it.

NOTES

1. Norman S. Hayner, "Variability in the Criminal Behavior of American Indians," *American Journal of Sociology* 47 (1942): 602–13.

2. Hans Von Hentig, "The Delinquency of the American Indian," *Journal of Criminal Law* 36 (1945): 84.

3. Omer Stewart, "Questions Regarding American Indian Criminality," *Human Organization* 23 (1964): 61–66.

4. Ibid.

5. Charles E. Reasons, "Crime and the Native American," in Charles E. Reasons and Jack L. Kuykendall, eds., *Race, Crime and Justice* (Pacific Palisades, Calif.: Goodyear Publishing Co., 1972), pp. 79–95.

6. Edwin Sutherland and Donald R. Cressey, *Principles of Criminology* (New York: Lippincott, 1966), p. 147.

7. Gary F. Jensen, Joseph H. Stauss, and V. William Harris, "Crime, Delinquency, and the American Indian," *Human Organization* 36 (1977): 252–57.

8. U.S. Department of Justice, Bureau of Justice Statistics, *Prisoners in State and Federal Institutions on December 31, 1984* (Washington, D.C.: Government Printing Office, 1987), p. 17.

9. Walter Echo-Hawk, "Native Prisoners, Tribal Religion, and the First Amendment," *Prison Law Monitor* 1 (1979): 205, 219.

10. Oklahoma Department of Corrections, *Annual Report—Fiscal Year 1978* (Oklahoma City, 1978).

11. Canada, Solicitor General, *Selected Trends in Canadian Criminal Justice* (Ottawa: Ministry of the Solicitor General, Programs Branch, 1981).

12. Gwynn Nettler, *Explaining Crime*, 3d ed. (New York: McGraw-Hill, 1984), p. 136.

13. D. A. Schmeiser et al., *The Native Offender and the Law* (Ottawa: Information Canada, 1974), p. 81.

14. Solicitor General, *Selected Trends*, p. 17.

15. M. J. Irvine, *The Native Inmate in Ontario: A Preliminary Study* (Ottawa: Ministry of Correctional Services, 1978).

16. Statistics Canada, *Correctional Institutions Statistics 1977* (Ottawa: Statistics Canada, 1979).

17. Nettler, *Explaining Crime*, p. 136.

18. Aside from substance abuse–related offenses such as those noted in Table 7.2, there is evidence that alcohol and drugs may also be a factor in other crimes, including murder, rape, robbery, and motor vehicle theft.

19. Thorsten Sellin, *Culture, Conflict, and Crime* (New York: Social Science Research Council, 1938), pp. 63–70.

20. Ronald B. Flowers, *Criminal Jurisdiction Allocation in Indian Country* (Port Washington, N.Y.: Associated Faculty Press, 1983).

21. Von Hentig, "Delinquency of the American Indian," pp. 82–83.

22. Warren H. Cohen and Phillip I. Mause, "The Indian: The Forgotten American," *Harvard Law Review* 81 (1968): 1818–58.

23. Theodore D. Graves and Minor Von Arsdale, "Values, Expectations and Relocation: The Navaho Migrant to Denver," *Human Organization* 23 (1966): 300–307.

24. Arthur S. Riffenburgh, "Cultural Influences and Crime among Indians— Americans of the Southwest," *Federal Probation* 28 (1964): 38–46.

25. Richard Jessor et al., *Society, Personality, and Deviant Behavior* (San Francisco: Holt, Rinehart & Winston, 1968).

26. Jerrold E. Levy, "Navajo Suicide," *Human Organization* 24 (1965): 308–18.

27. Alan C. Kerckhoff, "Anomie and Achievement Motivation: A Study of Personality Development within Cultural Disorganization," *Social Forces* 37 (1959): 196–202.

28. Hayner, "Variability."

29. Von Hentig, "Delinquency of the American Indian," pp. 75–84.

30. Stewart, "Questions Regarding American Indian Criminality."

31. Mhyra S. Minnis, "The Relationship of the Social Structure of an Indian Community, Its Adults and Juvenile Delinquency," *Social Forces* 41 (1963): 395–403.

32. Murray L. Wax, *Indian Americans: Unity and Diversity* (Englewood Cliffs, N.J.: Prentice-Hall, 1971), p. 151.

33. Riffenburgh, "Cultural Influences and Crime among Indian-Americans."

34. Edward P. Dozier, "Problem Drinking among American Indians," *Quarterly Journal of Studies on Alcohol* 27 (1966): 72–87.

35. Stewart, "Questions Regarding American Indian Criminality," p. 66.

8

Minorities and Organized Crime

Organized crime has long been thought of as an illegal underworld enterprise composed almost exclusively of traditional white ethnic groups such as Italians, Irish, and Jews. But recent evidence suggests that more racially distinctive groups such as blacks, Hispanics, and Asians are beginning to make their presence known in organized illicit activity.

DEFINING ORGANIZED CRIME

Before proceeding, we need to distinguish between "organized" and "unorganized" crime. There is often a fine line between the two. Organized crime suggests a systematic, business approach to criminality, usually on a wide scale; conversely, unorganized crime implies criminal activity that is unsystematic, unstructured, nonunited, loosely knit, or individualistic. Both can comprise the same types of illegitimate opportunities, activities, and goals, and membership can coexist in each.

What ultimately seems to set organized crime apart from other criminality is the public's, and often law enforcement's perception of it as a secret, all-powerful organization made up of a number of criminal syndicates, or families, who collectively or singularly are referred to as La Cosa Nostra, the Mafia, underworld, mob, syndicate, or racketeers. In fact, organized crime is not limited to the types of groups or individuals that we conjure up images of but can refer to anyone in the business of committing crime who has some sense of organization in the process. Yet this obviously would make the term too broad to differentiate this type of criminality from others.

A number of definitions have been applied to organized crime. We look at three of them here.

The state of California defines organized crime as consisting of two or more persons who, with continuity of purpose, engage in one or more of the following activities: (1) the supplying of illegal goods and services, i.e., vice, loansharking, etc.; (2) predatory crime, i.e., theft, assault, etc.[1]

The FBI's definition as formulated by criminologist Donald Cressey is that

an organized crime is any crime committed by a person occupying, in an established division of labor, a position designed for the commission of crime, providing that such division of labor also includes at least one position for a corrupter, one position for a corruptee, and one position for an enforcer.[2]

The Federal Bureau of Alcohol, Tobacco, and Firearms seeks to "deal with means and ends, acts and actors" in its definition of organized crime, which it refers to as

those self-perpetuating, structured, and disciplined associations of individuals, or groups, combined together for the purpose of obtaining monetary or commercial gains or profits, wholly or in part by illegal means, while protecting their activities through a pattern of graft and corruption.[3]

Generally the criminality of minority groups such as those examined in this book has rarely been associated with organized crime as it is typically defined, for a number of reasons, including the apparent lack of organization displayed by these minorities in their criminal activities, greater emphasis on established organized crime groups, and limited knowledge as to the involvement of racially distinctive groups in organized crime.

Because this approach of implied omission appears to sell short the organizational capabilities of certain racial minorities in the pursuit of crime, we shall create a definition of organized crime to apply to blacks, Hispanics, Asians, and other minorities distinguished by physical characteristics to read as follows:

The joint commission of crime by persons of racially distinctive minority membership (though such illicit activity need not be limited to members of the same race/ethnicity or minorities) that is consistent with known organized criminal activities such as providing illegal goods and services—narcotics, pornography, prostitution, extortion, loansharking, gambling—and involves some degree of organizational structure, secrecy, membership, methodology, success; and to whom the primary objective is economic gain.

This definition is deliberately broad in order to enable us to consider certain patterns of the criminality of minority groups in a context similar to that of those ethnic groups for which most definitions of organized crime were formulated.

BLACKS IN ORGANIZED CRIME

Many see blacks as part of a new wave of ethnic groups involved in organized criminal activity in the United States, although there is disagreement over the depth of this involvement. In his controversial book *Black Mafia*, written in the early 1970s, Francis Ianni refers to an "ethnic succession" taking place in organized crime:

The Irish came first . . . [and] were succeeded in organized crime by the Jews. . . . The Italians came next . . . [and] are leaving or being pushed out of organized crime by the next wave of migrants to the city: blacks and Puerto Ricans. . . . We shall witness over the next decade the systematic development of what is now a scattered and loosely organized pattern of emerging black control in organized crime into a black Mafia.[4]

Peter Reuter, author of *Disorganized Crime*, lends credence to Ianni's contention; he maintains that black and Hispanic challenges to Mafia power in their communities have not "generated any effort by the Mafia to assert control through superior violence."[5]

Others, however, remain skeptical about an ethnic succession in organized crime. Nicholas Gage denounces any notion that the Mafia is "an equal opportunity employer": "No door is more firmly locked to blacks than the one that leads to the halls of power in organized crime."[6]

This observation notwithstanding, clearly blacks have begun to make some strides in organized crime. Prison-spawned black gangs such as the Black Guerrilla Family are known to be involved significantly in drugs and extortion beyond the prison gates. New York City police officer David Durk comments that if nothing else the drug business has emerged as an equal opportunity employer.[7]

But how "equal" have blacks become in other aspects of organized crime? Most experts agree that blacks have yet to achieve equal status beyond the lower divisions of organized criminality. Many believe that in organized crime "at its lowest levels," blacks and Hispanics "now work side by side with Italian, Irish, and Jewish racketeers. In black or Hispanic areas these 'new' ethnics oversee the distribution of drugs, prostitution, and gambling in a symbiotic relationship with old-line racketeers."[8] Peter Lupsha posits that rather than an ethnic succession taking place, blacks and Hispanics have simply been "licensed" control of some street-level crime markets that Italian-American organized criminals have discarded due to the low profit and high risks involved.[9]

Although blacks apparently have yet to move into the mainstream of organized crime, their involvement at all in conjunction with their rate of crime, the highest in the nation, makes this a group to watch in the future of American organized crime.

HISPANICS IN ORGANIZED CRIME

Hispanic groups such as Mexicans, Puerto Ricans, Cubans, and Colombians have begun to emerge in organized criminal activity. This is particularly true in the burgeoning illicit drug market, as described by sociologist Howard Abadinsky:

Drug trafficking provided a financial base and served as a catalyst for the formation of black and Hispanic organized criminal groups. In many respects, the rise of black, Mexican, Cuban, and Colombian criminal organizations, whose business centers on heroin and cocaine trafficking, parallels the experience of other ethnic groups during the Prohibition era. Heightened ethnic awareness and organization resulted in Italian-American criminal operations being forced out of many black and Hispanic areas.[10]

Hispanics are also making their way into other areas of organized crime. For instance, recently a federal commission on organized crime reported that in New York City and New Jersey, a $45 million a year illegal gambling syndicate was being run by a group of Cuban-American racketeers.[11]

Unlike black organized crime groups, who are predominantly home grown, Hispanic involvement in American organized crime is composed of many members of groups based in Spanish-speaking countries. Mexico's most well-known organized syndicate, the Herrera family, is believed to oversee the production and distribution of Mexican "brown heroin" from "opium-growing plots in the Sierra Madre Occidental Mountains to the streets of Chicago—from 'farm to arm.' "[12] Exiled Cuban criminals play a major role in the importation of drugs into the United States.

Perhaps the closest Hispanic group to the Italian-American crime families, and, arguably more violent, are those emerging from Latin America. Whereas once Colombian organized criminals concentrated on the importation of liquor, automobiles, and electronic equipment, today they are believed to be the undisputed leaders in drug trafficking.[13] Government officials have identified a small group of Colombian kingpins who have established control over the smuggling of cocaine, marijuana, and counterfeit Quaaludes into this country. *Newsweek* has described this select group as nearly "as rich and powerful as the Colombian government itself."[14] These Colombian crime families use extreme violence, even against women and children, in pursuit of their illicit trade.[15]

In addition to those Hispanic organized criminals based and established outside the United States, some have their roots in American penitentiaries. The Mexican Mafia and La Familia are products, respectively, of California and Arizona's prison systems.[16] Formed initially as a measure of self-protection and their own cultural isolation, these groups eventually made their way into criminal activities beyond the prison gates, including extortion, drug trafficking, and criminal exploitation of the poor. The Hispanic victims of these gangs are especially vulnerable because "they are isolated by language, culture, and invisible neighborhood walls and by their distrust of law enforcement authorities."[17] Should these measures of victim silence fail, varying levels of intimidation usually do not, making it all but impossible for law enforcement to respond to this organized criminality.

What these various Hispanic organized criminal groups have in common (as opposed to black organized criminals), similar to the Italians, is the importance placed on kinship in the formation and maintenance of their criminal enterprises.[18] Where Hispanics and blacks are most similar in their organized criminal networks is their general low positioning in the social and economic structure, the nature of their organized crime, the significance of their street and prison ties, the participation of women, and the lack of tradition and distinct organizational patterns in their criminality.

CHINESE ORGANIZED CRIMINALS

Despite the low crime rate noted among Asians in the United States, Asian groups are neither new nor silent in organized crime. Recent evidence suggests that their involvement in organized criminal activity in this country is spreading at a dangerous rate. Some criminal justice officials contend that in a few years, the Asiatic-originated underworld will become the nation's number one organized crime problem.

Chinese-organized crime exists in two separate yet related factions. The faction more familiar to law enforcement officials are the Chinese Tongs, offspring of secret societies long in existence in China known as Triads. Their emergence in the United States came with the early immigrants from southeastern China who were routinely and severely persecuted by the dominant group in American society. The Tongs were formed in Chinatowns across the country largely as a result of this mistreatment. Tong actually means "town hall" or "large hall." These Tongs were benevolent societies whose purpose generally was to take care of their own, including food, rent, and protection against other clans; they also helped keep the crime rate low by settling disputes outside the U.S. civil and criminal justice systems.

It was, however, the criminal activities of these secret societies that formed the basis of their power. Tongs provided and profited from such illicit services as drugs, gambling, and prostitution. During the 1860s they controlled the drug trafficking in San Francisco's Chinatown and managed its houses of gambling and prostitution.[19] The Tongs also were notorious for their gang wars and killings as they competed with each other for control of the illegal services in Chinatowns.

Today Tongs call themselves "benevolent associations" or "merchant associations" and are engaged in legitimate business. Yet they also continue to engage in gambling, drug smuggling, and loan-sharking.[20] According to the President's Commission on Organized Crime, established in 1983 by President Reagan, in a "fight to break the power of the mob," Tongs that contain criminal elements are active throughout the United States and Canada.[21]

The second faction of Chinese membership in the ranks of organized crime in the United States is the Asian-based Chinese Triad societies, which have only recently begun to enter this country as "part of a new [to the United States] crime cartel that is emerging in the Far East and spreading" to North America.[22] Referred to by Fenton Bresler, author of *The Chinese Mafia*, as "a new and terrible menace on the scene of international crime," Triad societies emerged in the late seventeenth century in China as resistance fighters working to overthrow the Ch'ing Dynasty and restore the Ming Dynasty to the imperial Chinese throne.[23] Early Chinese novels often portrayed their members as Robin Hoods. The term *triad* derives from the original groups' sacred symbol, a triangle that is representative of heaven, earth, and man—the three basic forces of nature for Chinese people.

Modern Triads are far from Robin Hoods by most accounts. The Immigration and Naturalization Service has called the Chinese Triads notoriously ruthless: "Triads have been known to smuggle heroin from Asia by killing infants, placing heroin inside their dead bodies and using women posing as nursing mothers to carry the heroin across national borders."[24]

The Commission on Organized Crime has linked Chinese Triad societies to significant involvement in narcotics, prostitution, robbery, gambling, extortion, corruption of government officials, and murder in the United States, as well as having ties to La Cosa Nostra. These Chinese criminal gangs are believed to be responsible for 20 to 30 percent of the heroin being smuggled into the United States and are thought to be "engaged in huge money-laundering operations using American banks in Hong Kong to hide their illegal activities."[25]

Few details have emerged in studies on Asian crime on the alleged relationship between U.S. Tongs and Asia-based Chinese Triad societies; however, given their common roots, it is reasonable to assume the connection may be at least as potentially as serious as it is between U.S.- and Sicilian-based contingents of organized crime. Clearly Chinese organized crime is something we need to learn more about.

JAPANESE ORGANIZED CRIMINALS

The Japanese also have historical ties to organized crime in the United States. Beginning in the early 1900s, resident Japanese became active in illegal gambling operations, particularly in downtown Los Angeles's Little Tokyo community where the Tokyo Club controlled gambling all over the West. In the early 1930s, Japanese were drawn into the illicit drug trade in America after they had conquered the narcotics market in East Asia. These activities ceased operation following the attack on Pearl Harbor, the opening of Japanese internment camps, and the postwar anti-Japanese sentiments.

Japanese organized criminal activities have once again begun to attract the attention of American law enforcement (some would argue this is the first serious attention regarding crime in the United States accorded to this Asian group). The Japanese Yakuza or "mafia" are said to have more than 100,000 members in Japan and are entering this country with extensive gambling, extortion, sexual slavery, drug smuggling, and money laundering operations. David Kaplan and Alec Dubro, coauthors of the provocative book *Yakuza*, contend that this Japanese version of La Cosa Nostra is one of the largest, most powerful crime organizations in the world.[26]

The Yakuza dates back to seventeenth-century feudal Japan when its members were originally outcast samurai, or knights, and peasants, who were able to gain control over parts of Japan's urban communities due to the leadership of Japanese Robin Hoods such as the legendary Chobei Banzuiin. These gangs were referred to as *machi-yakko*, or "servants of the town."

Today Yakuza members regard themselves as modern samurai and have adopted the exotic customs of their ancestry, including extensive tattooing that often covers their bodies from the neck to the ankles and the self-amputation of a fingertip with a short sword to offer to the "don" as a measure of penitence for botched assignments.

Yakuza essentially means "good for nothing" and is derived from a blackjack-like Japanese card game in which the drawn cards 8, 9, and 3 are pronounced in Japanese: *Ya-Ku-Za*, or "a worthless hand." Yakuza members thus view themselves as worthless social outcasts. Similar to many of the American organized criminals, many Yakuza members were "born into poverty and graduated from juvenile delinquency into organized crime."[27]

The first Japanese Yakuza were believed to have come to Hawaii in the 1960s, where they extorted money from Japanese-Americans and tourists and set up illegal bookmaking operations. In recent years their illicit activities, as well as legitimate businesses, have expanded to Los Angeles, San Francisco, Arizona, Washington, Nevada, and New York, where they are said to be involved in high-stakes gambling operations as part of a joint Yakuza–Italian-American crime enterprise.

According to witnesses who testified during three days of hearings held by the President's Commission on Organized Crime to address the emerging organized criminality of Asian groups in this country, so far the Yakuza, unlike the Chinese Triad, has not solicited the membership of Asian-Americans; however, they do apparently use Japanese-Americans as guides and interpreters.[28]

VIETNAMESE ORGANIZED CRIMINALS

Although the Vietnamese entry into American organized crime is the newest among Asian groups, it threatens to be just as prominent in the long run. In the opinion of Arlington, Virginia, police detective James Badey: "If the Vietnamese criminal element is allowed to continue unchecked or only moderately checked we shall have, in the not too distant future, a well defined, highly sophisticated, organized crime machine which when compared to the [Mafia] will make the [Mafia] look like a fraternity of wimps."[29]

The President's Commission on Organized Crime has reported that in at least thirteen states, gangs of Vietnamese refugees are "expanding criminal operations" that include narcotics, gambling, prostitution, extortion, robbery, and smuggling.[30] The gangs include San Francisco's Black Eagle, Houston's Fishermen, Chicago's Eagle Seven, and Orange County's (California) Frogmen.

Criminologists and criminal justice officials disagree as to the organization of Vietnamese crime in the United States. Some believe there is at least a minimal connection between various gangs in different cities; others believe that a nationwide Vietnamese criminal organization exists, headed by former South Vietnamese generals.

Some experts reject both theories as "demeaning speculation based on American prejudices from the Vietnam War era."[31] They prefer to relate the criminality of Vietnamese exiles to a small number of youths in poorly organized gangs, similar to other urban delinquent gangs. As evidence, they point to the rate of Vietnamese crime, which is the lowest among both Asian and other ethnic groups in the United States.

Nevertheless, there has been a noticeable increase in household robberies by armed Vietnamese gangs in Orange County, California, a suburban area south of Los Angeles and the home of some 90,000 Vietnamese residents, the largest concentration in the nation. Some law enforcement officials argue that there has to be at least some form of structure to account for this increase. Louis Spalla, an Arizona Narcotics Strike Force officer and a former Vietnam veteran and adviser to South Vietnamese police, in a 1979 report wrote that a nationwide Vietnamese "Mafia-type" criminal syndicate, the Association, exists. He contended that it included former South Vietnamese soldiers who served as enforcers and were engaged in crimes ranging from drug smuggling and prostitution to extortion and murder.[32] The existence of organized Vietnamese criminal activity was further corroborated in late 1984 during hearings of the Commission on Organized Crime. One Vietnamese witness, identifying himself as a high-level operative of an unnamed Vietnamese gang, testified that he was trained in Los Angeles to use machine guns and perpetrate crimes.[33]

The evidence is still somewhat shaky about the existence and extent of Vietnamese organized crime, yet the consensus is that even if in an early stage, it does exist and will get stronger.

FIGHTING ORGANIZED MINORITY GROUP CRIME

The battle against the new ethnic minority groups' involvement in organized crime is being fought as part of the overall problem of organized crime. That is, the same law enforcement combat efforts waged against traditional organized criminal syndicates apply also to more recent groups. Yet only relatively recently have any effective measures been aimed at organized crime. The Transportation in Aid of Racketeering Enterprises Act (Travel Act) was one of the first prominent anti–organized crime measures.[34] The act prohibits "travel in interstate commerce or use of interstate facilities with the intent to promote, manage, establish, carry on, or facilitate an unlawful activity; it also prohibits the actual or attempted engagement in these activities."[35]

Under the Organized Crime Control Act of 1970, Title IX is perhaps its most effective weapon. The Racketeer Influenced and Corrupt Organizations Act (RICO) established new categories of offenses (as opposed to new crimes) in racketeering, which it defined as participation in at least two acts prohibited by twenty-four current federal and eight state statutes, such as the federal crimes of white slavery, counterfeiting, bribery, loan-sharking, mail fraud, wire fraud, and drug violations and the state crimes of murder, gambling, bribery, kidnapping, and extortion.[36] A person convicted under RICO could be subject to twenty years' imprisonment and a $25,000 fine.

In 1983, the government launched its "most ambitious drive against organized crime in two decades," the President's Commission on Organized Crime. It sought to determine the extent, range, and participants of organized crime in America and to evaluate judicial, legislative, and law enforcement ways to fight it.

Although the final report of the commission warned of emerging organized crime groups and the FBI and local law enforcement agencies are aware of minority member participants in organized crime, there is still only limited knowledge of the organized criminality of blacks, Hispanics, and Asians and, hence, limited emphasis on targeting legislative and law enforcement efforts toward controlling it. This is particularly true pertaining to Asian criminal organizations where language barriers, traditions, and codes of silence have made penetrating these groups virtually impossible.

Perhaps the continued dominance of organized crime in America by traditional white ethnic groups dictates that efforts at controlling this area of criminality be targeted toward this majority. However, history should serve as an example that the best way to fight criminal elements is to do so before they get too large and therefore unbreakable.

There has been an increased spotlight on new or nontraditional participants in the underworld of organized crime. Blacks, Hispanics, and Asians have shown the capacity for and capability of organizing for criminal motives, although the degree of organization varies from group to group or subgroup. We know little about the dynamics and dimensions of these groups in organized crime. Clearly this is an area of criminology that must be pursued. These groups have proved that in organized criminal activity they are no longer the silent minority.

NOTES

1. Task Force on Organized Crime, *Organized Crime* (Washington, D.C.: U.S. Government Printing Office, 1976), p. 214.

2. Donald R. Cressey, *Theft of the Nation* (New York: Harper & Row, 1969), p. 319.

3. Howard Abadinsky, *Organized Crime,* 2d ed. (Chicago: Nelson-Hall, 1985), p. 5.

4. Francis A. J. Ianni, *Black Mafia: Ethnic Succession in Organized Crime* (New York: Simon and Schuster, 1974), pp. 12–14.

5. Peter Reuter, *Disorganized Crime* (Cambridge: MIT Press, 1983), p. 136.

6. Nicholas Gage, *The Mafia Is Not an Equal Opportunity Employer* (New York: McGraw-Hill, 1971), p. 113.

7. David Durk and Ira Silverman, *The Pleasant Avenue Connection* (New York: Harper & Row, 1976).

8. Larry J. Siegel, *Criminology,* 2d ed. (St. Paul, Minn.: West Publishing Co., 1986), p. 392.

9. Peter A. Lupsha, "Individual Choice, Material Culture, and Organized Crime," *Criminology* 19 (1981): 3–24.

10. Abadinsky, *Organized Crime*, p. 154.

11. Eric Schmitt, "U.S. Panel Says Cuban Emigrés Run a Bet Ring," *New York Times* (June 25, 1985): B4.

12. Abadinsky, *Organized Crime*, p. 159.

13. Ibid., pp. 160–63.

14. Mark Whitaker, Elaine Shannon, and Ron Moreau, "Colombia's King of Coke," *Newsweek* (February 25, 1985): 19.

15. "The Evil Empire," *Newsweek* (February 25, 1985): 14–18.

16. See George Park, "The Organization of Prison Violence," in Albert K. Cohen, George F. Cole, and Robert G. Bayley, eds., *Prison Violence* (Lexington, Mass.: Lexington Books, 1976); Herbert Edelhertz, Roland J. Cole, and Bonnie Berk, *The Containment of Organized Crime* (Lexington, Mass.: Lexington Books, 1984), pp. 16–17.

17. Edelhertz, Cole, and Berk, *Containment of Organized Crime*, p. 17.

18. Ianni, *Black Mafia*, p. 201.

19. Milton Meltzer, *The Chinese Americans* (New York: Thomas Y. Crowell, 1980), p. 100.

20. Ivan Light and Charles Choy Wong, "Protest or Work: Dilemmas of the Tourist Industry in America Chinatowns," *American Journal of Sociology* 80 (1975): 1359.

21. Margot Hornblower, "Asian Mafia Seen Spreading," *Washington Post* (October 24, 1984): A3.

22. Jack Anderson and Joseph Spear, "Spread of Chinese Gangs Worries INS," *Washington Post* (January 25, 1986): C13.

23. Fenton Bresler, *The Chinese Mafia* (New York: Stein and Day, 1980), pp. 27–28.

24. Immigration and Naturalization Service "strategic assessment" bulletin, quoted in Anderson and Spear, "Spread of Chinese Gangs."

25. Fox Butterfield, "Chinese Organized Crime Said to Rise in the U.S.," *New York Times* (January 13, 1985): A2.

26. David E. Kaplan and Alec Dubro, *Yakuza: The Explosive Account of Japan's Criminal Underworld* (Reading, Mass.: Addison-Wesley, 1986).

27. Donald Kirk, "Crime, Politics and Finger Chopping," *New York Times Magazine* (December 12, 1976): 93.

28. Margot Hornblower, "Japanese Crime Group Expands," *Washington Post* (October 25, 1984): A19.

29. James R. Badey, written testimony before the President's Commission on Organized Crime, quoted in Margot Hornblower, "Vietnamese Criminal Gangs Cited by Mystery Witness," *Washington Post* (December 26, 1984): A2.

30. Hornblower, "Vietnamese Criminal Gangs." See also President's Commission on Organized Crime, *Organized Crime of Asian Origin* (Washington, D.C.: Government Printing Office, 1985).

31. Fox Butterfield, "The Shifting Picture of Crime by U.S. Vietnamese," *New York Times* (January 21, 1985): A13(L).

32. Ibid.

33. Hornblower, "Vietnamese Criminal Gangs."
34. 18 U.S.C. 1952 (1976).
35. Siegel, *Criminology*, p. 393.
36. Public Law No. 91–452, Title IX, 84 Stat. 941 (1970).

9

The Delinquency of Racial and Ethnic Minorities

Perhaps the most critical area of the criminality of minorities concerns youth. Indeed a disproportionate amount of study has been devoted to juvenile delinquents (as opposed to adult criminals), for several reasons. One is the belief that an understanding of the criminality of delinquents will get to the root of all criminal behavior. A second is the hope that such research might lead to ways to reduce delinquency and prevent juvenile delinquents from becoming adult criminals. Another explanation for the attention on adolescent crime is the diversity and controversy of juvenile antisocial behavior, ranging from status offenses in which juveniles are subject to labeling, arrest, and conviction to the more serious, more noticeable violent crime that seems to be plaguing urban centers to gang delinquency that many believe is the force behind most juvenile crime. Minorities as a group seem to be overrepresented in most juvenile arrest and crime data, as well as the literature.

MEASURING THE DELINQUENCY OF MINORITIES

There are two primary ways in which we learn about the scope of delinquency among minority groups: official arrest statistics and self-report surveys. Self-report surveys rely on asking young people if they have participated in criminal or delinquent behavior that led (or could have led) to arrest or referral to the juvenile court.

ARREST DATA

UCR arrest data for 1985 reflect a disproportionately high percentage of arrests of black, Hispanic, and Native American youths; Asians un-

Table 9.1
Total Arrests of Juveniles,[a] by Race/Ethnicity, 1985

Percent Distribution:

Offense Charged	By Race[b]					By Ethnic Origin		
	Total	White	Black	American Indian or Alaskan Native	Asian or Pacific Islander	Total	Hispanic	Non-Hispanic
TOTAL	100.0	74.9	23.2	.9	1.0	100.0	11.7	88.3
Murder & nonnegligent manslaughter	100.0	48.2	50.7	.2	.1	100.0	21.5	78.5
Forcible rape	100.0	48.3	50.6	.7	.2	100.0	9.4	90.6
Robbery	100.0	32.1	66.8	.3	.1	100.0	15.3	84.7
Aggravated assault	100.0	57.8	40.7	.8	.3	100.0	14.2	85.8
Burglary	100.0	75.9	22.5	.8	.2	100.0	13.2	86.8
Larceny-theft	100.0	70.8	26.7	1.2	1.0	100.0	10.0	90.0
Motor vehicle theft	100.0	69.1	28.9	1.1	1.0	100.0	12.6	87.4
Arson	100.0	84.7	13.6	1.0	.7	100.0	9.1	90.9
Violent crime[c]	100.0	46.3	52.4	.6	.7	100.0	14.5	85.5
Property crime[d]	100.0	72.1	25.7	1.1	1.2	100.0	11.0	89.0
Crime Index total[e]	100.0	69.2	28.6	1.0	1.1	100.0	11.3	88.7
Other assaults	100.0	65.2	32.8	.8	1.2	100.0	10.4	89.6
Forgery & counterfeiting	100.0	82.6	16.0	.9	.5	100.0	6.4	93.6
Fraud	100.0	54.1	44.3	.2	1.5	100.0	24.6	75.4
Embezzlement	100.0	74.3	23.7	.9	1.1	100.0	10.1	89.9
Stolen property; buying, receiving, possessing	100.0	65.7	33.1	.6	.6	100.0	13.0	87.0
Vandalism	100.0	83.0	15.5	.7	.8	100.0	9.5	90.5
Weapons; carrying, possessing, etc.	100.0	69.1	29.5	.5	1.0	100.0	16.0	84.0

132

Prostitution & commercialized vice	100.0	58.4	40.4	.9	.3	100.0	7.4	92.6
Sex offenses (except forcible rape & prostitution)	100.0	72.8	26.1	.5	.6	100.0	9.0	91.0
Drug abuse violations	100.0	77.0	21.5	.5	1.0	100.0	18.8	81.2
Gambling	100.0	24.4	59.5	.1	15.9	100.0	5.6	94.4
Offenses against family & children	100.0	76.5	22.1	.6	.8	100.0	10.5	89.5
Driving under the influence	100.0	95.6	2.7	1.2	.5	100.0	11.3	88.7
Liquor laws	100.0	95.1	2.8	1.6	.5	100.0	5.3	94.7
Drunkenness	100.0	93.3	5.0	1.5	.2	100.0	25.6	74.4
Disorderly conduct	100.0	74.1	25.0	.6	.3	100.0	11.3	88.7
Vagrancy	100.0	85.3	14.0	.4	.3	100.0	12.5	87.5
All other offenses (except traffic)	100.0	74.4	23.8	.5	1.3	100.0	14.3	85.7
Suspicion	100.0	81.8	17.0	.8	.5	100.0	11.1	88.9
Curfew & loitering law violations	100.0	74.3	23.6	.9	1.2	100.0	10.3	89.7
Runaways	100.0	84.7	13.1	.9	1.2	100.0	7.7	92.3

[a] Arrests of persons under age 18.

[b] Because of rounding, the percentages may not add to total.

[c] Violent crimes are offenses of murder, forcible rape, robbery, and aggravated assault.

[d] Property crimes are offenses of burglary, larceny-theft, motor vehicle theft, and arson.

[e] Includes arson.

Source: U.S. Federal Bureau of Investigation, *Crime in the United States: Uniform Crime Reports, 1985* (Washington, D.C.: Government Printing Office, 1986), pp. 183, 186.

der the age of 18 are arrested proportionately lower than their numbers in the population (Table 9.1). Although whites show by far the greatest percentage of total arrests—nearly 75 percent—-the figure falls below their percentage of the juvenile population.

On the other hand, blacks, who account for roughly 13 percent of all juveniles in this country, constituted 23.2 percent of the arrests of persons under age 18 in 1985. For violent crimes, this figure more than doubled—to 52.4 percent. Blacks under the age of 18 comprised 50.7 percent of all juvenile arrests for murder and nonnegligent manslaughter.

Detroit on the Spot

The city of Detroit is in the midst of one of its worst outbreaks of teen violence, specifically, black teen shootings. A youth was shot in Detroit every day on the average in 1986; the overwhelming majority of these shootings involved poor, inner-city black males as both victims and offenders.[1] In April 1987, city leaders closed Detroit's twenty-three high schools for two days to hold student-parent forums on the growing violence plaguing the city and also imposed a citywide curfew on teens.

Although teenage violence has become an epidemic throughout the country, its proportion in Detroit relative to population size is almost unprecedented. In the city, which already has the distinction of having the nation's highest city murder rate, forty-three youths under the age of 17 were slain in 1986. Through the first four months of 1987, more than one hundred persons under age 16 were shot, and at least ten of them died.[2]

Perhaps most frightening, most of the shootings appear unprovoked. Detroit differs in this respect from such other cities as New York and Los Angeles, where juvenile murders are predominantly associated with gang activity or drugs. Most criminologists and criminal justice officials are at a loss to explain this unusual phenomenon. Some experts suggest that crime in Detroit seems to be "feeding on itself" and that the violent-prone years of adolescence make this group most susceptible to committing crimes.

Where this violence and loss of young, mostly black lives will end, no one is sure. However, the spotlight is now on Detroit, which will serve as a model for examining and dealing with this problem elsewhere in the nation.

In fact, black youths are disproportionately represented in arrest data for all Crime Index offenses, with the exception of arson, as well as most Part II offenses.

Although the differential may not be as glaring, Hispanics and Native Americans also show alarming rates of arrest. Hispanics in 1985 accounted for 11.7 percent of juvenile arrests and 14.5 percent of the arrests for crimes of violence, including 21.5 percent of the murder and nonnegligent manslaughter arrests—this in comparison with their approximately 6 percent share of the juvenile population. Because many Hispanics are also included in UCR data as black, the disproportion of

Table 9.2
Most Frequent Arrests of Juveniles, by Offense and Race/Ethnicity, 1985

Rank	B L A C K	Rank	N A T I V E A M E R I C A N
1	Larceny-theft	1	Larceny-theft
2	All other offenses (except traffic)	2	Liquor laws
3	Burglary	3	All other offenses (except traffic)
4	Other assaults	4	Runaways
5	Disorderly conduct	5	Burglary
6	Robbery	6	Vandalism
7	Runaways	7	Other assaults
8	Drug abuse violations	8	Curfew & loitering law violations
9	Curfew & loitering law violations	9	Disorderly conduct
10	Vandalism	10	Motor vehicle theft

Rank	H I S P A N I C	Rank	A S I A N
1	All other offenses (except traffic)	1	Larceny-theft
2	Larceny-theft	2	All other offenses (except traffic)
3	Burglary	3	Runaways
4	Drug abuse violations	4	Burglary
5	Runaways	5	Other assaults
6	Vandalism	6	Curfew & loitering law violations
7	Disorderly conduct	7	Drug abuse violations
8	Other assaults	8	Vandalism
9	Liquor laws	9	Liquor laws
10	Drunkenness	10	Motor vehicle theft

Source: Adapted from U.S. Federal Bureau of Investigation, *Crime in the United States: Uniform Crime Reports 1985* (Washington, D.C.: Government Printing Office, 1986), pp. 183, 186.

Hispanic crime could be even greater. A scan of the offenses shows that only for the crimes of liquor law violations and gambling does the Hispanic percentage of arrest fall below their proportion of the population.

Native American youths, who represent around 0.6% percent of the juvenile population, show a higher percentage of arrests in a number of offenses, including property crime, alcohol-related offenses, and prostitution and runaways. Because of the low number of total arrests of Native American juveniles, their high rate of crime often goes unnoticed.

It is unclear why Asian youths, who represent a greater percentage of the juvenile population than Native Americans, have such a low arrest rate in comparison with other minority groups, although part of the reason is believed to be the closeness of the Asian community, which handles many of these disputes. The only offense for which Asian arrests exceeded their population representation was gambling.

These arrest distributions have proved to be consistent for a number of years.

Another measure of the nature and incidence of juvenile crime among these minority groups is the offense pattern of most frequent arrests for each group. Table 9.2 lists the top ten offenses for which black, Native American, Hispanic, and Asian juveniles were arrested in 1985. For each group, larceny-theft was in the top two offenses for most frequent arrest among all offenses. Burglary was the third offense blacks and Hispanics were most frequently arrested for. By and large, however, each group was arrested most often for Part II offenses, specifically status offenses or related ones, such as runaways, curfew violations, vandalism, and disorderly conduct.

A closer analysis of each group's pattern of frequency could indicate basic ethnic differences regarding the type of crimes most frequently committed by specific minority groups. For instance, black youths appear to be more likely to be arrested for juvenile criminal violations as opposed to status offenses, whereas Hispanics seem more prone to substance abuse–related arrests. Or the nature of each group's arrests could be related more to discriminatory treatment by law enforcement, differential opportunity, or other factors.

Limitations of Arrest Data

We have already examined weaknesses of official statistics in general and with respect to minorities. A major drawback to arrest data for the purpose of this chapter is the lack of a good breakdown by age of minority juvenile arrestees. For instance, perhaps a more effective analysis of the arrest patterns of various ethnic groups would result by comparing the arrests and crime distribution of those between, say, ages 16 and 18 with those ages 14 to 16, or, better, looking at specific crime and arrest patterns for each age group up to age 18.

Also, no official measurement of delinquency combines age, gender, and race/ethnicity, a neglect that hampers studying these groups effectively. Such an approach may be necessary in the future to allow criminologists and researchers better to assess, understand, and apply theories to the criminal behavior of groups and subgroups of delinquent minority members.

SELF-REPORT DATA

Self-report surveys have been viewed by many criminologists as a necessary alternative to official data and their limitations in measuring the extent of juvenile delinquency. Most such studies have focused on high school and college students who are surveyed as to whether they have ever or within certain time frames violated juvenile or criminal laws. Generally self-report studies reveal that law violations among youths are far more widespread and frequent than indicated by official statistics. In fact, self-reported information suggests that virtually everyone in the general population has committed at least one violation of the law, although most such violations are petty or status-type offenses such as truancy, alcohol use, fighting, and shoplifting.

Self-report studies often focus on class differences in delinquent behavior rather than differences in race/ethnicity. When race is measured, it is almost entirely related to black-white delinquency comparisons. Thus, there is no way to assess the nature and extent of the delinquency of other minority groups in comparison with each other and black and white delinquents.

When black and white delinquents have been studied through self-report measures, the results have been inconsistent though generally nonsupportive of official findings. Early studies by Leroy Gould[3] and William Chambliss and Richard Nagasawa[4] found that in spite of the significantly higher rate of official black delinquency than white delinquency, self-report data revealed that white youths show a rate slightly higher than that of blacks. More recent studies, such as that conducted by Michael Hindelang, Travis Hirschi, and Joseph Weis, reveal that blacks are more likely to report serious offenses, whereas blacks and whites are similar in their rate of trivial offense involvement.[5] Others have found black delinquency to be more frequent than that of whites;[6] and still others report the differential rate of frequency of black and white delinquent acts to be negligible.[7]

The consensus of such studies seems to be that the discrepancy between blacks and whites in official statistics is not substantiated by self-report data, indicating that class biases likely do exist within the criminal justice system and could be applied as well when looking at the official delinquent patterns of other minority group members, particularly Native Americans and Hispanics.

Shortcomings of Self-Report Data

Undoubtedly the primary failure of self-report studies for our purpose is the lack of attention paid to racial and ethnic groups aside from blacks and whites. Even on the rare occasions when other minority groups are included in self-report measurements, it is usually only as an addendum to the major emphasis on black or white delinquency. This omission of serious study of racial and ethnic minorities through self-reports undermines greatly their effectiveness in establishing the characteristics of all juvenile offenders.

Other weaknesses of self-report data include their dependence on respondent honesty, relatively small sample groups, communication problems, measurement difficulties, and lack of qualified researchers.

JUVENILE GANG DELINQUENCY

Little research has been carried out on the delinquency of juvenile gangs since the 1950s and 1960s; yet the number, membership, and degree of violent delinquent gangs in the United States has risen steadily. Recently Walter Miller, who has studied juvenile gang membership in this country extensively, identified 2,200 gangs nationally consisting of about 96,000 members spread out over 300 communities.[8]

The relationship between gang membership and delinquency appears particularly significant among racial and ethnic minority members of the lower classes. In Los Angeles County, criminal justice officials estimated that in 1986 there were between 450 and 500 juvenile street gangs representing most ethnic groups, with a total membership of 45,000 to 50,000.[9]

Said the head of the Los Angeles city attorney's gang unit, "These gangs are extremely violent today. They're killers. We literally have dead bodies all over the place."[10] An organizer for a Los Angeles group that works to keep youths from joining gangs has recently described gang violence in the city as reaching an all-time high. A city attorney spokesman notes caustically: "We're not talking about kids with zip guns. We're talking about kids with Uzis."[11] The number of gang-related homicides in Los Angeles County illustrates the severity of its gang problem. Between 1980 and 1985, there were, respectively, 351, 267, 205, 214, 355, and 269 such homicides.[12]

Although juvenile gangs are not new to Los Angeles—they developed in the early 1900s upon the arrival of Mexican immigrants to the city—their numbers and membership have increased drastically since the early 1970s. Some attribute this increase to Hispanics and Southeast Asian immigrants banding together as a measure of self-defense and the formation of social ties traditionally provided by families.[13]

The nature of juvenile gangs has also undergone significant changes from earlier years. Whereas once their primary occupation was protection and control of their territory, they have expanded into drug dealing, extortion, and other crimes. Robert Ruchhoft, a veteran of the police department's Gang Activities Section in Los Angeles, sees these changes especially in black and Asian gang delinquency. Black gangs, he notes, have stepped up from traditional turf wars and knife fights to drug distribution and hired killers or, as he put it, their delinquency is "disorganized crime on the threshold of organized crime."[14]

Asian gangs are the latest menace in Los Angeles County. Their members are the offspring of the many thousands of Vietnamese, Filipinos, and Koreans who have immigrated to the city. Asian gangs differ markedly from their black and Hispanic counterparts, who "communicate, boast and threaten by spray-painting graffiti on walls and seem to thrive on both negative and positive publicity."[15] In contrast, Asian gangs tend to be more secretive, shunning the limelight. Specializing in extortion and robbery of Asian residents, Ruchhoft contends that Asian gangs are "the closest thing we've got to real organized crime in Los Angeles."[16] Although the overall rate of Asian crime is low, the criminality and violence of juvenile gangs of Asian origin have increased in recent years, as seen in the following:

Chinatown Juvenile Gangs: An Increasingly Serious Problem

There are recent indications that Chinese youth gangs are becoming a greater problem in Chinatowns throughout the United States, though this is generally not reflected in Asian arrest or incarceration statistics. For instance, in 1966, Chinese juvenile delinquents in New York's Chinatown rose to more than 200, after having never exceeded 10 per year prior to 1966.[17] Many of these youths were believed to have been part of juvenile gangs.

In the San Francisco Bay Area, a number of Chinese juvenile street gangs have been identified, such as the Hwa Ching and the Yu Li, some claiming more than 200 members.[18] These youths fight each other, snatch purses, and engage in robbery, extortion, and murder. In some instances, gang members work for criminal Chinese Tongs; they also operate in defiance of traditional Chinatown criminal elements, resulting at times in open warfare between the old and the new.[19]

This upsurge in Chinese juvenile delinquency is explained by the overcrowding, mental illness, substance abuse, and a feeling of alienation from their host cities that characterize most Chinatowns, leaving many Chinese believing they must deal with their problems alone. Many Chinese immigrant youths are experiencing language barriers, unemployment, low-paying jobs, and difficult adjustments to cultural and social differences of both white America and traditional Chinese communities. Many of these juveniles have banded together in street gangs whose penchant for violence and other serious crimes as well as a seeming disregard for others is plaguing a number of Chinatowns.[20]

There is still far too little known about Chinese or other Asian delinquent gangs to elaborate on the problem. Clearly it requires more study and the attention of law enforcement.

Although the ethnic diversity of juvenile gang membership in Los Angeles County may be atypical, the ethnic dominance of delinquent gangs by minority groups and the concentration of serious criminal involvement in lower-class urban areas are evident throughout the country. At the same time, there is evidence that middle- and upper-class white delinquent gangs are not less violent. Rather, members of these gangs may benefit from class biases prevalent in the criminal justice system and labeling mechanisms of society.

CAUSAL THEORIES OF JUVENILE GANG DELINQUENCY

There has been a paucity of recent theoretical research on delinquent gangs; yet many criminologists contend that juvenile gangs, specifically minority member gangs, account for a great deal of all lower-class crime. In a survey of gang behavior between 1973 and 1977, Miller found that gangs and other groups of youth delinquents committed more than 50 percent of all youth crimes.[21] Thus it is important to review the three most influential theories of juvenile gang delinquency to date.

Reaction-Formation Theory

Albert Cohen advanced his reaction-formation theory in his 1955 book, *Delinquent Boys: The Culture of the Gang*.[22] Influenced largely by Merton's social structural theory of anomie, Cohen's theory sought to explain the disproportionate involvement of lower-class youths in delinquent behavior as seen through official data. He posits that the delinquency of lower-class youths represents a necessary response or reaction to the norms and values of the middle class.

Cohen, like Merton, cites such values as seeking success through working hard; disciplining oneself; having optimism for the future; deferment of gratification; being responsible; being ambitious; respecting property; using one's skills to progress; and controlling violence and aggression. Although lower-class youths learn these values from their parents, the media, teachers, and ex-members of the lower class, they are generally at a disadvantage in institutional settings, such as the school, where they are measured by middle-class standards. Furthermore, lower-class adolescents are too young to have a family or well-paying job; thus, they lack legitimate opportunities to attain culturally prescribed goals.

As a result of these blocked opportunities to achieve societal goals legitimately, Cohen theorizes that lower-class juveniles undergo a type of culture conflict, which he refers to as "status frustration" or a "reaction-formation against a middle-class organized status dilemma in which the lower-class boy suffers status frustrations in competition with middle status boys."[23] This causes many of these youths to band together in juvenile gangs and participate in conduct that is "nonutilitarian, malicious, and negativistic."[24]

Cohen sees this as a delinquent subculture where the values are just the opposite of middle-class values. Because of an emotional attachment to middle-class goals that are unattainable, these youths reject such goals and instead establish their own standards by which to achieve success and, with it, status, self-esteem, and solidarity.

Cohen therefore associates juvenile delinquent gangs with the lower class and the rejection of middle-class values and attributes this delinquent subculture to the structural failures of the system (that is, the family and the institutional settings).

There is much merit in Cohen's work; he was among the first to associate the school with delinquency. Nevertheless, his reaction-formation theory can be criticized. Foremost is that he offers no conclusive empirical evidence in support of his propositions. Also his focus is solely on the delinquent gang subculture of the lower class and therefore is not applicable to the criminality of the individual delinquent or of gang delinquency of the middle and upper classes. The implication is that it is only lower-class youth groups, or primarily minority member delinquent gangs, that we need be concerned about.

Other faults with Cohen's theory lie in the reaction-formation concept itself. There is little evidence to support the contention that lower-class youths repudiate middle-class values. Nor is it fair or sensible to group all delinquents or gang members in behavior patterns described as nonutilitarian, malicious, and negativistic, just as it would be impractical to suggest that nonlabeled delinquents are all sensible, utilitarian, and law abiding. And there is no explanation for why some delinquents leave gangs as they grow older and join the mainstream and its values, while other delinquent youths become adult criminals.

On the whole, Cohen's theory fails because its social-psychological premise cannot be validated scientifically.

Differential Opportunity Theory

In their renowned *Delinquency and Opportunity: A Theory of Delinquent Gangs* (1960), Richard Cloward and Lloyd Ohlin contributed substantially to the study and understanding of criminal subcultures.[25] Their theory of differential opportunity was inspired by Merton's theory of anomie and Sutherland's differential association theory.

Cloward and Ohlin follow Merton's structuralist formulation of cultural goals and the unequal access of some to the socially structured means of attaining them. They go one step further by positing that one's access to both legitimate and illegitimate means is influenced by the social structure. That is, while differential opportunity exists in reaching cultural goals through legitimate means, differential opportunity is also present in the use of illegitimate means for attaining cultural goals.

Differential opportunity theory concentrates on the difference between what lower-class youths desire and what they have access to, assuming that "discrepancies between aspirations and legitimate chances of achievement increase as one descends in the class structure."[26] Because lower-class youths are not able to lower their aspirations as learned from the larger society, their lack of access to approved means to reach culturally defined goals results in deep frustration and deviation to illegitimate means to attain these cultural goals.

Cloward and Ohlin postulate that two types of opportunities are distributed unequally: (1) access to "learning structures," or the "appropriate environments for the acquisition of the values and skills associated with the performance of a particular role," and (2) access to "performance structures," or the opportunity to group with those sharing a related problem of adjustment and the opportunity to obtain peer approval for one's behavior.[27] The theory of differential opportunity contends that it is the social structure of a community that determines the access lower-class juveniles will have to learning and performance structures. Thus, the type of delinquent subculture and type of juvenile gang in a given area are dependent on the community social structure.

According to the researchers, depending on the available means, three kinds of subcultural responses to blocked legitimate opportunity exist:

Criminal gangs. These gangs use illegitimate routes to seek material gain, power, and prestige. This response occurs primarily in stable lower-class neighborhoods where there is an established link between juvenile delinquents and organized adult criminals. Youths observe and learn the necessary values and skills of criminal participation (primarily property crimes) as they become adult criminals.

Conflict gangs. Conflict gangs enable juveniles to achieve prestige in their peer groups. These gangs develop in communities lacking both legitimate and stable illegitimate opportunities for success. Consequently, they may create their own goals of success (for example, being viewed as tough) and the means by which to achieve them (such as the gang violence, robberies, and assaults that typify conflict gangs).

Retreatist gangs. These gangs develop when juveniles are blocked from or abandon legitimate and illegitimate opportunities to attain success. Retreatist juveniles generally fall into patterns of substance use and abuse and usually develop secondary criminal behavior to support their habit (such as prostitution, con artistry, and selling drugs). They achieve personal status with those they are around by trying to be the "coolest" person.

Cloward and Ohlin's differential opportunity theory appears more solid than Cohen's theory, for its recognition of various kinds of delinquent gang subcultures may be more representative of actual juvenile gang behavior than Cohen's view of delinquent acts as purposeless, destructive, or vile. (Cohen later acknowledged that his original delinquent subculture theory was too simplistic and that a more complex proposition was needed.)[28]

Nevertheless, Cloward and Ohlin's model has limitations. Similar to Cohen, the authors focus only on lower-class juvenile gang delinquency, disregarding the individual delinquent or gang delinquency of middle- and upper-class adolescents. Also, although they contend that the types of juvenile gangs in an area are determined by the type of community social structure, they do not explain why some communities have a number of different types of gangs at once. Furthermore, some dissenters question the validity of a retreatist gang, pointing out that alcoholics and drug addicts tend not to be part of a gang of organized deviants.

Cloward and Ohlin's work has received some empirical support as well as conflictive analysis. Its shortcomings aside, differential opportunity theory has succeeded in influencing the study of delinquency and some social policies.

Lower-Class Culture Theory

A third prominent approach to the delinquency of juvenile gangs was formulated around the same time as Cohen's and Cloward and Ohlin's by Walter Miller.[29] As opposed to Cohen's theory that lower-class gang delinquency is the result of rejection of middle-class values, Miller theorized that gang delinquency in lower-class neighborhoods results from positive attempts by youths to achieve goals determined by the values, or focal concerns, of the lower-class culture.

Miller mentions six lower-class focal concerns, or areas of interest, that put forth widespread, continual attention and emotional involvement:

- *Trouble* is in reference to circumstances that result in unwanted involvement with law enforcement. Miller sees keeping out of trouble and getting into trouble as a daily concern of people of the lower class. Although lower-class members seek to avoid law violations, they may admire those who do break laws.

- *Toughness* relates to masculinity, physical superiority, daring, and bravery.

- *Smartness* is the ability to outsmart, outwit, or con others while avoiding being deceived or duped.

- *Excitement* refers to the need for thrills and risks.

- *Fate* concerns interest or feelings connected with luck, fortunes, and jinxes. Miller contends that members of the lower class often perceive themselves as having little to no control over their lives.

- *Autonomy* is closely related to fate and is in reference to a need to be in control of one's own life.

Miller regards the delinquent gang as a social setting in which juveniles can attain prestige through actions in accordance with lower-class focal concerns.

The most critical weaknesses of this theory are that it fails to explain how these focal concerns originated, and it does not differentiate between lower-class law violators and nonlaw violators or, for that matter, juveniles and adults insofar as their focal concerns. Since not all members of the lower class engage in crime, does that mean that noncriminals have different focal concerns from criminals?

Also, Miller gives no indication of the difference, if any, in focal concerns and criminal behavior from one class to another. Furthermore, Miller's suggestion that the lower-class culture, which he terms the "generating milieu" of delinquency, accounts for the 15 percent of the population that is the "hard-core lower class" and directly influences another 25 to 45 percent of the population is based on 1950s' estimates. These proportions are likely exaggerated today because there are proportionately fewer Americans at the poverty level and more as part of the middle class.

Miller's recent work on juvenile gangs has been more effective in examining the problem and prevalence of gang behavior.

Juvenile delinquency among minority group members continues to be a pressing societal problem. Black, Hispanic, and Native American youths are particularly overrepresented in delinquency statistics, although Asian youths are exhibiting a growing problem of delinquency. Most minority member delinquency is of the petty crime and status offense variety; however, it is the more violent and property offenses that draw the most attention and fear.

Gang delinquency involving minority groups appears to be on the rise and of a more violent nature than in the past. Yet there has been little theoretical or scientific study in recent years to address this problem. Related concerns also require further attention, such as the relationship of and differences between the delinquency of individuals and gang delinquency, lower and other class delinquency, the delinquency of minority members and nonminority members, and the role of the criminal justice system in the official attention given to the various classes of delinquents.

NOTES

1. Isabel Wilkerson, "Crime-jaded Detroiters Jolted by Surge in Teen Violence," *Sacramento Bee* (May 9, 1987): A2.

2. James Risen, "Detroit Shuts High Schools in Wake of Teen Shootings," *Sacramento Bee* (April 18, 1987): A13.

3. Leroy Gould, "Who Defines Delinquency: A Comparison of Self-Reported

and Officially-Reported Indices of Delinquency for Three Racial Groups," *Social Problems* 16 (1969): 325–36.

4. William Chambliss and Richard Nagasawa, "On the Validity of Official Statistics: A Comparative Study of White, Black, and Japanese High School Boys," *Journal of Research in Crime and Delinquency* 6 (1969): 71–77.

5. Michael J. Hindelang, Travis Hirschi, and Joseph G. Weis, "Correlates of Delinquency: The Illusion of Discrepancy between Self-Report and Official Measures," *American Sociological Review* 44 (1979): 995–1014.

6. Derbert S. Elliot and Suzanne S. Ageton, "Reconciling Race and Class Differences in Self-Reported and Official Estimates of Delinquency," *American Sociological Review* 45 (1980): 95–110.

7. Jay R. Williams and Martin Gold, "From Delinquent Behavior to Official Delinquency," *Social Problems* 20 (1972): 209–29.

8. Walter B. Miller, cited by John E. Conklin, *Criminology*, 2d ed. (New York: Macmillan, 1986), p. 193. See also Walter Miller, "Gangs, Groups and Serious Youth Crime," in David Schichor and Delos Kelly, eds., *Critical Issues in Juvenile Delinquency* (Lexington, Mass.: Lexington Books, 1980).

9. Jim Morris, "Gangs at War in LA Streets," *Sacramento Bee* (October 19, 1986): A1.

10. Ibid.

11. Ibid.

12. Ibid.; Judith Cummings, "Increase in Gang Killings on Coast Is Traced to Narcotics Trafficking," *New York Times* (October 29, 1984): A1, A10.

13. Conklin, *Criminology*, p. 193.

14. Robert Ruchhoft, quoted by Morris, "Gangs at War," p. A24.

15. Morris, "Gangs at War," p. A24.

16. Ruchhoft, quoted by Morris, "Gangs at War."

17. Chang Pao-min, "Health and Crime among Chinese-Americans: Recent Trends," *Phylon* 42 (1981): 363–67.

18. Ivan Light and Charles Choy Wong, "Protest at Work: Dilemmas of the Tourist Industry in American Chinatowns," *American Journal of Sociology* 80, no. 6 (1975): 1353.

19. Ibid., pp. 1359–60.

20. W. Wong, "San Francisco Killings Jolt Nationwide Myth of Carefree Chinatown," *Wall Street Journal* (November 16, 1977): 1, 15.

21. Miller, "Gangs, Groups and Serious Youth Crime."

22. Albert K. Cohen, *Delinquent Boys: The Culture of the Gang* (New York: Free Press, 1955).

23. Cohen, *Delinquent Boys*, pp. 36–44.

24. Ibid., p. 25.

25. Richard A. Cloward and Lloyd E. Ohlin, *Delinquency and Opportunity: A Theory of Delinquent Gangs* (New York: Free Press, 1960).

26. Ibid., p. 80.

27. Ibid., p. 148.

28. Albert Cohen and James Short, "Research on Delinquent Subcultures," *Journal of Social Issues* 14 (1958): 20.

29. Walter B. Miller, "Lower Class Culture as a Generating Milieu of Gang Delinquency," *Journal of Social Issues* 14, no. 3 (1958): 5–19.

IV

RACE AND THE SYSTEM OF CRIMINAL JUSTICE

10

Differential Enforcement of the Law

We have noted the high rate of arrest and conviction among blacks, Hispanics, and Native Americans. A major question often posed by theorists, criminologists, and other professionals is how large a role discriminatory treatment within the criminal justice system plays in the overrepresentation of these groups in crime and crime figures. Some suggest that biases play only a small part in the high crime rate of minority members. Others contend that discrimination and racism contribute substantially to the disproportionate involvement of minorities, especially those of the lower class, in the system of criminal justice.

POLICE PRACTICES

The subject of differential enforcement of the law usually starts with the police, generally the first line of the criminal justice system minority members come into contact with. As a result, it is at this stage that the disposition of such involvement (and its implications) is most critical to the person of minority status. Dependent largely on the law enforcement action taken, minorities can be drawn further into the system or possibly avoid it and subsequent decisions, which may also be a reflection of discriminatory policies and personalities.

Police Discretion

In the course of their duties, police officers often have wide latitude. This discretion, or power to use personal judgment in determining the disposition of a matter, is essentially selective law enforcement by authorized members of the criminal justice system. Ideally such discretion is based on the police officer's best judgment of a situation, such as whether an alleged incident warrants the arrest of a suspect or whether the course of action decided on would be in the public's best interests. Police officers' daily actions are rarely reviewed administratively or judicially (other than clear violations of an arrestee's constitutional rights), so these discretionary powers can potentially cross over from discretion to racism, discrimination, personal likes and dislikes, violence, and other forms of illegal or unauthorized enforcement of the law.

Generally broad police discretion is most applicable to minor offenses. For more serious or violent crimes, police usually are somewhat limited in the options available to them as to whether to arrest a suspect, settle a dispute unofficially, and so on.

A number of factors have been associated with the discretionary powers of police officers in deciding the fate of suspects, including community attitudes and values; the customs, policies, and procedures of particular police departments; peer pressure; individual perception; and the circumstances of the situation. For our purposes, a key area of police discretion revolves around decision making based on race and/ or ethnicity and related areas such as class, age, and sex.

There has been no clear consensus on the role these factors play in an officer's decision to invoke the power of arrest. Empirical studies, however, support the contention that police discretion is more likely to result in the arrest of minority group members, lower-class persons, and the young; the wealthy, the politically well associated, and majority group members are less likely to suffer from unfavorable police disposition.[1]

Class differences have also been shown to be prominent in police decision making. One study found that police discretion in domestic disturbances is largely a product of the neighborhood in which the disturbance occurred.[2] The police were more prone to act formally in domestic cases occurring in poor neighborhoods than in higher-income areas. A police officer's exercise of discretion in an interpersonal dispute also tended to vary with the socioeconomic status of the community. This study suggested that police judgment was based less on the offense and more on the socioeconomic position of the neighborhood where the incident took place.

Limiting police discretion and its sometimes subjective enforcement of the law has been tackled from several different angles. The courts have restricted the degree of discretion police can use during interrogations and investigations.[3] Police administrators have sought to establish guidelines and controls for officer performance in the exercise of duty, including creating special units to supervise police work and setting parameters of police efficiency.[4]

Yet success in narrowing the discretion of police officers has been limited because of the number of factors involved (such as different policies in different police departments, differences in how one officer interprets such policies from another officer, and the variance in specific encounters in which discretion may come into play), making it a near-impossible task. At present, it appears that the best way to manage police discretionary powers is to presume officers will be in compliance with the general guidelines. This is not always the case.

Police Discrimination

The issue of police discrimination is a critical component in the discretionary powers of police officers. Many feel that police discretion is often based on race/ethnicity and social class, both of which tend to make minority group members more susceptible to discriminatory treatment by police; however, studies on this subject have shown mixed results.

Early findings showed that police discrimination was a factor in disposition decisions involving minority group members. An observational study in the mid-1960s of police in Boston, Chicago, and Washington, D.C., discovered that a considerable amount of prejudice existed among the police, with around 75 percent of the officers described as "very" or "considerably" prejudiced against blacks, based on the officers' impulsive behavior and comments.[5]

More recent work has supported this contention. One study that compared the police and courts with respect to the disposition of juvenile arrestees found that there was more racial bias by the police in requiring juveniles to appear in court than there was racial bias in the court disposition of the juvenile. This racial bias increased the likelihood of a minority youth's having a record. It also contributed to further criminal involvement by affecting future police and court actions.[6]

Some studies, such as the one undertaken by Richard Hollinger, have concluded that police bias was associated more with the socioeconomic status of the person involved and not race/ethnicity.[7] However, even here race/ethnicity is an important factor since minority groups are overrepresented in the lower classes; therefore, the police, in making decisions based on class, would presumably be influenced as well by the racial and ethnic status of the arrestee.

There has been research as well that has found that police racial discrimination against minorities has focused more on the minority complainant than the minority suspect. For instance, one study showed that when a complainant was involved, the police were more likely to make an arrest when the complainant was white.[8] This study suggests that minority victims are less likely to receive law enforcement help or a satisfactory disposition of their situation than are white victims.

On the other hand, some researchers, such as Donald Black and Albert Reiss, have found that minority youths tend to be arrested more than white youths in part because the minority complainant (usually adults of the same race) was more likely than white complainants to insist on arresting the suspect rather than simply issuing a warning.[9] This finding seems to contradict the prior one. In both instances, however, minority members appear to be the victims of discrimination, for the implication is that white complainants are taken more seriously than nonwhite complainants and when arrests are made, no matter who the complainant is, minority members are more likely to be arrested.

There is also evidence against the racial discrimination theory of police behavior. Research conducted in the South has found that racial factors are less influential in police decisions to invoke arrest powers than such other factors as prior criminal record, seriousness of the crime, demeanor, and socioeconomic status.[10]

In a recent study of police discretion and racial discrimination, it was found that the race of a suspect was of little consequence in discretionary arrest decisions in crimes in which there was no complainant.[11] The exception to this was that officers were more likely to arrest black females in the absence of a complainant than white females.

Another study using victimization data and arrest statistics concluded that there was practically no selection bias in criminal justice for rape or robbery but that such bias was present for assault, particularly aggravated assault.[12]

In general, the consensus seems to be that racial prejudice is influential in various police encounters with minority members with respect to disposition of the matter. Ironically, racial bias in decision making has been sanctioned by the courts. Although racial discrimination violates constitutional rights, courts have upheld using race for identification purposes in helping police narrow their searches for suspects. Also, courts have upheld governmental use of race as a factor in establishing probable cause in searches for illegal aliens and profiles of drug couriers.[13]

Police Violence

The use of excessive force, violence, and other modes of police power has also been associated with police discrimination against minorities. Blacks appear to be a target of this type of mistreatment but are not the only racial and ethnic minority to face violent police discrimination. Native Americans living on or near reservations have long complained about abusive, discriminatory treatment by police officers in the course of arrest and nonarrest. As far back as 1931, a government report concluded that Mexican-Americans were more likely than other groups to be subjected to severe and illegal police practices, overt racism, language barriers, and discrimination by those who administer the law.[14] More recently, the U.S. Commission on Civil Rights found that the same type of harsh, prejudicial police treatment of Hispanics existed in the five southwestern states where the study was focused.[15]

Unnecessary police violence and brutality against minorities has a long history in this country; discriminatory treatment against blacks, Native Americans, Hispanics, and Asians has at times been the rule and not the exception. This sort of nationally condoned behavior has also extended to law enforcement practices against those viewed as lesser people or deviants.

During the 1940s, the police use of violence became a national topic of concern as rioting resulted in extreme police reprisal. The 1943 race riot in Detroit, which left thirty-four people dead, prompted Thurgood Marshall of the National Association for the Advancement of Colored People to refer to the Detroit police as a "gestapo."[16] Twenty-five years later, during the Democratic National Convention in Chicago, the unnecessary use of police force, this time against protestors, again became a major issue.

Today a major area of concern is the unnecessary or selective use by the police of deadly force in apprehending suspects or offenders. Deadly force generally refers to a police officer's shooting and killing a suspect fleeing arrest or attacking another person or an officer. Evidence suggests that minority members, especially blacks, are considerably more likely to be killed by the police than are whites. Catherine Milton and colleagues found that blacks accounted for 79 percent of those shot in the seven cities they studied as compared to their 39 percent representation of the population of those cities.[17] Similarly, Betty Jenkins and Adrienne Faison discovered that between 1970 and 1973, 52 percent of those killed by police were black and 21 percent Hispanic.[18] A more recent study of police shootings in Memphis, Tennessee, supports these findings, concluding that blacks were more likely to be shot by police than whites even if differences in the type of criminal behavior were considered.[19]

Some researchers dispute the higher rate of racial minority member police killings. In a study of Chicago police shootings between 1974 and 1978, it was found that the police were generally equally likely to shoot blacks, Hispanics, and whites; hence there was no finding of racial discrimination in the use of force.[20] However, the methodology used in this study did not consider the shootings of each of these groups in relation to their population figures; if it had, the results undoubtedly would have been different.

In James Fyfe's study of New York City shootings between 1971 and 1975, racial bias was also dismissed as a motivation.[21] Yet Fyfe's conclusions were based on the finding that police were more likely to shoot suspects who attacked officers. He also noted that many of the shootings resulted from scenes in which police officers themselves were injured or killed and that minority group members were more likely than whites to assault police with weapons.

A study by Albert Reiss found that police aggression was manifested more in verbal abuse and harassment than physical violence.[22] According to Reiss, there was little disparity in the police treatment of whites and blacks; when force was present, its selective use was more likely to be against those showing disregard or disrespect for police authority after arrest.

On the whole, there can be little question that police violence, sometimes deadly, does exist and that members of minority groups are more likely to be discriminated against in this regard than white members of society. Variations in the degree and incidence of police violence against minorities are often a matter of not only personal discretion and discrimination but differences from city to city in the relative power of minority members, police department organization, and departmental administrative directives.[23]

There have been both legal and law enforcement administration efforts to control the use of deadly force by police. In 1985, the U.S. Supreme Court took measures to restrict police use of deadly force when it banned the shooting of unarmed or nonthreatening fleeing felony suspects.[24] The Court's decision was based on the concept that shooting a suspect under those circumstances constituted illegal seizure of the person's body under the Fourth Amendment. According to the Court, police could not justify shooting a fleeing felon unless it became "necessary to prevent the escape, and the officer has probable cause to believe that the suspect poses a significant threat of death or serious physical injury to the officers or others."

Internal review and departmental policymaking have also been successful in contributing to declining incidences of use of deadly force by police officers. The New York Police Department established the Firearm Discharge Review Board to evaluate shooting circumstances. A study of the effectiveness of this policy found that the frequency of police shootings had been reduced substantially following formation of the review board.[25]

Although both police group violence and individual police brutalities against minority members are not as blatant as in the past and therefore do not get as much media attention, it is still not uncommon for police officers to use excessive force in arresting minority suspects, particularly when arrestees are verbally abusive, the victims are not minorities, the crime has taken place in a predominantly white area, or the complainant is white.

DISCRIMINATION IN THE COURTS

If minority group members are at a disadvantage at the law enforcement stage of the criminal justice system with respect to the differential enforcement of the law, they are equally likely to be the victims of racial bias in the courtroom. The concept of equal treatment under the law has generally proved to be more of a theoretical assumption than a reality. Minorities have been shown to be discriminated against in every phase of the court process.

Minority members facing courtroom dispositions are predominantly poor, thus, their attorney will likely be appointed by the court. Such an attorney usually becomes available only after the fact—that is, after an arrest, repossession or seizure of property, or self-incrimination. Furthermore, there is evidence to suggest that lawyers who represent the poor are more likely to be unethical, unattentive, inadequate, and self-serving than private attorneys.[26] Thus, there exists a congruous relationship between poverty and being a member of a racial minority in court proceedings as in law enforcement involvement.

Minority group members are less likely to make bail and thus are more likely to be convicted.[27] Upon conviction, they generally are given longer, more severe sentences, are less likely to be put on probation, and after serving time, are less likely to receive parole.

Racism and Jurors

Simulated juror experiments have shown the presence of antiminority feelings among the subjects.[28] In actual trials, juror discrimination has been far more direct. Proportionately, persons of minority status are found guilty much more often than whites.[29] The disparity rises for serious crimes and crimes in which the victim is white.

Juror prejudices also exist in the voir dire procedure, the questioning period when prospective jurors are asked "to speak the truth" with regard to the possibility of bias and prejudgment in a particular case. Ideally voir dire is supposed to ensure that the jury selected is fair and impartial. This is not always the result. Part of the fault lies in the format of the voir dire examination, which is typically at the discretion of the judge. Variance in who conducts the voir dire, the conditions in which potential jurors are questioned, and the role of attorneys may affect the answers that individual prospective jurors give. For example, research shows that when an entire jury pool of people (numbering fifty or more) are asked if they are racially prejudiced, few people are willing to single themselves out by answering yes.[30] Hence, it is reasonable to assume some jurists are acknowledged (if only to themselves) racists.

Surveys of ex-jurors have found that many people deliberately are dishonest during voir dire questioning because they want to serve on the jury.[31] In other instances potential jurors feel compelled to be untruthful when the interviewer (often a judge) intimidates them so that they respond in a socially desirable way.

Also, people are often not aware of their racial biases. Numerous unobtrusive studies of prejudice and discrimination indicate that anti-black sentiments are more common than suggested by survey data.[32] "The diffuseness of racial attitudes makes it possible for jurors to be convinced that they are impartial with regard to race while in fact they hold a variety of prejudicial assumptions."[33]

A final area in trial juries where racism is especially conspicuous concerns the dearth of proportionate jury representation of minority members. Although juries are supposed to reflect the community from which they are chosen, minorities are typically underrepresented on them, although an important recent Supreme Court decision does offer hope at least in this area of courtroom discrimination. In a reversal of *Swain v. Alabama,* in which the Court ruled that a defendant "is not constitutionally entitled to a proportionate number of his race on the trial jury," the Supreme Court moved to forbid the tactic of peremptory challenges by prosecuting attorneys or "challenges without cause, without explanation and without judicial scrutiny," to eliminate prospective jurors strictly because of their race.[34] In essence, the decision held that prosecutors can no longer routinely challenge minority members without sound justification. Although it is unclear whether this decision will affect the outcome of trials of minorities, their unfavorable situation certainly could not get any worse.

Judges, Sentencing, and Racial Discrimination

Judges wield enormous power over those brought before them in criminal courts. Although it would seem that the stature of their position would ensure compliance with the fair and impartial doctrine asked of jurors with respect to all defendants, the evidence shows that judicial racial prejudice is just as prominent and carries more weight since it is at this stage of the judicial system where sentences are typically handed out. Numerous studies lend credence to the proposition that minority members are discriminated against at every stage of the judicial process.[35]

Where discriminatory treatment is most felt by minorities and where the literature has been most extensive is at sentencing. Minority members—blacks in particular—have been shown to receive longer, more severe sentences than whites. A recent study by a group at Rand Corporation found this to be true in their examination of California Bureau of Criminal Statistics data and self-report surveys of prisoners in California, Texas, and Michigan.[36] L. Foley and C. Rasch's study of female felony defendants revealed that blacks received harsher sentences than whites for property crimes.[37] A study by M. Farnworth and P. Horan showed a correlation between race and sentence severity, but contended that other variables also affected sentence outcome such as appointed counsel, past criminal record, and the type of offense committed.[38]

Other data suggest that minorities are dealt with more severely in sentencing when their victims are white, especially for crimes of rape and murder. In a study in Maryland, J. Howard found that black males convicted of raping white women were proportionately most likely to receive the death penalty among rapists. He established that no black was executed for raping a black woman.[39] Marvin Wolfgang and Marc Riedel's study of capital rape convictions between 1945 and 1965 demonstrated that when nonracial factors were held constant, judges imposed death sentences on a considerably higher proportion of blacks than whites.

According to the authors:

Whether or not a contemporaneous offense has been committed, if the defendant is black and the victim is white, the defendant is about eighteen times more likely to receive the death penalty than when the defendant is in any other racial combination of defendant and victim.[40]

Wolfgang and Riedel concluded that this racial disparity in death penalty sentencing is a matter of racial discrimination.

Further support for the discriminatory relationship between the offender's race and the race of the victim can be seen in W. Bowers and G. Pierce's recent study of discrimination in sentencing. They found that black offenders with white victims received harsher sentences than other offenders.[41] A study by G. LaFree reached the same conclusion.[42]

Minorities and the Death Penalty

The topic of racial discrimination has been debated most often where it concerns the death penalty. Capital punishment will be looked at more closely in chapter 11; for now, it is enough to know that between 1930 and 1985, 3,909 executions took place in the United States. More than 50 percent of those executed were black. If D. Bell's strong statement made in 1973 suggesting that blacks have little reason to trust the American judicial system is true, it is certainly most pertinent when assessing blacks and the penalty of death.[43]

In 1986, nearly half the death row inmates were black, Hispanic, Native American, or Asian, with blacks comprising more than 40 percent of the total under death sentences, a figure well above their 12 percent representation in the general population.[44] Blacks have long been disproportionately sentenced to death, most notably for rape and murder.

This imbalance led to the 1972 U.S. Supreme Court ruling in *Furman v. Georgia* that the death penalty was discriminatory and thus a violation of the Eighth Amendment's cruel and unusual punishment clause.[45] The ensuing ban on executions and the easing of the outcries against racial discrimination in an area where there was no second chance after the fact proved to be short-lived, however. In 1976, the Supreme Court upheld the death penalty in three states where the laws were revised to reduce discriminatory treatment, which in effect reinstated the potential for renewed racial bias in death sentences across the country.[46]

The evidence suggests that history is repeating itself. Minorities, particularly blacks, are still overrepresented on death row compared to whites. At the end of 1985, 903 whites, 672 blacks, 11 Native Americans, and 5 Asians had been sentenced to death, 99 of them of Hispanic origin.[47] All of the prisoners had been convicted of murder, which in fact represents a positive change from capital punishment of earlier years when so many blacks were sentenced to death for rape.

The likelihood that a minority member will receive the death penalty is greater if the victim is a white person. A study of murders from January 1977 to December 1984 in states that have the death penalty found that murderers of whites are not only prosecuted more frequently but are eleven times more likely to be executed than the killers of blacks.[48] There have been forty-four death row convicts executed for killing whites in the twelve states that have used capital punishment since 1977, compared to four executions for killers of blacks. Nationally, the study reported, killers of whites are three times more likely to receive the death sentence than those who murder blacks in the thirty-two states in which the penalty of death has been imposed. In these states, killers of whites face a one in nine chance of receiving the death penalty, whereas killers of blacks have less than a one-in-twenty chance of being sentenced to death.

Although most homicides are intraracial, it is the interracial murders in which the disparity in sentencing widens and is most open to charges of racism. For instance, in Texas a white person is twelve times more likely to get the death penalty for killing a white person than for killing a black person. The situation is virtually reversed for blacks killing whites. Between 1977 and 1984, thirteen blacks were executed for killing whites; yet not a single white has been put to death in Texas for killing a black.

Recently this discrepancy was challenged in the Supreme Court by Warren McCleskey, a black man sentenced to death in 1978 in Georgia for murdering a white police officer. His appeal was based on the contention that the Georgia death penalty discriminated against racial minorities who killed whites in a violation of the constitutional protections against cruel and unusual punishment. He presented studies prepared by David Baldus, a professor of law at the University of Iowa, who examined 2,000 Georgia murder cases occurring during the 1970s. Baldus, holding about 230 nonracial variables constant, demonstrated that blacks who killed whites were much more likely to receive the death penalty than whites who killed blacks.[49]

In what opponents of the death penalty called a major defeat, the Supreme Court ruled that Georgia's death penalty did not discriminate against blacks who killed whites. Although the Court acknowledged the existence of a "discrepancy that appears to correlate with race," it argued that this "does not constitute a major systemic defect. Any mode for determining guilt or punishment has its weaknesses and the potential for misuse."[50]

Hence, the Court appears to be condoning racial discrimination in death sentence disparity and in the process opening up a new era of debate and heated reaction, as illustrated by William Robinson of the Lawyers Committee for Civil Rights, who commented, "We are terribly disappointed. The Supreme Court had a chance to require that the death penalty be imposed more fairly and without regard to race. It did not serve the nation well."[51]

There can be little doubt that minority members face some form of discriminatory treatment in every phase of the criminal justice system, from the police to the courts to death row, that puts them at greater risk for being arrested, convicted, and given harsher sentences than whites. Blacks, lower-class members, and the undereducated are especially prone to this unequal justice.

Police, jurors, and judges have an enormous amount of discretion and power in deciding the fate of those before them. It is presumed that this power will be utilized fairly; this is often, either by design or otherwise, not the case. Racial prejudice and discrimination in the system of criminal justice is but a reflection of that in society.

NOTES

1. Nathan Goldman, *The Differential Selection of Juvenile Offenders for Court Appearance* (New York: National Council on Crime and Delinquency, 1963); Irving Piliavin and Scott Briar, "Police Encounters with Juveniles," *American Journal of Sociology* 70 (1964): 206.

2. Douglas A. Smith and Jody R. Klein, "Police Control of Interpersonal Disputes," *Social Problems* 31 (1984): 468–81.

3. Larry J. Siegel, *Criminology*, 2d ed. (St. Paul, Minn.: West Publishing Co., 1986), p. 503.

4. Jerome Skolnick and J. Richard Woodworth, "Bureaucracy, Information and Social Control: A Study of a Morals Detail," in David Bordua, ed., *The Police: Six Sociological Essays* (New York: Wiley, 1960); John Gardner, *Traffic and the Police: Variations in Law Enforcement Policy* (Cambridge: Harvard University Press, 1969).

5. John E. Conklin, *Criminology*, 2d ed. (New York: Macmillan, 1986), pp. 355–56.

6. Dale Dannefer and Russell K. Schutt, "Race and Juvenile Justice Processing in Court and Police Agencies," *American Journal of Sociology* 87 (1982): 1113–32.

7. Richard C. Hollinger, "Race, Occupational Status and Pro-Active Police Arrest for Drinking and Driving," *Journal of Criminal Justice* 12 (1984): 173–83.

8. Douglas A. Smith, Christy A. Visher, and Laura A. Davidson, "Equity and Discretionary Justice: The Influence of Race on Police Arrest Decisions," *Journal of Criminal Law and Criminology* 75 (1985): 234–49.

9. Donald J. Black and Albert J. Reiss, Jr., "Police Control of Juveniles," *American Sociological Review* 35 (1970): 63–78.

10. Conklin, *Criminology*, p. 355.

11. Smith, Visher, and Davidson, "Equity and Discretionary Justice."

12. Michael J. Hindelang, "Race and Involvement in Common Law Personal Crimes," *American Sociological Review* 43 (1978): 101.

13. Sherri Lynn Johnson, "Race and the Decision to Detain a Suspect," *Yale Law Journal* 93 (1983): 214–58.

14. National Commission on Law Observance and Enforcement, "Report on Crime and the Foreign Born: 1931," in C. E. Cortes (advisory ed.), *The Mexican American and the Law* (New York: Arno Press, 1974).

15. U.S. Commission on Civil Rights, *Mexican Americans and the Administration of Justice in the Southwest* (Washington, D.C.: Government Printing Office, 1970).

16. Samuel Walker, *Popular Justice* (New York: Oxford University Press, 1980), p. 197.

17. Catherine H. Milton, Jeanne W. Halleck, James Lardner, and Gary L. Abrecht, *Police Use of Deadly Force* (Washington, D.C.: Police Foundation), 1977.

18. Betty Jenkins and Adrienne Faison, *An Analysis of 284 Persons Killed by New York City Policemen* (New York: Metropolitan Applied Research Center, 1974).

19. James J. Fyfe, "Observations on Police Deadly Force," *Crime and Delinquency* 27 (1981): 376–89.

20. William Geller and Kevin J. Karales, "Shootings of and by Chicago Police; Uncommon Crises. Part I: Shootings by Chicago Police," *Journal of Criminal Law and Criminology* 72 (1981): 1813–66.

21. James J. Fyfe, "Race and Extreme Police-Citizen Violence," in R. L. McNeely and Carl Pope, eds., *Race, Crime and Criminal Justice* (Beverly Hills: Sage, 1981).

22. Albert Reiss, *The Police and the Public* (New Haven, Conn.: Yale University Press, 1971).

23. William B. Waegel, "The Use of Lethal Force by Police: The Effect of Statutory Change," *Crime and Delinquency* 30 (1984): 121–40.

24. Tennessee v. Garner, 105 S.Ct. 1694 (1985).

25. James J. Fyfe, "Administrative Interventions on Police Shooting Discretion: An Empirical Examination," *Journal of Criminal Justice* 7 (1979): 309–23.

26. See, for example, G. LaFree, "Variables Affecting Guilty Pleas and Convictions on Rape Cases: Toward a Social Theory of Rape Processing," *Social Forces* 58 (1980): 837–50; H. E. Kelly, "A Comparison of Defense Strategy and Race as Influences in Differential Sentencing," *Criminology* 14 (1976): 241–49.

27. Studies show that people who do not make bail are more likely to be convicted than those who do, which also is intrinsically tied in to the discrimination of those unable to afford private attorneys or public support.

28. Stephanie Nickerson, Clara Mayo, and Althea Smith, "Racism in the Courtroom," in John F. Dovidio and Samuel L. Gaertner, eds., *Prejudice, Discrimination, and Racism* (Orlando, Fla.: Academic Press, 1986), p. 273.

29. Ibid.

30. P. Hare, *Handbook of Small Group Research,* 2d ed. (New York: Free Press, 1976).

31. D. Schatz, "The Trials of a Juror," *New York State Bar Journal* 49 (1977): 8-201, 232–36.

32. F. Crosby, S. Bromley, and L. Saxe, "Recent Unobtrusive Studies of Black and White Discrimination and Prejudice: A Literature Review," *Psychological Bulletin* 87 (1980): 546–63.

33. Nickerson, Mayo, and Smith, "Racism in the Courtroom," p. 268.

34. Swain v. Alabama, 380 U.S. 202 (1965).

35. See, for example, G. Kleck, "Racial Discrimination in Criminal Sentencing: A Critical Evaluation of the Evidence with Additional Evidence on the Death Penalty," *American Sociological Review* 46 (1981): 783–804; C. Spohn, J. Gruhl, and S. Welch, "The Effect of Race on Sentencing: A Re-examination of an Unsettled Question," *Law and Society Review* 16 (1982): 71–88.

36. J. Petersilia, *Racial Disparities in the Criminal Justice System* (Santa Monica, Calif.: Rand Corporation, 1983).

37. L. A. Foley and C. E. Rasch, "The Effect of Race on Sentence: Actual Time Served and Final Disposition," in J. Conley, ed., *Theory and Research in Criminal Justice: Current Perspectives* (Cincinnati: Anderson, 1979).

38. M. Farnworth and P. Horan, "Separate Justice: An Analysis of Race Differences in Court Processes," *Social Science Research* 9 (1980): 381–99.

39. J. C. Howard, "Racial Discrimination in Sentencings," *Judicature* 59 (1975): 120–25.

40. Marvin E. Wolfgang and Marc Riedel, "Race, Judicial Discretion, and the Death Penalty," *American Academy of Political and Social Science* 407 (1973): 132.

41. W. J. Bowers and G. L. Pierce, "Arbitrariness and Discrimination Under Post-Furman Capital Statute," *Crime and Delinquency* 26 (1980): 563–635.

42. G. LaFree, "The Effect of Sexual Stratification by Race on Official Reactions to Rape," *American Sociological Review* 45 (1980): 842–54.

43. D. A. Bell, Jr., "Racism in American Courts: Cause for Black Disruption or Despair?" *California Law Review* 761 (1973): 193.

44. "Black-and-White Issue? The Supreme Court Wrestles with the Death Penalty and Race," *U.S. News & World Report* (October 20, 1986): 24.

45. *U.S. Law Week,* June 29, 1972.

46. The three states successful in reinstating the death penalty in 1976 were Florida, Texas, and Georgia.

47. U.S. Department of Justice, Bureau of Justice Statistics, *Capital Punishment, 1985* (Washington, D.C.: Government Printing Office, 1986).

48. The study was released by the *Dallas Times Herald* in 1985.

49. John Johnson, "Justices Reject Racial Bias Argument," *Sacramento Bee* (April 23, 1987): A1.

50. Ibid., p. A26. See also 481 U.S. 95 (1987).

51. William Robinson as quoted in John Johnson, "Justices Reject Racial Bias," p. A26.

11

Incarceration of Minorities

Just as minorities as a group are overrepresented in arrests and convictions, so too are they disproportionately incarcerated. The racial discrimination we observed in the previous chapter is just as evident when minority members are put behind bars. Yet ironically, in some instances, minority group prisoners enjoy an advantage over the dominant group of prisoners that they do not have on the outside. Because the vast majority of institutionalized minorities are male (93 percent of the jail inmates and 96 percent of those in prison), it is this segment of the racial and ethnic minority population that we will focus most on.

MINORITIES IN PENITENTIARIES

Ethnic and racial minority members account for more than 56 percent of the federal and state male prisoners in the United States. At the end of 1983, blacks comprised the greatest number of prisoners at 45.7 percent, followed by Hispanics at 9.5 percent, and Native Americans and Asians, who both constitute less than 1 percent of the prison population (Table 11.1). Only blacks show a higher percentage of state institution imprisonment than federal.

Proportionately blacks are more likely to be institutionalized than whites in every state, aside from those in which the black population is extremely low. In some states, blacks are ten times more likely to be imprisoned than whites.[1] Furthermore, states with a higher proportion of blacks in the general population tend also to have higher incarceration rates on the whole.[2]

The rate of incarceration per 100,000 population is significant not only for blacks, who have the highest rate, but for Native Americans and Hispanics as well.[3] Despite their small numbers of imprisoned, Native

Table 11.1
Minority Male Prisoners in Federal and State Institutions, by Race/Ethnicity, 1983

	Total[a]	Black	Native American	Hispanic	Asian	Percentage of Minority Groups Incarcerated				
						Total[b]	Black	Native American	Hispanic	Asian
United States	418,084	191,020	3,833	39,744	1,503	56.5	45.7	.9	9.5	.4
Federal Institutions	30,172	9,685	634	7,181	181	58.5	32.0	2.1	23.8	.6
State Institutions	387,912	181,335	3,199	32,563	1,322	56.2	46.7	.8	8.4	.3

[a]Includes white prisoners and those of undetermined race.
[b]Hispanics may also be included in the black percentage.

Source: Adapted from U.S. Department of Justice, Bureau of Justice Statistics, *Prisoners in State and Federal Institutions on December 31, 1983* (Washington, D.C.: Government Printing Office, 1986), Tables 7, 9.

Americans have the second highest rate of imprisonment among all racial and ethnic groups. Their overrepresentation in penitentiaries is especially prevalent in states where there are a large number of Native Americans (for instance, Oklahoma and South Dakota). Native American inmates have been predominantly convicted for alcohol-related offenses.

Hispanics have the highest incarceration rate in federal institutions. Prisoners of Hispanic origin are imprisoned in federal and state facilities at a rate higher than non-Hispanic whites and Asians. Approximately one of every sixteen prisoners in the United States is Hispanic. Hispanic prisoners are more likely than other groups to be incarcerated for drug-related offenses.

Asians in this country have the lowest rate of imprisonment among all groups. There is, however, evidence that Asian crime is on the increase, and in a few years corrections data will reflect this rise, although it is unlikely that this group will challenge other minority groups in overall rates of imprisonment in the near future.

In general, minority prisoners are more likely to be imprisoned for violent crimes than whites and less likely to be imprisoned for crimes of property. They also are more likely than white prisoners to have been impoverished upon arrest, to be lower educated, and to be of lower occupational status. The rate of recidivism among minority prisoners is only slightly higher than among first-time minority prisoners.

Trends in the Incarceration of Minorities

Historically, minority groups have long been disproportionately incarcerated as compared to whites. Given the persecution and racism most disadvantaged racial and ethnic minorities have had to endure in the United States, it should come as no surprise that this also manifested itself in the early prison treatment of minorities. This was particularly true for blacks who not only were subjected to official segregation policies in most North and South prisons but also were victimized by discrimination and prejudice in other ways. For example, blacks once routinely worked the least desired jobs and felt class pressures of both white inmates and correctional officers if they attempted to fight the status quo.[4]

The rise in the minority crime rate in the North came about due to the mass migration of minorities from the Deep South, resulting in an increase in street crime, or the types of offenses most likely to lead to imprisonment. On the average day in 1960, one of every twenty-six black males aged 25 to 34 was imprisoned.[5]

Traditionally, correctional institutions have not catered to the religious and cultural needs of prisoners. Many Hispanics, for instance, speak little English, and thus have experienced communication problems with nonbilingual corrections officers. Outside attention to this denial of the special needs of ethnic and racial minorities surfaced in the 1960s with the rise in the number of Black Muslims in correctional institutions. The Muslims' assertion that their religious and constitutional rights were being violated led to federal court challenges to the discriminatory practices in jails and penitentiaries across the country.[6] After much litigation, a series of Supreme Court decisions upheld the Muslims' right to their own religious practices.[7] Paradoxically, where once the Muslims were perhaps the most feared inmate group by correctional authorities, today, with their religious grievances appeased, they are seen as a stabilizing element in prisons, where more violent, disorganized youth gangs have emerged.[8]

The Black Muslim prisoners' strong show of solidarity and perseverance paved the way for better organization of other inmate groups and further court decisions that allowed Native Americans and other minority groups to have their special needs provided for by correctional administrators, including cultural and dietary needs associated with religious practices and nonreligious practices.[9]

Today it is recognized that the cultural and religious appeasement of minority groups is critical to prison stability. Yet although minorities in prison may have gained certain liberties, they continue to be discriminated against as prisoners in other ways. For instance, the lack of proportionate representation of minorities on correctional staffs can be seen as discriminatory toward minority prisoners, for it maintains an atmosphere of racial inferiority and a lack of identification with the staff, both of which seem to be a strong statement against affirmative action and civil rights. This will need to change in the future if stability in the prison system is to become the rule rather than the exception.

Black inmates seem to be especially targeted for oppressive treatment within prisons. Some evidence indicates they are more likely than white inmates to be considered dangerous, resulting in harsher treatment by prison officials, including searches, closer surveillance, and other discretionary treatment.[10] Studies by Robert Johnson[11] and Hans Toch[12] found discrimination to be among the greatest concerns of black prisoners, who see the prison structure itself and those who run it as part of the centuries of subjugation and racism they have had to endure.

Race Relations

The relationship between members of the same minority group, as well as with other prison groups, is a major part of prison life and a constant source of concern for correctional officials. Since the Black Muslims won concessions in the 1960s, black and Hispanic inmates have progressively become more powerful within the prison subculture, usually at the expense of white inmates.

A number of researchers have explored the issue of race relations in U.S. prisons. In most studies, it was found that a high degree of racial and intraracial polarization exists within the prisoner subculture.[13] This has been viewed as a critical component in the nature of racial and ethnic divisions, which have been characterized by conflict, tension, avoidance, and violence. James Jacobs describes each racial block as promoting "its own culture and values" and attaining "what supremacy can be achieved at the expense of the others."[14]

Although intrarace relations have at times been tumultuous in penitentiaries—there were violent hostilities between rival California Hispanic prisoner gangs as examined by George Park,[15] and Jacobs' study of Stateville Penitentiary in Illinois found that blacks were divided into three "warring super gangs"[16]—it is the interracial race relations that have attracted the most attention.

In virtually all instances in the past two and a half decades, black prisoners have been shown to be the dominant force in most prison systems, followed by Hispanic inmates. Together they have heavily infringed upon what once was a white prisoner domain.

John Irwin examined the early changes in race and ethnic relations and the power structure in the California penal system, which has shown the most racial polarization. After blacks began to replace their criminal identities with those based on racial differences, Hispanics followed suit. Within this shift, white prisoners were not always looked upon as the enemy. Notes Irwin,

The blacks and Chicanos, as they focus on the whites as their oppressors, seem to be excluding white prisoners from this category and are, in fact, developing some sympathy for them as a minority group which itself is being oppressed by the white establishment and the white police.[17]

Yet soon racial violence became so commonplace that California corrections officials were forced to segregate their maximum security "adjustment center" facilities in order to reduce the victimization of prisoners.

Generally black and Hispanic prisoners do not need a numerical advantage over white prisoners to dominate them. Even with as small as 25 percent of the inmate population, the greater social solidarity of minority groups puts them in a superior position to control the larger white group of prisoners. This edge in racial and ethnic minority group superiority is rooted in the long-time oppression and discrimination of these groups in America. Minorities' victimization and frustrations provide them with a common means by which they can relate, giving them a purpose for cooperating with each other. Solidarity within minority groups becomes especially high when many prisoners are members of the same racial and ethnic street gangs, as is the case in California, New York, and some other states.[18]

This racial dominance that minority groups enjoy within prison societies can be seen clearly in prison rape. Blacks are typically the aggressors and whites the victims.[19] Alan Davis relates blacks' raping whites to revenge for the discrimination blacks face outside the prison system, where the white numerical advantage is clearly in the whites' favor, and a need for blacks to assert their masculinity under conditions in which homosexual rape is the most forceful means for establishing dominance over others.[20] When black gangs are well organized, they can rape isolated white victims with little fear of retaliation, though there are fewer blacks in the prison.[21]

Perhaps the most comprehensive study of race relations in the prison culture was undertaken by Leo Carroll from 1970 to 1971.[22] Carroll found that although minority and white prisoners were forced into demographic integration in the maximum security institution he examined, there remained mutual dislike, mistrust, fear, and suspicion. The majority of racial interaction was of a limited and superficial nature and confined to work detail. In more appropriate settings for social interaction, such as the gymnasium and dining hall, the groupings were generally intraracial. According to Carroll:

Neither their rejection by society, nor their proximity within the prison, nor their common subordination to the authority of the custodians, nor the integrationist policies of the Warden, nor the material deprivations they suffer are sufficient to produce a cross-racial solidarity among prisoners.[23]

Cooperation between racial groups was largely confined to common goals such as avoiding a race riot and sex and drug needs. Even then hostilities, suspicion, and distrust remained high.

In the past, prison officials used racism and segregation as a control strategy. They believed that if division between various racial and ethnic prisoners resulted in their spending most of their time jockeying for position within the prisoner society subculture, they would have less time to think about escaping, placing demands on the administration, or other more volatile preoccupations; thereby the prison could be kept tranquil.[24] Today prison administrators—faced with the possibilities of major race riots, unwanted outside attention, and loss of control of their institutions as minority prisoner societies continue to grow in numbers and organization in challenging the white prisoners' control—put much effort into seeking to reduce racial tension inside the prison walls rather than encouraging it as a means to protect themselves.

Although prison officials find it easier to control their prisons when they are confronted with individuals in competition for dominance, survival, and other objectives, individualism has to a large extent been displaced by competing factions organized into power blocs and fueled by racial, religious, and political strength. Blacks and other ethnic minorities more often than not set the tone for prisoner race relations and prison stability.

CAPITAL PUNISHMENT AND MINORITIES

Minorities have typically constituted around half of the prisoners under sentence of death annually, well in disproportion to their representation in the general population. Of even greater concern is the actual carrying out of the sentence.

The evidence indicates that minorities are more likely to be executed than whites and less likely to have their sentences commuted. Since 1930, the federal government has maintained data on state and federal executions. Between 1930 and 1967, 3,859 prisoners were executed in the United States, 54.6 percent of them minorities.[25] Hayward Burns puts this disparity in proper perspective:

Not only is it less likely that a white person will be sentenced to the electric chair, gas chamber, gallows or firing squad, but the workings of executive and administrative discretion are such that, once condemned to die, a white person is more likely to have his sentence commuted to life imprisonment by a governmental executive, board of pardons or similar agency.[26]

According to Marvin Wolfgang, of those sentenced to death, between 10 and 20 percent more black prisoners are executed than white prisoners.[27] Although white offenders committed the majority of murders between 1930 and 1967, blacks were executed more often for murder. The discrepancy is even wider for the crime of rape and other crimes, with roughly five minority prisoners being executed for every white inmate. Of the 455 persons executed for rape during this period, a staggering 89.5 percent were racial minorities.[28]

Blacks have been the most victimized by differential execution treatment for sex crimes, particularly when the victim was white. National prison statistics reveal that since 1930, of the nineteen jurisdictions to execute men for rape, nearly one-third, or six states, have put only blacks to death.[29] In some years blacks were the only persons executed for rape in the nation.

This disparity in sentences of death for rape has been shown to be associated to the race of the victim. Black rapists have been far more likely to be put to death when their victims were white females rather than black females, whereas the death penalty has been imposed on white rapists exclusively when their victims were also white. In Florida between 1960 and 1964, while around the same percentage of black and white males involved in intraracial rape were sentenced to death (between 4 and 5 percent), 54 percent of the black males convicted of raping white women received the death penalty compared to none of the white men convicted of raping black women.[30] Even taking into account differential factors (eighty-four black males and eight white males were convicted of interracial rape during the period), such a disparity in death sentences can be explained only by racial discrimination.

Since the Supreme Court reinstated the death penalty in 1976, there is some indication that the discrimination against minorities has lessened. Between 1977 and 1985, of the fifty persons executed, 66 percent were white and 34 percent black.[31] Part of this reduction in black executions is attributed to the absence in executions for rape, which once was almost solely a black male phenomenon. Some believe, however, that race is still a prominent factor in both the death penalty and actual execution.[32] This seems particularly true for high-profile cases in which a minority member murders a white.[33] Nor can it be ignored that the percentage of minorities sentenced to death or executed continues to be considerably disproportionate to their percentage of the population. While justice may be served in individual cases, there is little reason to believe that it is being served equally with respect to race/ethnicity and the death penalty.

MINORITIES IN JAILS

Minority members are also overrepresented in jails in relation to their general population figures. As of June 30, 1986, minorities constituted some 60 percent of the nation's inmate population in jails.[34] Among the 92 percent male inmates, 41 percent were black, 14 percent Hispanic, and 1 percent other minority groups.

Jail inmates of minority status tend to be predominantly from poor backgrounds and disadvantaged educationally and occupationally. They also experience many of the problems typical of prison life, such as power struggles, homosexuality, rape, drug abuse, overcrowding, unsanitary conditions, idleness, stress, and frustration.

In general, the privileges and treatment accorded minority prison inmates do not always follow suit for those in jails. The one advantage minority jail inmates may have over those in prisons is the usually closer proximity of jails for visitation, if the rules permit. Additionally, the average jail inmate tends to be incarcerated for a shorter length of

Table 11.2
Percentage Distribution of Minority Female Prisoners, by Race/Ethnicity, 1983

	Total[a]	Black	Hispanic	Native American	Asian
United States	56.7	48.0	7.0	1.3	.4
Federal Institutions	62.1	43.4	16.6	1.2	.9
State Institutions	56.1	48.5	6.0	1.3	.3

[a]Some Hispanics may also be included in the black prisoner percentage.

Source: Adapted from U.S. Department of Justice, Bureau of Justice Statistics, *Prisoners in State and Federal Institutions on December 31, 1983* (Washington, D.C.: Government Printing Office, 1986), Tables 8, 9.

time, for less serious crimes, or simply for detainment while awaiting trial, sentencing, or appeals.

Regardless of the reason for being jailed, minority inmates are proportionately more likely to be in jail than nonminorities and discriminated against once there.

INCARCERATED MINORITY WOMEN

Although there are considerably fewer minority women in U.S. jails and prisons than minority men, their disproportion in relation to their representation in the population is comparable to that of their male counterparts. Annually, minority women account for more than half the incarcerated women in this country.

Studies by Ruth Glick and Virginia Neto[35] and the U.S. General Accounting Office[36] estimated that around 50 percent of the incarcerated women were black and more than 9 percent Hispanic in comparison to their approximately 11 percent and 5 percent, respectively, of the general population. Incarceration data for jails and prisons support this overrepresentation of minority women inmates.

According to the 1986 Annual Survey of Jails, females made up 8 percent of all jail inmates nationally.[37] Minority women annually comprise more than half the females jailed on any given day.

Women account for even less of the total prison inmate population— 4 percent. Yet, as we can see in Table 11.2, at the end of 1983, females of minority status comprised more than 56 percent of the imprisoned females in federal and state institutions nationally. Black, Hispanic, and Native American women are disproportionately represented, and Asian women are underrepresented. Forty-eight percent of the imprisoned women were black. A substantial disparity can be seen in the percentage of Hispanic women in federal institutions and state facilities, with the higher percentage of Hispanics as federal prisoners.

Black and Hispanic female inmates tend to be imprisoned most often for drug-related crimes, murder, robbery, and larceny; Native American women are more likely to be incarcerated for alcohol-related offenses and forgery/fraud.[38] As a group, minority women prisoners are less likely than white women prisoners to be able to afford bail or private attorneys. They are also more likely to be single, poor, less educated, and have dependents. Similar to white female inmates, minority women offenders tend to have poor health, substance-abuse problems, family pressures, and few rehabilitative or vocational programs as prisoners.

Racial and ethnic minority female prisoners face the same discriminatory treatment as their male counterparts. Not only are they more likely to be incarcerated than white females, but they are subjected to more forms of racism, sexism, and labeling in prison.

Racism has been used in women's prisons as a control strategy. A study of a Midwest women's prison revealed that staff members often redefined nonracial situations as racially motivated in order to promote racial tensions and divert attention away from activities disruptive to the institution.[39] This strategy of pitting minorities against whites was toned down if it appeared a race riot might result. Favors would be extended to respective leaders of different racial groups, and for a time incidents would be redefined as nonracially motivated.

Although some improvements have been made in the correctional treatment of minority women, their special cultural need and reintegration into society have been inadequately addressed in most institutions.

Minority female prisoners also are disadvantaged in other forms of penal punishment. They are disproportionately likely to be on death row in this country. Between 1930 and 1967, black women accounted for 37.7 percent of the women executed. In 1984, 25 percent of those women under sentence of death were black.

MINORITY JUVENILES IN CUSTODY

Juveniles of minority group status are also overrepresented in correctional facilities.[40] On February 1, 1985, more than half the juveniles in public juvenile custody facilities were of nonwhite racial or ethnic status.[41] Black juveniles made up 37 percent of those held in public institutions, well above their approximately 13 percent of the juvenile population at large. Hispanics accounted for 13.3 percent of those housed in public facilities; better than twice their 6 percent proportion of the population. Juvenile custody figures group other minority member juvenile prisoners together; however, other data suggest that Native Americans, too, are overrepresented in juvenile custody facilities, and Asian juveniles are underrepresented.[42]

Proportionately, juveniles of minority status are also more likely to be in adult jails and prisons than white juveniles and are given stiffer sentences.[43] Studies show that juvenile minority members are more likely to be discriminated against at every decision point within the system of juvenile justice than white youths, leading up to and including being institutionalized and often for longer periods of time.[44]

Minority member juvenile inmates typically come from poor backgrounds, broken homes, and high-crime urban areas; they are 15 years old on the average, will not complete high school, and have previously served time in a juvenile correctional facility.

The prisoner societies that exist in adult prisons are also established in juvenile facilities, although usually they are not as highly developed because of the shorter average stay of juvenile offenders. Similar to minority adult prisoners, minority youth inmates are successful in reversing the traditional white-black order in society in occupying the higher rungs of the institutional ladder.[45] Nor is it necessary for them to have an edge numerically; their strength in solidarity and intimidation is generally superior to that of white incarcerated juveniles.

On the other hand, minority juvenile inmates are themselves victimized and discriminated against through juvenile correctional administrative policies that for the most part ignore the needs particular to minority prisoners, such as special cultural programs and proportionate recruitment of minority staff members. As a result, these youths often leave the juvenile justice system bitter, confused, without positive role models, and unprepared to lead a productive life.

Minorities are disproportionately more likely than whites to be incarcerated, given harsher sentences, including the death penalty, and discriminated against in other ways by the criminal justice and correctional systems. The one advantage minority prisoners seem to enjoy over white prisoners is strength in solidarity. This enables minority inmates to dominate their white counterparts in the power plays that characterize prison societies.

During the 1960s, minorities began to gain some rights in prison with respect to their cultural, religious, and dietary needs. Yet other gains have been slow to come about, such as adequate vocational and rehabilitative programs to reflect racial and cultural differences, proportionate minority staff, and an atmosphere more conducive to preparing minority inmates to return to a society where they are already at a disadvantage.

NOTES

1. Frank M. Dunbaugh, "Racially Disproportionate Rates of Incarceration in the United States," *Prison Law Monitor* 1 (1979): 205, 219–22.

2. Jack H. Nagel, "Crime and Incarceration: A Reanalysis," Fels Discussion Paper No. 112, School of Public and Urban Policy, University of Pennsylvania, 1977.

3. See Table 7.4.

4. John Irwin, *Prisons in Turmoil* (Boston: Little, Brown, 1980).

5. Eric O. Wright, *The Politics of Punishment: A Critical Analysis of Prisons in America* (New York: Harper & Row, 1973).

6. See for example, Sewell v. Pegelow, 304 F.2d 670 (1962); Knuckles v. Prasse, 435 F.2d 1255 (1970).

7. See, for example, Cooper v. Pate, 378 U.S. 546 (1964).

8. See Keith Butler, "The Muslims Are No Longer an Unknown Quality," *Corrections Magazine* 4 (1978): 55-65.

9. Clair Cripe, "Religious Freedom in Prisons," *Federal Probation* 41 (1977): 31-35; Lawrence French, "Corrections and the Native American Client," *Prison Journal* 59 (1970): 49-60.

10. B. S. Held, D. Levine, and V. D. Swartz, "Interpersonal Aspects of Dangerousness," *Criminal Justice and Behavior* 6 (1979): 49-58; L. Carroll and M. E. Mondrick, "Racial Bias in the Decision to Grant Parole," *Law and Society Review* 11 (1976): 93-107.

11. Robert Johnson, *Culture and Crisis in Confinement* (Lexington, Mass.: Lexington Books, 1976).

12. Hans Toch, *Living in Prison: The Ecology of Survival* (New York: Free Press, 1977).

13. Robert Minton, ed. *Inside Prison American Style* (New York: Random House, 1971); Wright, *Politics of Punishment*.

14. James B. Jacobs, *New Perspectives on Prisons and Imprisonment* (Ithaca, N.Y.: Cornell University Press, 1983), p. 68.

15. George Park, "The Organization of Prison Violence," in Albert K. Cohen, George F. Cole, and Robert G. Bayley, eds., *Prison Violence* (Lexington, Mass.: Lexington Books, 1976).

16. James B. Jacobs, *Stateville: The Penitentiary in Mass Society* (Chicago: University of Chicago Press, 1977).

17. John Irwin, *The Felon* (Englewood Cliffs, N.J.: Prentice-Hall, 1970), p. 82.

18. James B. Jacobs, "Race Relations and the Prisoner Subculture," in Norval Morris and Michael Towry, eds., *Crime and Justice: An Annual Review of Research*, vol. 1 (Chicago: University of Chicago Press, 1979).

19. Leo Carroll, *Hacks, Blacks, and Cons: Race Relations in a Maximum Security Prison* (Lexington, Mass.: D.C. Heath, 1974); Alan J. Davis, "Sexual Assaults in a Philadelphia Prison System and Sheriff's Vans," *Transaction* 6 (1968): 8-16.

20. Davis, "Sexual Assaults."

21. Carroll, *Hacks, Blacks, and Cons*.

22. Ibid.

23. Ibid., p. 195.

24. Jessica Mitford, *Kind and Usual Punishment* (New York: Random House, 1971).

25. U.S. Department of Justice, Bureau of Justice Statistics, *Capital Punishment, 1985* (Washington, D.C.: Government Printing Office, 1986).

26. Haywood Burns, "Can a Black Man Get a Fair Trial in This Country?" in Robert Yin, ed., *Race, Creed, Color, or National Origin* (Itasca, Ill.: F. E. Peacock, 1973), p. 222.

27. Marvin Wolfgang, cited by ibid.

28. Marvin E. Wolfgang and Marc Riedel, "Race, Judicial Discretion, and the Death Penalty," *American Academy of Political and Social Science* 407 (1973): 123.

29. National prison data cited by Burns, "Can a Black Man Get a Fair Trial?"

30. Burns, "Can a Black Man Get a Fair Trial?"

31. Bureau of Justice Statistics, *Capital Punishment, 1985.*

32. Several studies have shown a strong relationship between race, death row, and execution. Studies by David Baldus, and Samuel Gross and Robert Mauro, in which blacks were found to be more likely to receive the death penalty than whites, are cited in "Black-and-White Issue? The Supreme Court Wrestles with the Death Penalty and Race," *U.S. News & World Report* (October 20, 1986): 24.

33. A good example is the recent case of Willie Jasper Darden, a black man who was convicted of killing a Lakeland, Florida businessman during a robbery in 1973. After years of appeals and publicity and despite recent evidence that suggested he may have been innocent, Darden was put to death in Florida's electric chair on March 15, 1988. See also Darden v. Wainwright, 513 F. Supp. 947; 11 Cir., 699 F. 2d 1031 (1986).

34. U.S. Department of Justice, Bureau of Justice Statistics, *Jail Inmates 1986* (Washington, D.C.: Government Printing Office, 1986).

35. Ruth M. Glick and Virginia V. Neto, *National Study of Women's Correctional Programs* (Washington, D.C.: Government Printing Office, 1977).

36. U.S. General Accounting Office, *Female Offenders: Who Are They and What Are the Problems Confronting Them?* (Washington, D.C.: Government Printing Office, 1979), p. 8.

37. Bureau of Justice Statistics, *Jail Inmates 1986.*

38. Glick and Neto, *National Study.*

39. Elouise J. Spencer, "The Social System of a Medium Security Women's Prison" (Ph.D. diss., University of Kansas, 1977).

40. In addition to juvenile custody facilities, juveniles are also incarcerated in jails and prisons for varying lengths of time. Although most statistics suggest that the juvenile inmate population outside juvenile detention facilities is fairly small, it is estimated that as many as 600,000 youths annually may spend time in adult jails. Proportionately, most of these youths are of minority groups.

41. U.S. Department of Justice, Bureau of Justice Statistics, *Children in Custody* (Washington, D.C.: Government Printing Office, 1986), p. 3.

42. See chapters 7 and 9.

43. There is some evidence to suggest that minority youths are more likely

than white juveniles to be sentenced to death and executed. See Burns, "Can a Black Man Get a Fair Trial?"

44. Ronald B. Flowers, *Children and Criminality: The Child as Victim and Perpetrator* (Westport, Conn.: Greenwood Press, 1986), pp. 171–82.

45. Ibid., pp. 90–91.

V

THE FUTURE OF CRIME, CRIMINAL JUSTICE, AND MINORITY GROUPS

12

Looking Ahead in Addressing Minorities, Crime, and Criminal Justice

Over the course of our examination into minorities and criminality, it has been well established that minority members as a group are disproportionately represented as victims and offenders of crime and have been subjected to discriminatory treatment throughout the criminal justice system. This disadvantage in American society is a result of the historical oppression and racism minorities faced at the hands of the white dominant group, and has been sustained through discriminatory government policies and an unequal social, economic, and political structure that has traditionally favored the powerful majority. The resulting overrepresentation of minority groups in the lower classes has made them most susceptible to involvement in criminality and mistreatment by those empowered to control crime.

Although minorities have gained a number of rights previously denied them through civil and criminal court decisions over the years, these efforts have done little to change the relative position minority group members hold in society. Minorities continue to be more likely than whites, with respect to their numbers in the total population, to come into contact with crime either as victims or offenders and with the criminal justice system, where the treatment they receive is generally less favorable than for whites.

As we look to the future, we must ask what can be done to change a disadvantaged pattern that has been all too consistent over the years. Here we will look briefly at important trends and their significance with respect to minorities, crime, and the system of criminal justice and consider the implications for a more positive approach to dealing with the unresolved issues of today so that tomorrow we might succeed in balancing the scales of justice and lowering the incidence of minority participation in crime.

CIVIL RIGHTS

The landmark Civil Rights Act of 1964 promised to put an end to, or at least curtail, the overt bigotry and racism that characterized much of our history with regard to minorities. The primary section of the act read: "All persons shall be entitled to the full and equal enjoyment of the goods, services, facilities, privileges, advantages, and accommodations of any place of public accommodation . . . without discrimination or segregation on the ground of race, color, religion, or national origin." The early results of the act were encouraging; many businesses and school districts tended to conform to the law, and many that did not were subject to federal pressure (such as antidiscrimination suits and loss of federal funding). It appeared as if racial discrimination was clearly on the wane.

More than two decades later, however, it has become apparent that where old problems in civil rights have vanished, new problems have emerged, and in other instances, progress has stalled considerably. Passage of such legislation as the Voting Rights Act of 1965, the Fair Housing Act of 1968, and equal employment opportunity acts and other affirmative action programs have been successful in providing minorities with opportunities and guarantees previously denied them. Minority group members have made significant inroads in school desegregation, higher education, business, income, and public office.

Recent trends threaten to undermine this progress. The Reagan administration has appeared less than supportive of the civil rights movement compared to earlier administrations. Cutbacks in programs for the poor, an apparent unwillingness to enforce civil rights laws and programs, and even administration attempts to rewrite civil rights legislation give rise to concern about the future of minority groups and race relations.

Further criticism has been leveled at the White House for its support of tax breaks for schools that discriminate against racial minorities and for altering the philosophy of the U.S. Commission on Civil Rights by appointing new members who favor Reagan's opposition to busing and racial quotas. Notes Ralph Neas, director of the Leadership Conference on Civil Rights, in a sentiment shared by many: "For three decades, the Department of Justice has been the champion of civil rights for women, blacks, Hispanics and other minorities. But the Reagan Administration and its Justice Department have sought to do the reverse."[1]

Whether the Reagan White House should bear most of the burden of blame or not, what is clear is that in the important areas of education, housing, and employment, the progress of minorities has been slowed or level in recent years, and in some instances, drawn backward, despite continuing affirmative action challenges in court.[2] Blatant racial discrimination may no longer exist in most circles; instead, a more subtle, equally defeating form of racism has emerged, promoting continued denial of full civil rights to racial and ethnic minorities.

As equal access to opportunity is hindered or denied, minorities are likely to continue to swell in the lower classes, where fear, disillusion, and desperation will contribute to a growing crime rate and increased racial tensions. Controlling this trend will require an increased racial/ ethnic balance in criminal justice system employment and administrative funding and education for better police-community relations, as well as a greater liaison between criminal justice agencies, the various levels of government, and other social services.

RACE RELATIONS

The correlation between civil rights and race relations is clear. As minorities gain civil rights, the dominant group effectively loses some. As the dominant group maintains its grip on racism and discrimination, minorities as a result suffer. Because there has never really been a point in our history when a proper balance has been achieved for everyone, race relations have varied from extreme turbulence to strained tensions.

Although race relations have improved markedly since the early 1960s, recent trends in civil rights and affirmative action, combined with the reemergence of white supremacist groups and individuals, have once again threatened to divide the country into "separate but equal" factions. The 1980s have seen a rash of violent encounters and criminal acts from such groups as the Ku Klux Klan and neo-Nazi contingents, as well as more recent groups or individuals of various ethnic and racial backgrounds. Much of this violence is blamed on a combination of factors—including fear, ignorance, the economy, and renewed hatred of those who are different. Civil rights groups argue that the Reagan administration's negligent enforcement of federal civil rights has resulted in "widespread contempt for the law."

If sporadic episodes of violence and racism are allowed to go unchecked or with only peripheral attention, they will get worse and perhaps lead to the types of race riots that were common in the 1960s. Complicating racial tensions are their implications for the criminal justice system. Race relations in general also tend to affect the relations of racial and ethnic groups in jails and prisons throughout the country. An already tense and often volatile relationship between prisoner groups is exacerbated when racial relations outside the prison deteriorate. The criminal justice system is likely to face increased pressure to act as a peacemaker and control force both inside and outside the correctional system. How it handles this role could set the direction of race relations.

Influencing the criminal justice system's response to civil rights and race relations is the makeup of criminal justice agencies and race relations within them. As more racial minorities are made an integral part of management and staff in criminal justice careers, the criminal justice system will be more effective in controlling crime.

Ultimately more affirmative action programs and equal opportunity laws, as well as their strict enforcement, will play a major role in the nature of race relations. Clearly the path ahead is a long and possibly frustrating one.

THE UNDERCLASS OF AMERICA

In spite of the success of civil rights in many areas related to the socioeconomic structure, there still exists a growing, possibly permanent, underclass in the United States made up predominantly of minorities. This underclass, explored in detail in Ken Auletta's *The Under Class*, consists of a subculture of people caught in a vicious cycle of poverty, joblessness, illiteracy, broken homes, welfare, substance abuse, crime, and violence.[3] These individuals are cut off from the mainstream of society and lack the qualities needed to climb out of this underclass. A perspective of life in this world "beyond hope and suffering," lacking values and income, can be seen in the following grim depiction:

It is a world where men are without jobs and women are without husbands. Some are career criminals. Others broker numbers and hustle stolen goods. Many are addicted to drugs and alcohol.

Dominating underclass life is the continuous threat of violence. Homicide is the leading cause of death for young [adult] men. High crime rates are accompanied by pervasive fear on the streets. . . . To many community leaders, the underclass is increasingly outside the law.[4]

The implications of this underclass in terms of crime and its control are frightening. As this class of society continues to grow, so too does crime and the incidence of violence. This has a rippling effect on racial discrimination and tensions, exaggerated fears and media focus, and law enforcement.

The system of criminal justice often becomes as much a part of the problem as a solution. Minority members of the underclass generally resent law enforcement intrusion, reflected in their frequent outcries of police brutality. This heightened tension manifests itself in the relationship between minority and white criminal justice employees, particularly the police. Minority police find themselves caught in the middle—wanted by neither their white coworkers, who see them as "interlopers who are interrupting a chain of succession that has been in operation for decades," nor their own racial and ethnic groups, who see them as traitors.[5]

Despite such intraracial hostilities in criminal justice agencies, their role in controlling urban crime will become increasingly important. Their success in preventing and combating crime will be reflected in the racial harmony in this country, as well as the economic and social direction it will go in. A positive law enforcement approach to the dilemma of urban crime will require policies that promote community relations rather than alienation, deemphasize the popular identification of crime with racial and ethnic minorities, and develop better systems of preventative law enforcement.

EMPLOYMENT OF MINORITIES IN THE CRIMINAL JUSTICE SYSTEM

We have noted the importance of minority personnel in the criminal justice system. How has the system responded to this need? On the surface, largely as a result of affirmative action and equal opportunity legislation, improvements have been made in minority staffing of criminal justice agencies in recent years. However, when viewing the overall employment picture of minorities in the criminal justice system, it becomes clear that they continue to be seriously underrepresented on virtually all fronts.

Minorities constitute only approximately 4 percent of the police personnel in this country.[6] Their numbers improve in correctional positions to 21 percent; however, only about 12 percent of those in higher management positions in correctional institutions are minorities compared to just over 8 percent in police agencies.[7] Members of minority groups are also in disproportion in other criminal justice–related institutions such as law, the judiciary, and higher education.[8]

What is the reason for this underrepresentation? It would be an oversimplification to suggest it is solely a matter of discriminatory practices of criminal justice agencies. This is a major stumbling block, but other prominent contributors to insufficient minority criminal justice personnel can be seen in the continuing litigation over affirmative action programs versus seniority systems and charges of reverse discrimination; budgetary constraints; racism and discrimination in other areas in the public and private sector; lack of "qualified" minority applicants; the dilemma of marginality whereby the potential minority employee must consider the prospect of condemnation from both peers and members of his or her racial/ethnic group; and the lure of other profes-

sional careers that are better paying, more prestigious, and less hazard-
ous.

Nevertheless, it is hard to look beyond the basic fabric of the criminal
justice system, which has long discriminated against minorities as victim, offender, and professional. This has made it doubly difficult to
increase the levels of minority employment. Supreme Court decisions
such as in the *Bakke* case, in which the Court held that preferential
treatment on the basis of race can be considered as long as a quota
system is not used, the creation of the federal Equal Employment Opportunities Commission and state commissions, and incentive programs such as that mandated by the Law Enforcement Assistance Administration have been supportive of affirmative action and have
contributed to its success in the employment of minorities in the criminal justice system.[9]

The battle lines remain drawn, however. Some judicial decisions (for
example, *Memphis Fire Department v. Stotts* in which the Supreme Court
ruled that nonbiased seniority systems had precedence in maintaining
jobs over minority workers of less seniority, despite affirmative action
mandates) and nondecisions in recent years appear to be going against
the affirmative action grain and employment and promotional opportunities for minorities.[10] Furthermore, minorities successful in the criminal justice system employ often find themselves at odds with their
white coworkers and white-dominated unions in an atmosphere of distrust, hostility, discrimination, alienation, and resistance to change. To
this end, minorities have formed such organizations as the Minority
Correctional Officer Association (MCOA) and the National Black Police
Association (NBPA) to represent their needs and fight ongoing racial
discrimination in the system.

Minorities working in the criminal justice system are also handicapped by their often-perceived role of being a traitor to members of
their own race or ethnic group, charges of abuse of power by minority
groups or favoritism by their white colleagues, and the need to be ac-
cepted by the system and prove they belong. This range of emotions
and situations ultimately increases tensions between minority workers
and other minorities they come into contact with, as well as with their
nonminority coworkers.

Nevertheless, the continued growth of minority representation in the
criminal justice system remains vital and will in all likelihood continue
in the coming years. Overall, minorities represent an important stabilizing force in quelling racial tensions involving minorities both incarcerated and in society. Also, because minorities generally share a common background of discrimination and injustice, those in the criminal
justice disciplines are more likely to be able to understand the situations of other minorities. They thus have a perspective of familiarity

that is necessary to counterbalance discriminatory practices in the system and enable them to dispense equal justice and protection to racial and ethnic minorities.

RESEARCH: KEY TO THE FUTURE

There has been a paucity of useful research on minorities in the areas of criminality and victimization. For various reasons, researchers have been reluctant to pursue this important study. As a result, an important educational component in understanding the history and dynamics of the American minority has been largely neglected. In order to understand better and interpret the relationship between minority groups and crime and influence social policies and attitudes toward minorities, it is imperative that more historical and scientific research be applied toward studying the minority in this country. In particular, minority group members must participate in the studies of minorities. Also needed is greater federal and private grant support to encourage and make possible such study.

LEGISLATIVE NEEDS

Legislative efforts on the state and federal levels must be stepped up to ensure that minorities are treated equally and fairly by the criminal justice system. For instance, the imbalance in death penalty sentences and other possible discriminatory practices within the system of criminal justice suggest that the entire criminal code and the means by which people are arrested, convicted, and sentenced may need to be overhauled. At the very least, better checks and balances are needed so that those disadvantaged in society will not expect the same treatment in criminal justice.

The violation of minorities' civil rights requires greater attention by legislators. Discrimination, racism, and prejudice that manifests itself through hiring, employment, housing, and educational practices are equally criminal and can also be associated with minority involvement in crime and the criminal justice system.

CRIMINAL JUSTICE EDUCATION

The criminal justice system is not as effective as it could be because of insufficient academic requirements across the board for its personnel. Because of the changing needs of society, further criminological study is needed at the college and university level to supplement the occupational work in such areas as law enforcement, corrections, and the courts. Additional education should be required in racial and ethnic studies, sociology, and psychology. Graduate studies should be encouraged across the board. This work will better prepare the criminal justice workers to deal more effectively with the cultural and racial differences of minorities and nonminorities alike and lower the barriers that contribute to negative race relations and discriminatory practices.

Higher education also has a responsibility to bring more minorities into the disciplines of criminal justice and criminology on both the undergraduate and graduate levels. The paucity of minority educators and college graduates in this area of study is contributing significantly to the underrepresentation of minorities in the system of criminal justice. Greater active recruiting of minorities by colleges and universities across the country, less disadvantageous selection policies for minority faculty, and more receptive utilization of affirmative action programs are sorely needed to begin to offset the imbalance in criminal justice higher education.

THE CRIMINAL JUSTICE SYSTEM

A number of reforms are needed in the system of criminal justice with respect to its involvement with minorities. The most significant are the following:

- The methodology used for gathering law enforcement statistics needs to be revised to reflect greater detail of all racial and ethnic groups and more useful comparisons between them, including gender and age differences. More emphasis should be placed on crimes that are frequent and white offender dominated, such as white-collar crimes.
- Qualification systems in the criminal justice system need to be overhauled in order to ensure nondiscriminatory hiring and promotion of all ethnic and racial group members.
- More minority member employees representing all racial and ethnic groups are needed on all levels of the criminal and juvenile justice system, particularly in law enforcement, corrections, and the judicial system.
- Both elected and hired criminal justice employees need further screening as to their racial values and ability to work fairly with citizens of all races and ethnicities.
- Criminal justice administrators need to develop better rules and regulations limiting the degree of discretionary powers at the disposal of its members when deciding the disposition of individual cases.
- A more effective system is needed in ensuring that criminal juries are fair and impartial. Multiple interviews and background checks of prospective jurors and more racially balanced juries are crucial.
- A greater interaction is needed among police officers, community leaders,

and social services so that each better understands the role of the other in working together to control crime.

- More police are needed in the most troubled urban areas, and better response time to complaints is urged.

- Alleged police misconduct and violation of citizens' rights needs to be investigated more thoroughly and dealt with appropriately internally and by government agencies.

- Correctional institutions need to incorporate into their rehabilitation and environment vocational and educational programs designed to reflect the racial and cultural differences of minority prisoners.

- Minority prisoner consultation on prison activities and stability is needed to promote better race relations and a better liaison among administration, staff, and prisoners.

- Too little attention is given in correctional facilities to preparing minority inmates for a successful return to society. Prisoners must be taught job-related skills, counseled, and educated.

- The often volatile and shameful conditions in jails and prisons throughout the United States create circumstances conducive to violence, victimization, illness, and other problems. Corrections and government officials need to find ways to make incarceration more humane for prisoners—if for no other reason than to quell tensions for both prisoners and staff.

VICTIMIZATION STUDIES

Victimization surveys fall short of utilizing their full potential in the study of minority victims. Key recommendations for improvement are as follows:

- Every racial and ethnic minority needs to be given individual and comparative attention. For example, Native Americans and Asians are currently grouped together, giving no real perspective on their victimization.

- The racial and ethnic definitional variables used in victimization data need to become more compatible for purposes of comparing Hispanics with other minority group victims.

- Further emphasis should be placed on offender data that are comparable to the victimization data recommended.

- Victimization studies need to include more of the personal and household crimes currently ignored.

- The role of differential treatment and perception of minority group respondents by interviewers needs to be examined.

CRIMINOLOGICAL STUDIES

The criminologist has an important role in our understanding of crime and criminals, but this role is often neglected. In other instances, it is misused. The pursuit of minority studies in criminology needs:

- More empirical research into theories of criminal behavior.
- Less emphasis on flawed official statistics with regard to minority crime.
- Further comparative analyses of the victimization and criminality of minorities as addressed by different disciplines.
- Greater attention to the role of differential treatment of minorities in the criminal justice system.
- More research into the criminality of the middle and upper classes in comparison with the lower class.
- Additional exploration of the relationship between race/ethnicity and class and race/ethnicity and sex.

COMMUNITY AND SOCIAL SERVICES

The community and its services are an integral part of controlling the criminality of minorities and offering assistance to minority victims. In order for such services to be more effective, what is needed is:

- Better trained, more efficient, and sensitive staff in various social services.
- Adequate representation of every racial and ethnic group in community and social service employ.
- Better referral services and coordination with other agencies.
- Updated newsletters and educational material pertaining to crime, victims, and advances in the fields of criminal justice and victimology.
- More community forums to discuss crime and other related issues.
- A greater emphasis on reaching out to adolescents, who are in the most vulnerable position to be both victim and offender.

BLACKS

As our nation's largest and most conspicuous racial minority, blacks have the highest crime and victimization rates and are arguably the most discriminated against. They have also been the most studied racial minority group. Yet the problems blacks face continue to grow. The following measures would seem to be necessary:

- Government subsidies and incentives need to be made available to employers to hire more black youths and adults, particularly of the lower classes, thereby providing more legitimate opportunities to counteract illegitimate ones.
- Black inner-city youths need more positive role models. Unfortunately, most such role models are confined to either athletes or criminals. Black youths need more accessible middle-class black professionals to look up to. It may take more hiring and more participation of established blacks in the black community to lower its crime rate and offer potential delinquents a positive alternative.
- More study and follow-up research is needed in exploring black criminal subcultures in relation to the economic structure, the crime of other minority groups, and the black experience.
- More legitimate enterprises and better housing are needed in lower-class urban areas to help create a better sense of community and to lower the crime rate.
- City and community officials and law enforcement need greater involvement in promoting safe streets, a work ethic, and stiffer penalties for law violations.

HISPANICS

Hispanics are fast becoming the largest ethnic group in the country. Numerically they rank second to blacks in crime and victimization. Because Hispanic involvement in crime is similar to that of blacks, the same implications for prevention or control apply. However, Hispanics differ from blacks in that they are a more heterogeneous group and therefore require additional efforts at understanding and tackling the problems they face:

- In-depth study is needed of the differences and relationship between Hispanic subgroups and Hispanic illegal aliens.
- The language barrier many Hispanics face should be addressed in exploring their criminality.
- We need to evaluate Hispanics' perceptions of their rights, civil liberties, and relationship to the criminal justice system.
- Criminal and victimization data must be revised to reflect better the racial and ethnic composition of Hispanics.
- Further study and criminal justice involvement is needed on the role of the illegal Hispanic in American victimization and crime, as well as criminal exploitation by non-Hispanic employers and others.
- The discriminatory issue at various stages of the law enforcement, court, and prison systems needs a great deal more attention as it relates to the Hispanic rate of arrest, conviction, and incarceration. (The same holds true for other racial and ethnic groups.)

ASIANS

Asian-American groups are similar to Hispanics in that there actually are several distinct Asian populations in this country, Chinese and Japanese being the largest. Although Asians, unlike Hispanics, have low criminal involvement, there is some evidence that Asian crime may be hidden more because of Asians' close communities and therefore does not show up as much in the statistics. Additionally, Asian youths are becoming more active in delinquency, and organized Asian criminals are forming a niche in American society.

Nevertheless, the overall low Asian crime rate as compared to other racial groups is somewhat mystifying. It is something we may be able to learn from and apply to other minority groups. Therefore we need to establish:

• Why the Asian crime rate is so low.
• What the difference is in the crime and victimization rates of individual Asian groups.
• What effect, if any, Asian victimization has had on their involvement in crime.
• How Asian crime in this country compares to that elsewhere.
• How the recent rash of Asian delinquency and organized Asian crime has affected the closeness of the Asian community.
• How the life-styles and socioeconomic factors of Asians differ from other American racial and ethnic groups.

NATIVE AMERICANS

Native Americans are perhaps the worst-off group in this country. They have the second highest crime rate nationwide relative to population size and are poorer, less educated, and in poorer health than the nation as a whole. They also have the highest rate of alcohol use and abuse. They are mostly either ignored or thought of in stereotypical terms as depicted in movies and television.

Perhaps the fairest solution to the Native American problem would be the return of their land stolen from them. However, since that would displace millions of people, a more reasonable solution is to create more government programs and legislation designed to allow Native Americans to become self-governing or effectively assimilate into the American culture. For their high rate of crime:

• Greater efforts must be made to understand why alcohol is so much a part of Native American crime compared to most other racial groups.
• More comparative study is needed on the crime of urban and reservation

Native Americans, as well as Canadian Indians, and the circumstances under which they live.

- Native American leaders and community and government officials need to establish greater communication with and better solutions in dealing with Native American crime.
- The role of Native American exploiters of their land and rights must be studied and investigated in terms of both prosecution and understanding of its effect on the Native American experience.
- Greater attention nationwide should be placed on the Native American heritage and the plight of Native Americans. It is time that we give them something back.

An understanding of minorities and their role in crime can best be achieved by examining the issues rather than turning our back on them. This book has sought to do the former. But clearly much remains to be learned about the minority community and criminality. We have taken that all important initial step.

NOTES

1. Ralph Neas as quoted in "King's Dream: How It Stands 20 Years Later," *U.S. News & World Report* (August 29, 1983): 48.
2. See Civil Rights Act, 28 U.S.C. (1983).
3. Ken Auletta, *The Under Class* (New York: Random House, 1982).
4. "A Nation Apart," *U.S. News & World Report* (March 17, 1986): 20.
5. Anthony V. Bouza, "Police Unions: Paper Tigers or Roaring Lions?" in William A. Geller, ed., *Police Leadership in America: Crisis and Opportunity* (Chicago: American Bar Foundation, 1985), p. 275.
6. This percentage also includes female police personnel. See Terry Eisenberg et al., *Police Personnel Practices in State and Local Government* (Washington, D.C.: Police Foundation, 1973), p. 35.
7. *The National Manpower Survey of the Criminal Justice System: Corrections* (Washington, D.C.: Superintendent of Documents, 1978), pp. 49-54; Eisenberg et al., *Police Personnel Practices*, p. 34.
8. See "Minority and Women Judges," *U.S. News & World Report* (January 20, 1986): 11; Robert M. O'Neil, "Preferential Admissions: Equaling the Access of Minority Groups to Higher Education," *Yale Law Journal* 80 (1971): 728.
9. Bakke v. Regents of the University of California, 98 S.Ct. 2733 (1978); See also P.L. 92-261.
10. Memphis Fire Department v. Stotts, 104 S.Ct. 2576 (1984). See also Detroit Police Officers' Association v. Young, 608 F.2d 671 (6th Cir. 1979), cert. denied, 452 U.S. 938 (1981).

Selected Bibliography

Abadinsky, Howard. *Organized Crime*. 2d ed. Chicago: Nelson-Hall, 1985.

Auletta, Ken. *The Under Class*. New York: Random House, 1982.

Bartollas, Clemens, Stuart J. Miller, and Paul B. Wice. *Participants in American Criminal Justice: The Promise and the Performance*. Englewood Cliffs, N.J.: Prentice-Hall, 1983.

Bondavalli, Bonnie J., and Bruno Bondavalli. "Spanish-Speaking People and the North American Criminal Justice System." In R. L. McNeely and Carl E. Pope, eds., *Race, Crime, and Criminal Justice*. Beverly Hills: Sage, 1981.

Bowker, Lee H. *Corrections: The Science and the Art*. New York: Macmillan, 1982.

Bresler, Fenton. *The Chinese Mafia: The Most Frightening New Organization in International Crime*. New York: Stein and Day, 1980.

Butler, Keith. "The Muslims Are No Longer an Unknown Quality." *Corrections Magazine* 4 (1978): 55–65.

Butterfield, Fox. "The Shifting Picture of Crime by U.S. Vietnamese." *New York Times* (January 21, 1985): A13(L).

Carroll, Leo. *Hacks, Blacks, and Cons: Race Relations in a Maximum Security Prison*. Lexington, Mass.: D. C. Heath, 1974.

Cloward, Richard A., and Lloyd E. Ohlin. *Delinquency and Opportunity: A Theory of Delinquent Gangs*. New York: Free Press, 1960.

Cohen, Albert. *Delinquent Boys: The Culture of the Gang*. New York: Free Press, 1955.

Cohen, Warren H., and Phillip I. Mause. "The Indian: The Forgotten American." *Harvard Law Review* 81 (1968): 1818–58.

Conklin, John E. *Criminology*. 2d ed. New York: Macmillan, 1986.

"Crime: An Equal-Opportunity Employer." *Newsweek* 106 (December 30, 1985): 22.

Cripe, Clair. "Religious Freedom in Prisons." *Federal Probation* 41 (1977): 31–35.

Daniels, Roger. *Anti-Chinese Violence in North America*. New York: Arno Press, 1978.

Dannefer, Dale, and Russell K. Schutt. "Race and Juvenile Justice Processing in Court and Police Agencies." *American Journal of Sociology* 87 (1982): 1113–32.

Davidson, Theodore. *Chicano Prisoners: The Key to San Quentin*. New York: Holt, Rinehart & Winston, 1974.

Dunbaugh, Frank M. "Racially Disproportionate Rates of Incarceration in the United States." *Prison Law Monitor* 1 (1979): 205–22.

Elias, Robert. *The Politics of Victimization*. New York: Oxford University Press, 1986.

Estrada, Leo F., F. Chris Garcia, Reynaldo F. Macias, and Lionel Maldonado. "Chicanos in the United States: A History of Exploitation and Resistance." *Daedalus* 110 (1981): 103–31.

Flowers, Ronald B. *Criminal Jurisdiction Allocation in Indian Country*. Port Washington, N.Y.: Associated Faculty Press, 1983.

Fyfe, James J. "Race and Extreme Police-Citizen Violence." In R. L. McNeely and Carl Pope, eds., *Race, Crime and Criminal Justice*. Beverly Hills: Sage, 1981.

Geller, William A., ed. *Police Leadership in America: Crisis and Opportunity*. Chicago: American Bar Foundation, 1985.

Georges-Abeyie, Daniel, ed. *The Criminal Justice System and Blacks*. New York: Clark Boardman, 1984.

Glick, Ruth M., and Virginia V. Neto. *National Study of Women's Correctional Programs*. Washington D.C.: Government Printing Office, 1977.

Hardy, Kenneth A. "Equity in Court Dispositions." In Gordon P. Whitaker and Charles D. Phillips, eds., *Evaluating Performance of Criminal Justice Agencies*. Beverly Hills: Sage, 1983.

Hayner, Norman S. "Variability in the Criminal Behavior of American Indians." *American Journal of Sociology* 47 (1942): 602–13.

Hornblower, Margot. "Asian Mafia Seen Spreading." *Washington Post* (October 24, 1985): A3.

Hunley, Steve, and Joseph L. Galloway. "American Indians: 'Beggars in Our Land.'" *U.S. News & World Report* 94 (May 23, 1983): 70–72.

Ianni, Francis A. J. *Black Mafia: Ethnic Succession in Organized Crime*. New York: Simon & Schuster, 1974.

Irwin, John. *Prisons in Turmoil*. Boston: Little, Brown, 1980.

Jacobs, James B. *New Perspectives on Prison and Imprisonment*. Ithaca, N.Y.: Cornell University Press, 1983.

Johnson, Robert, and Hans Toch, eds. *The Pains of Imprisonment*. Beverly Hills: Sage Publications, 1982.

Johnson, Sherri L. "Race and the Decision to Detain a Suspect." *Yale Law Journal* 93 (1983): 214–58.

Kaplan, David E., and Alec Dubro. *Yakuza: The Explosive Account of Japan's Criminal Underworld*. Reading, Mass.: Addison-Wesley, 1986.

Long, Elton, James Long, Wilmer Leon, and Paul B. Weston. *American Minorities: The Justice Issue*. Englewood Cliffs, N.J.: Prentice-Hall, 1975.

McCoy, Candace. "Affirmative Action in Police Organizations." In James J. Fyfe, ed. *Police Management Today: Issues and Case Studies*. Washington, D.C.: International City Management Association, 1985.

McKee, Jesse O., ed. *Ethnicity in Contemporary America: A Geographical Appraisal.* Dubuque, Iowa: Kendall/Hunt, 1985.

Marsh, Frank H., and Janet Katz, eds. *Biology, Crime and Ethics: A Study of Biological Explanations for Criminal Behavior.* Cincinnati: Anderson Publishing Co., 1985.

Mednick, Sarnoff, and Karl O. Christiansen. *Biosocial Bases of Criminal Behavior.* New York: Gardner Press, 1977.

Meltzer, Milton. *The Chinese Americans.* New York: Thomas Y. Crowell, 1980.

Merton, Robert K. *Social Theory and Social Structure.* Glencoe, Ill.: Free Press, 1957.

Miller, Eleanor M., and Lynne H. Kleinman. "Political Economy and the Social Control of Ethnic Crime." In Lionel Maldonado and Joan Moore, eds., *Urban Ethnicity in the United States.* Beverly Hills: Sage, 1985.

Miller, Stuart C. *The Unwelcome Immigrant: The American Image of the Chinese, 1785–1882.* Berkeley: University of California Press, 1969.

Miller, Walter B. "Lower Class Culture as a Generating Milieu of Gang Delinquency." *Journal of Social Issues* 14 (1958): 5–19.

Mindel, Charles H., and Robert W. Habenstein, eds. *Ethnic Families in America: Patterns and Variations.* New York: Elsevier, 1976.

Moore, J. W. *Homeboys: Gangs, Drugs and Prison in the Barrios of Los Angeles.* Philadelphia: Temple University Press, 1978.

Morris, Jim. "Gangs at War in LA Streets." *Sacramento Bee* (October 19, 1986): A1.

Nettler, Gwynn. *Explaining Crime.* 3d ed. New York: McGraw-Hill, 1984.

Nickerson, Stephanie, Clara Mayo, and Althea Smith. "Racism in the Courtroom." In John F. Dovidio and Samuel L. Gaertner, eds., *Prejudice, Discrimination, and Racism.* Orlando, Fla.: Academic Press, 1986.

Pao-min, Chang. "Health and Crime among Chinese Americans: Recent Trends." *Phylon* 42 (1981): 363–67.

President's Commission on Organized Crime. *Organized Crime of Asian Origin.* Washington, D.C.: U.S. Government Printing Office, 1984.

Radelet, Louis A. *The Police and the Community.* 4th ed. New York: Macmillan, 1986.

Reasons, Charles E. "Crime and the Native American." In Charles E. Reasons and Jack L. Kuykendall, eds., *Race, Crime and Justice.* Pacific Palisades, Calif.: Goodyear Publishing Co., 1972.

Reid, Sue Titus. *Crime and Criminology.* 2d ed. New York: Holt, Rinehart & Winston, 1979.

Reuter, Peter. *Disorganized Crime.* Cambridge: MIT Press, 1983.

Riffenburgh, Arthur S. "Cultural Influences and Crime among Indians—Americans of the Southwest." *Federal Probation* 28 (1964): 38–46.

Romero, Leo M., and Luis G. Stelzner. "Hispanics and the Criminal Justice System." In Pastora San Juan Cafferty and William C. McCready, eds., *Hispanics in the United States: A New Social Agenda.* New Brunswick, N.J.: Transaction Books, 1985.

Sellin, Thorsten. *Culture, Conflict and Crime.* New York: Social Science Research Council, 1938.

Sheley, Joseph F. *America's "Crime Problem": An Introduction to Criminology*. Belmont, Calif.: Wadsworth, 1985.

Shover, Neal. *A Sociology of American Corrections*. Homewood, Ill.: Dorsey Press, 1979.

Siegel, Larry J. *Criminology*. 2d ed. St. Paul: West, 1986.

Silberman, Charles. *Criminal Violence, Criminal Justice*. New York: Random House, 1978.

Smith, Douglas A., Christy A. Visher, and Laura A. Davidson. "Equity and Discretionary Justice: The Influence of Race on Police Arrest Decisions." *Journal of Criminal Law and Criminology* 75 (1985): 234–49.

Southern Commission on the Study of Lynchings. *Lynchings and What They Mean*. Atlanta: Southern Commission on the Study of Lynchings, 1931.

Staples, Gracie Bonds. "Self-Inflicted Death Plagues US Blacks." *Sacramento Bee* (December 8, 1986): A14.

Stewart, Omer. "Questions Regarding American Indian Criminality." *Human Organization* 23 (1964): 61–66.

"Sudden Rise of Hate Groups Spurs Federal Crackdown." *U.S. News & World Report* 98 (May 6, 1985): 68.

Sutherland, Edwin H. *Principles of Criminology*. Philadelphia: Lippincott, 1939.

Taub, Richard P., D. Garth Taylor, and Jan D. Dunham. *Paths of Neighborhood Change: Race and Crime in Urban America*. Chicago: University of Chicago Press, 1984.

Taylor, Dalmas A. "Toward the Promised Land." *Psychology Today* 18 (June, 1984): 46–50.

Thornberry, Terrence P. "Race, Socioeconomic Status and Sentencing in the Juvenile Justice System." *Journal of Criminal Law and Criminology* 64 (1973): 90–98.

Toppin, Edgar A. *A Biographical History of Blacks in America since 1528*. New York: David McKay, 1971.

Vander Zanden, James W. *American Minority Relations*. 4th ed. New York: Alfred A. Knopf, 1983.

Von Hentig, Hans. "The Delinquency of the American Indian." *Journal of Criminal Law* 36 (1945): 75–84.

Waddell, Jack O., and O. Michael Watson, eds. *The American Indian in Urban Society*. Boston: Little, Brown, 1971.

Waegel, William B. "The Use of Lethal Force by Police: The Effect of Statutory Change." *Crime and Delinquency* 30 (1984): 121–40.

Wax, Murray L. *Indian Americans: Unity and Diversity*. Englewood Cliffs, N.J.: Prentice-Hall, 1971.

White, Jack E. "When Brother Kills Brother." *Time* (September 16, 1985): 2–36.

Wilson, James Q., and Richard J. Herrnstein. *Crime and Human Nature*. New York: Simon & Schuster, 1985.

Wolfgang, Marvin E. "Race and Crime." In H. J. Sklare, ed., *Changing Concepts of Crime and Its Treatment*. London: Pergamon, 1966.

Wolfgang, Marvin E., and Marc Riedel. "Race, Judicial Discretion, and the Death Penalty." *American Academy of Political and Social Science* 407 (1973): 119–32.

Yetman, Norman R., ed. *Majority and Minority: The Dynamics of Race and Ethnicity in American Life*. 4th ed. Boston: Allyn and Bacon, 1985.

Yin, Robert K., ed. *Race, Creed, Color, or National Origin: A Reader on Racial and Ethnic Identities in American Society*. Itasca, Ill.: F. E. Peacock, 1973.

Supplementary References

Although there continues to be a lack of substantive research and written material on minorities in general and with respect to victimization, criminality, and the system of criminal justice, the following books and articles provide additional reading sources that make a contribution to the understanding and knowledge of various aspects of minorities, crime, discrimination, and criminal justice.

"A Nation Apart." *U.S. News & World Report* 100 (March 17, 1986): 18–28.

Alex, Nicholas. *Black in Blue: A Study of the Negro Policeman.* New York: Appleton-Century-Crofts, 1969.

Allport, Gordon W. *The Nature of Prejudice.* New York: Addison-Wesley, 1958.

Bayley, David H., and Harold Mendelsoh. *Minorities and the Police: Confrontation in America.* New York: Free Press, 1969.

Blackburn, Sara, ed. *White Justice: Black Experience Today in America's Courtrooms.* New York: Harper & Row, 1971.

Bonger, William A. *Race and Crime.* Montclair, N.J.: Patterson Smith, 1969.

Brown, Claude. *Manchild in the Promised Land.* New York: Macmillan, 1965.

Burley, R. M. *Ethnic and Racial Groups: The Dynamics of Dominance.* New York: Cummings Publishing Co., 1978.

Christianson, Scott. "Racial Discrimination and Prison Confinement: A Follow-Up." *Criminal Law Bulletin* 16 (1980): 616–21.

Clark, Kenneth B. *Dark Ghetto: Dilemmas of Social Power.* New York: Harper & Row, 1965.

Conant, Ralph W. *The Prospects for Revolution: A Study of Riots, Civil Disobedience and Insurrections in Contemporary America.* New York: Harper & Row, 1971.

Cooper, John L. *The Police and the Ghetto.* New York: Kennikat Press, 1980.

Countryman, Vern. *Discrimination and the Law.* Chicago: University of Chicago Press, 1965.

Denfeld, Duane, and Andrew Hopkins. "Racial-Ethnic Identification in Prisons: 'Right On from the Inside.'" *International Journal of Criminology and Penology* 3 (1975): 355–66.

Dorsen, Norman. *Discrimination and Civil Rights.* Boston: Little, Brown, 1969.

Fox, James G. *Organizational and Racial Conflict in Maximum Security Prisons.* Lexington, Mass.: Lexington Books, 1972.

Fox, Vernon. "Racial Issues in Corrections." *American Journal of Corrections* 34 (1972): 12–17.

Freedman, Morris, and Carolyn Banks, eds. *The Minority Experience in America.* Philadelphia: J. B. Lippincott, 1972.

Grimshaw, Allen D., ed. *Racial Violence in the United States.* Chicago: Aldine-Atherton, 1969.

Kantrowitz, Nathan. "The Vocabulary of Race Relations in a Prison." *Publication of the American Dialect Society* 51 (1969): 23–34.

Kephart, William M. *Racial Factors and Urban Law Enforcement.* Philadelphia: University of Pennsylvania Press, 1957.

Killian, Lewis, and Charles Grigg. *Racial Crisis in America: Leadership in Conflict.* Englewood Cliffs, N.J.: Prentice-Hall, 1964.

Kleck, G. "Racial Discrimination in Criminal Sentencing: A Critical Evaluation of the Evidence with Additional Evidence on the Death Penalty." *American Sociological Review* 46 (1981): 783–804.

Kluchesky, Joseph T. *Police Action on Minority Problems.* New York: Freedom House, 1946.

Lincoln, C. Eric. *The Black Muslims in America.* Boston: Beacon Press, 1961.

Lohman, Joseph D. *The Police and Minority Groups.* Chicago: Chicago Park Police, 1947.

McNeely, R. L., and Carl E. Pope, eds. *Race, Crime and Criminal Justice.* Beverly Hills: Sage Publications, 1981.

Marden, Charles F., and Gladys Meyer. *Minorities in American Society.* New York: American Book Co., 1962.

Owens, Charles E., and Jimmy Bell. *Blacks and Criminal Justice.* Lexington, Mass.: Lexington Books, 1977.

Petersilia, Joan. *Racial Disparities in the Criminal Justice System.* Santa Monica, Calif.: Rand Corp., 1983.

Ransford, Edward. *Race and Class in American Society: Black, Anglo, Chicano.* Cambridge, Mass.: Schenkman, 1977.

Rothman, David. "Decarcerating Prisoners and Patients." *Civil Liberties Review* 1 (1973): 8–30.

Segal, Ronald. *The Race War.* New York: Viking Press, 1966.

Simpson, George E., and J. Milton Yinger. *Racial and Cultural Minorities.* New York: Harper & Brothers, 1953.

Uhlman, Thomas M. *Racial Justice: Black Judges, Black Defendants and the American Legal Process.* Lexington, Mass.: Lexington Books, 1979.

U.S. Commission on Civil Rights. *Social Indicators of Equality for Minorities and Women.* Washington, D.C.: U.S. Government Printing Office, 1978.

U.S. National Advisory Council on Criminal Justice. *The Inequality of Justice: A Report on Crime and the Administration of Justice in the Minority Community.* Washington, D.C.: U.S. Government Printing Office, 1980.

Wagler, Charles, and Marvin Harris. *Minorities in the New World.* New York: Columbia University Press, 1958.

Weckler, J. E., and Theo E. Hall. *The Police and Minority Groups*. Chicago: International City Managers' Association, 1944.

Widick, B. J. *Detroit: City of Race and Class Violence*. Chicago: Quadrangle Books, 1972.

Wintersmith, Robert. *Police and the Black Community*. Lexington, Mass.: Lexington Books, 1974.

Witt, James W. *The Police, the Courts and the Minority Community*. Lexington, Mass.: Lexington Books, 1979.

Wolfgang, Marvin E., and Bernard Cohen. *Crime and Race*. New York: Institute of Human Relations Press, 1970.

Wright, Eric O. *The Politics of Punishment: A Critical Analysis of Prisons in America*. New York: Harper & Row, 1973.

Index

Abadinsky, Howard, 122
Act of March 3, 1871, 5
Adoption studies, 60-61
Affirmative Action, 180-84
Ageton, Suzanne, 73
Aggravated assault, 22, 40, 97, 152
Aichorn, August, 63
Alcoholism, 58, 67
Alcohol-related offenses, 97, 105-6, 108, 113-14, 116-17, 135, 137, 165, 172. *See also* Substance abuse
Aleuts, 3, 111. *See also* Native Americans
American Indians, 3, 10, 50, 92, 112-13. *See also* Native Americans
American Revolution, 4
American Violence and Public Policy (Comer), 88
Amir, Menachem, 87
Anomie, theory of, 65-66, 115, 140-41
Apache, 4
Arrests: by age, 41, 134, 136; Crime Index, 41, 48-49, 54, 83, 134; distribution of, by race/ethnicity, 40-41, 131-36; of juveniles, 131-36; limitations of data, 49-51, 136; for Part II crimes, 46, 48, 134-36; patterns of, 46, 48, 54, 87, 135-36; police discre-
tion and, 149-52; property crime, 41, 54, 135-36; for racial violence, 34; rate of, 40-41, 46, 86, 89, 92, 96, 105-11, 134; ratio of, 46, 108, 110-11; statistics, 49, 152; trends, 48-49; violent crime, 40, 49, 54, 134. *See also* Crime; Delinquency, juvenile
Arson, 40
Asians, 14-17, 34, 39-41, 46, 48-49, 106, 123-28, 131-36, 138-39, 190; arrest rate of, 39, 41, 46, 49, 106, 108, 135; Chinatowns, 15, 124, 139; crime rate of, 75, 116, 123-24, 126, 190; and delinquency, 131-33, 135-36, 138-39, 144; and discrimination, 15, 17, 153; exploitation of, 14, 16; gangs, 124-27, 138-39; incarcerated, 111, 163-65, 172-73; and organized crime, 119-20, 123-25; persecution of, 14-17; rate of incarceration, 112, 165; victimization of, 14-17, 23, 25, 33-35, 190. *See also specific national-ity*; Juveniles; Organized crime; Victimization
Assault, 22, 27, 40, 73, 97, 108, 142, 152
Assimilation, 5-6, 13, 17, 114, 190
Atavistic theories, 58
Auletta, Ken, 182

Badey, James, 126
"Bad seed" theory, 59-60
*Bakke v. Regents of the University of
California,* 184
Baldus, David, 159
Banzuiin, Chobei, 125
Beasley, Ulysses, 84
Becker, Howard, 70
Bell, D. A., 157
Biological theories, 58-62, 64-65, 76;
    ineffectiveness of, 62, 76
Black, Donald J., 152
Black experience in American theory,
    88-89
Black fratricide, 85
Black Guerrilla Family, 121
Black Mafia (Ianni), 121
Black Muslims, 166
Blacks, 7-10, 14, 25, 30, 32-33, 39-54,
    57, 64, 74-76, 83-92, 119-23, 128,
    131, 134, 136-38, 144, 149, 151, 157-
    58, 166-72, 188-89; arrests of, 39,
    40-41, 46, 48-49, 54, 83, 86, 89, 92,
    96, 105-6, 131, 134, 149; and civil
    rights, 8, 10, 33, 166, 180; convic-
    tion rate of, 83, 86, 92, 149, 157;
    and crime, 9, 22, 51, 75, 83-92, 122;
    and crime theories, 57, 64, 74, 76,
    88-92; criminal justice system and,
    84, 87, 89; and delinquency, 131-
    34, 136-38, 144; discrimination
    against, 8, 86, 151-54, 156-59, 165-
    66; and emancipation, 8; gangs,
    121, 134, 138, 167-68; incarceration
    rate of, 112, 163; inmates, 88, 157,
    166, 170; and intraracial crime, 83-
    85, 89; and Jim Crow, 8; juvenile,
    86-87, 134, 172; men, 31, 33, 85, 87,
    158; as offenders, 39, 51, 57, 83,
    100, 134, 157; and organized crime,
    119-23, 128; prisoners, 86-88, 97,
    163, 166-67, 169; and racial vio-
    lence, 8-9, 84; segregation and, 8-9;
    and self-destructive behavior, 85-
    86, 92; and slavery, 7-8, 10, 88, 92;
    victimization of, 7-10, 22-23, 25, 27,
    30, 33-35, 51-54, 83-84, 85, 92, 158;
    and violent crime, 40-41, 49, 74, 83-
84, 92, 108. *See also* Crime; Crimi-
    nals; Discrimination; Minorities;
    Prejudice; Prisoners; Racial dis-
    crimination
Block, Richard, 100
Body-type theories, 59, 91
Bonger, Willem, 73
"Born criminal," 58
Bowers, W. J., 157
Brain disorder research, 61
Bresler, Fenton, 124
Bribery, 127
Broken homes, 69, 74-75, 100, 182;
    theories, 74-75
Brown v. Board of Education, 8
Bureau of Criminal Statistics, 156-57
Bureau of Indian Affairs, 5
Bureau of Justice Statistics, 22, 27, 99
Bureau of the Census, 3, 22, 95, 99,
    106
Burglary, 22, 25, 27, 30, 40, 97, 100
Burns, Hayward, 169

Canadian Indians, 112-13. *See also*
    Native Americans
Capital punishment, 157-59, 169-70,
    172. *See also* Courts; Discrimination
Carroll, Leo, 168
Carter administration, 98
Causes of Delinquency (Hirschi), 68
Census of Population, U.S., 46, 106
Chambliss, William, 90, 137
Cherokees, 4
Cheyenne, 4-5
Chicanos, 10, 88, 95, 167. *See also*
    Hispanics; Mexican-Americans
Chicasaws, 4
Children, 9, 61, 74, 123. *See also*
    Crime, theories of; Juveniles
Chinatowns, 15, 124, 139
Chinese, 14-19, 34, 39, 92, 123-26,
    139. *See also* Asians
Chinese Exclusion Act of 1882, 14, 16
Chinese Mafia, The (Bresler), 124
Chinese Tongs, 123-25, 139. *See also*
    Delinquency, juvenile; Organized
    crime

Chinese Triad Societies, 123-26. *See also* Minorities; Organized crime

Ch'ing Dynasty, 124

Choctaws, 4

Civil justice system, 124

Civil rights, 8, 10, 33, 166, 180-81, 185

Civil Rights Act of 1964, 8, 180

Cloninger, C. Robert, 61

Cloward, Richard A., 67, 141-43

Cohen, Albert K., 67, 73, 140-43

Cohen, Warren H., 114

Colonialism, 17, 99

Colombians, 101-2, 122

Columbus, 7

Comer, James P., 88-89

Commercialized vice, 40, 46

Commission on Civil Rights, U.S., 153, 180

Commission on Organized Crime, President's, 122, 124, 126-28

Conflict theories, 89-90

Conformity, 66

Control theory, 68-69

Cooley, Charles H., 70

Correctional facilities, 86-87, 97, 111-13, 172. *See also* Prisons

Correctional officers, 165, 183. *See also* Criminal justice system, employment of minorities in

Corruption, 124

Counterfeiting, 22, 127

Courts, 114, 131, 151-52, 155-59, 166, 170, 179, 181, 184, 189; civil, 179; criminal, 156, 179; discrimination in the, 151-52, 155-59; juvenile, 131, 151; state, 114; Supreme Court, 154, 156, 158-59, 166, 170, 184; tribal, 114. *See also* Criminal justice system; Law enforcement; Laws

Creeks, 4

Cressey, Donald R., 106, 120

Crime, 3, 9, 13, 15, 39-54, 74, 100-102, 119, 127, 169, 179, 182; and age, 41, 62, 134; arrests for, 34, 39-49, 96-97, 106-11, 131-36; delinquency, 59, 61, 63-64, 68-69, 126, 131-44; extent of, 39-46, 131-36;

gender differences in, 62, 163, 170-71; hidden, 21-22; household, 22, 25-27, 30, 84; international, 124; juvenile, 131, 135-36; laws, 34; minorities and, 3, 39-54, 75-76, 119-28, 131-44; nature of, 39; offenders, 40, 51, 53-54, 100; patterns of, 46, 48, 68, 135-36; personal, 22, 31, 100; property, 22, 40-41, 74, 108, 135, 142, 157; racial differences in, 88-92, 158; rates, 22, 27, 39, 41, 46, 48, 50, 62, 65-67, 72-73, 87-88, 90-92, 116, 122, 149, 165; statistics, 40-51, 72-73, 131-36; street, 62, 71-72; theories, 57-76, 88-92, 99, 113-17, 140-44; trends, 27, 30, 35, 48-49; underreported, 33, 50; unreported, 22, 33, 84, 100; urban, 183; victimization, 3-17, 21-35, 83-86, 96, 99-100; victimless, 133; violent, 4, 9, 14-15, 21-22, 33, 41, 51, 60-62, 74-75, 83-84, 92, 100, 108, 134; white-collar, 50, 91, 186. *See also* Arrests; Asians; Blacks; Native Americans; Organized crime

Crime, organized. *See* Organized crime

Crime and Human Nature (Wilson and Herrnstein), 90

Crime and the Man (Hooton), 59

Crime Index, 39-41, 46, 48-50, 54, 83, 97, 108, 134

Crime in the United States: Uniform Crime Reports, 39. *See also* Uniform Crime Reports (UCR)

Crime Risk Index, 27

Criminal behavior, 13, 58-69, 73, 75, 97, 131, 136, 153, 188

Criminal elements, 124, 126, 139

Criminal justice, 95, 101-2, 123, 126, 134, 152

Criminal justice system, 71, 73, 84, 87, 89, 99, 102, 113, 124, 138-39, 144, 149, 155, 159, 173, 179, 181-87; discriminatory treatment within, 99, 103, 113, 149, 159, 179, 185, 188; employment of minorities in, 181, 183-85

Criminal law, 90, 114-15, 136. *See also*
  Laws
Criminals, 49, 59, 61, 64-65, 67, 69,
  71, 92, 122, 141. *See also* Crime; Of-
  fenders; Prisoners
*Criminal Victimization in the United
  States*, 22. *See also* National Crime
  Survey (NCS)
Criminal Violence, Criminal Justice (Sil-
  berman), 87
Critical theory, 71-72
Crutchfield, R. D., 75
Cuban refugees, 13, 97-98. *See also*
  Cubans
Cubans, 10, 12-13, 95-98, 102, 122.
  See also Hispanics
Cultural conflict theories, 114-15
Culture, Conflict and Crime (Sellin),
  114
Current Population Survey, 10

Davidson, Theodore, 96
Davis, Alan J., 168
Dawes Act of 1887, 5
Death penalty, 157-59, 172-73
Death row, 157-59
Delinquency, 39, 59, 64, 69, 73-74,
  131-44; gangs, 126, 131, 134, 138-
  44; juvenile, 59, 61, 68, 126, 131-44;
  latent, 63; measurement of, 131-37;
  race and class variations in, 64,
  131-41; and self-report data, 131,
  136-37; statistics, 131-35, 144; theories of, 59, 61, 63-64, 68-69, 74, 140-
  44. *See also* Crime; Gangs; Juveniles; Violent crimes
*Delinquency and Opportunity: A Theory
  of Delinquent Gangs* (Cloward and
  Ohlin), 141
*Delinquent Boys: The Culture of the
  Gang* (Cohen), 140
Department of Justice, U.S., 22, 34,
  86, 99, 180
Differential association theory, 67-68,
  141
Differential enforcement of the law,
  48, 73, 149-59. *See also* Courts;
  Criminal justice system; Discrimination; Police; Racism

Differential opportunity theory, 141-
  43
Discrimination, 7-10, 12, 14, 17, 72,
  75-76, 86-87, 89, 92, 113-14, 136,
  149-59, 163, 165-66, 179, 183-85. *See
  also* Criminal justice system; Law
  enforcement; Minorities; Racial dis-
  crimination; Victimization
Disorderly conduct, 108, 136
Disorganized Crime (Reuter), 121
Dozier, Edward P., 116
Driving under the influence, 46, 106
Dropping out, 66
Drugs, 116, 121-22, 124, 134; abuse,
  46, 97, 108, 170; smuggling, 124-25,
  127; trafficking, 122-24, 138. *See also*
  Alcohol-related offenses; Orga-
  nized crime; Substance abuse
Drunkenness, 46, 106
Dubro, Alec, 125
Durk, David, 121
Durkheim, Emile, 65-67

Economic deprivation, 73-74
Economic determinism, 115-16
Economic theories, 74, 90-91
Ego, 63
Eighth Amendment, 158
Eisenhower, Dwight, 6
Eisenhower administration, 6
Elliot, Delbert, 73
Embezzlement, 40, 48
English Convict, The (Goring), 58
Equal Employment Opportunities
  Commission, 184
Eskimos, 3. *See also* Native Americans
Ethnicity, 27, 32, 50-51, 62, 136-37,
  151, 170, 188. *See also* Race
Ethnic minorities, 3, 15, 32, 75-76, 95-
  96, 108, 137-38, 165-66, 172, 181,
  185; and crime, 39-54, 95-103; and
  delinquency, 131-44. *See also* His-
  panics; Minorities; Racial minorities
Exploitation, 4, 10-12, 14, 71-72, 102,
  123. *See also* Victimization
Extortion, 120, 123-27, 138-39

Fair Housing Act of 1968, 180
Faison, Adrienne, 153

Family, breakdown in structure of, 74
Fanon, Frantz, 89
Franworth, M., 157
Federal Bureau of Alcohol, Tobacco, and Firearms, 120
Federal Bureau of Investigation (FBI), 21, 39, 50, 96, 120, 128
Federal Detention Center (Oakdale, Louisiana), 97
Females, 85, 98, 111, 171-72; black, 85-86, 152, 172; Hispanic, 100, 172; inmates, 171-72; Native American, 111; white, 86, 152, 172
Ferracuti, Franco, 90
Filipinos, 17, 138. *See also* Asians
Firearm Discharge Review Board, 154
Foley, L. A., 157
Forgery and counterfeiting, 50, 172
Fourth Amendment, 154
Fraud, 22, 40, 46, 172
Freud, Sigmund, 62-63
Furman v. Georgia, 158
Fyfe, James J., 153

Gadsden Purchase, 11
Gage, Nicholas, 121
Gambling, 48, 120-22, 124-27, 135
Gangs, 96, 121, 123-27, 131, 134, 138-44, 166-68; Asian, 138-39; black, 134, 138, 167-68; Chinese, 124, 139; conflict, 142; criminal, 124, 142; delinquent, 126-27, 138-39; Filipino, 138; Hispanic, 96, 138, 167; Japanese, 125; Korean, 138; prison, 96, 121, 123, 166-68; retreatist, 142; street, 168; Vietnamese, 126-27, 138; violent, 138-39. *See also* Delinquency, juvenile; Organized crime
Genetic theories, 59-61, 91
Gentleman's Agreement of 1907, 16
Glick, Ruth M., 171
Glueck, Eleanor T., 59, 74
Glueck, Sheldon, 59, 74
Goring, Charles, 58
Gould, Leroy, 137
Gove, W. R., 75

Haskell, Martin R., 66
Hayner, Norman S., 105, 116

Hereditary theories, 59-61, 92
Herrera family, 122. *See also* Organized crime, Hispanics in
Herrnstein, Richard, 64, 90
Hindelang, Michael J., 64, 73, 137
Hirschi, Travis, 64, 68, 73, 137
Hispanics, 10-14, 23-25, 27, 34, 40-41, 46-49, 75, 87-89, 95-103, 115, 119-23, 131-36, 138, 189; arrests of, 39, 40-41, 46, 48, 49, 54, 87, 96, 99, 106, 108, 111, 134, 149; and crime, 95-103, 135; and crime theories, 57, 76, 99; on death row, 157-58; delinquency of, 131-36, 138, 144; and discrimination, 12, 14, 89, 99, 103, 152-53, 165-66; drug abuse violations, 46, 97; exploitation of, 10-13; gangs, 96, 138; Hispanos, 10; illegal aliens, 11-12, 101-2; and immigration, 11-12; incarcerated, 88, 97-99, 112, 163-67, 170-73; Latin machismo, 96-97; and organized crime, 119-23, 128; prisoners, 96-98, 163, 167; and unemployment, 99-100, 102; victimization of, 10-14, 23, 25, 27, 31-35, 53, 96, 99-102; women, 31, 96, 123, 171-72. *See also* specific nationality; Minorities; Victimization
Hispanos, 10
Hollinger, Richard C., 151
Homicide, 85, 87, 158. *See also* Murder
Homosexuality, 168, 170
Hooton, Ernest A., 59
Horan, P., 157
Household crimes, 22, 25-27, 30, 35, 84, 100, 126-27. *See also* Crime
Howard, J. C., 157

Ianni, Francis, 121
Id, 63
Immigration Act of 1956, 16
Immigration and Naturalization Service, 124
Immigration Reform and Control Act of 1986, 12
Imperialism, 17, 99

Incarceration, 9, 83, 86-87, 97-99, 111-
13, 127, 163-74; of Asians, 163-65,
172; of blacks, 9, 83, 86-87, 163-72;
of Canadian Indians, 112-13; of
Hispanics, 97-99, 163-67, 171-72; of
juveniles, 172-73; of minorities,
163-74; of minority women, 171-72;
of Native Americans, 111-12, 163-
66, 172. *See also* Prisoners
Indian Alcoholism Commission, Los
Angeles, 7
Indian Americans (Wax), 116
Indian Intercourse Act of 1832, 116
Indian Removal Act of 1830, 4
Indians, 3-7; Canadian, 112-13, 191.
See also Alcohol-related offenses;
Native Americans; Prisoners
Indian Self-Determination Act of
1975, 6
Inmates, 88, 97, 99, 111-13, 157, 163-
74; American Indian, 113; black,
88, 157, 166, 170; Canadian Indian,
113; on death row, 157-58; female,
171-72; Hispanic, 157, 166-67, 170;
jail, 97, 111, 113, 163, 170-71; juve-
nile, 99, 173; male, 163, 170; minority, 170-71, 173-74; Native Americans, 111-13, 157-58; prison, 112-13,
171; white, 165, 167, 169; women,
171
Innovation, 66-67
Intelligence quotient (IQ) theories,
64, 91
Irish, 119, 121
Irwin, John, 167
Italians, 119, 121-23, 126. *See also* Organized crime

Jacobs, James B., 167
Jails, 86, 97, 111-14, 163, 166, 170-71,
181; discrimination in, 166; females
in, 171; males in, 163, 170; minorities in, 86, 97, 111, 170-71. *See also*
Prisoners; Prisons
Japanese, 14-17, 39, 125-26; in organized crime, 125-26; relocation of,
15-17. *See also* Asians

Japanese Yakuza, 125-26. *See also* Or-
ganized crime
Jenkins, Betty, 153
Jensen, Arthur, 64
Jensen, Gary F., 106
Jessor, Richard, 115
Jews, 119, 121
Jim Crow, 7, 8
Johnson, Robert, 96, 166
Jurors, 155-56. *See also* Courts; Racial
discrimination
Juvenile court, 131, 151. *See also* Delinquency, juvenile; Juveniles
Juveniles, 74, 86-87, 98-99, 131-44,
172-73; Asian, 131, 135-36, 138-39,
173; black, 86-87, 131, 134, 136,
138, 172; and crime, 131, 135-36;
custody facilities, 86-87, 98-99, 111,
172-73; delinquent, 131-44; and
gang delinquency, 138-44; Hispanic, 98-99, 131, 134-36, 138, 172;
inmates, 99, 173; Native American,
131, 134-36, 173; offenders, 137. *See
also* Crime; Delinquency, juvenile

Kaplan, David E., 125
Kidnapping, 127
Koreans, 138. *See also* Asians; Delin-
quency, juvenile
Ku Klux Klan, 34, 181

Labeling theory, 69-71
La Cosa Nostra, 119, 124-25. *See also*
Organized crime
La Familia, 96, 123, *See also* Prison
gangs
La Free, G., 157
Lander, B., 73
Larceny, 22, 25, 27, 100, 172
Larceny-theft, 40-41, 97, 136
Latin Americans, 10. *See also* Hispan-
ics; Organized crime, Hispanics in
Latin machismo, 96-97. *See also* Crim-
inal behavior; Prisoners, Latin
Law enforcement, 22, 34, 50-51, 99,
101, 119, 123, 125, 127-28, 139, 155,
182-83, 185-86, 189; administration,
154; bias in, 90, 150-53; differential,

48, 73, 90, 149-59; discriminate, 89, 101, 136, 151; and organized crime, 119, 123, 125, 127-28

Law Enforcement Assistance Administration, 184

Laws, 12, 34, 74, 114, 136, 153, 180-81; civil rights, 180; criminal, 90, 114-15, 136; federal, 114; juvenile, 136; state, 114; tribal, 114; violations of, 69, 74, 136. *See also* Courts

Lawyers Committee for Civil Rights, 159

Leadership Conference on Civil Rights, 180

Liquor law violations, 40, 46, 106, 135

Loansharking, 120, 124, 127

Loitering, 108

Lombroso, Cesare, 58-59

Looking-glass self, concept of, 70

Lower class, 13, 62, 64, 66-67, 71-74, 89-90, 139-44, 149, 151, 159, 179, 188-89. *See also* Social class

Lower-class culture theory, 143-44

Lupsha, Peter A., 121

Machismo, 96-97

Mafia, 119, 121; black, 121; Mexican, 123

Mail fraud, 127

Males: adoptees, 61; black, 84-86, 97, 157, 165, 170; Hispanic, 97-98, 100; Native American, 111; prisoners, 163, 170; white, 86, 97. *See also* Juveniles; Men

Manslaughter, 113. *See also* Murder

Marielitos, 13, 97. *See also* Cubans; Hispanics

Marshall, Thurgood, 153

Marxist criminology, 71

Mause, Phillip J., 114

McCleskey, Warren, 158-59

Memphis Fire Department v. Stotts, 184

Men: black, 31, 33, 85, 87, 158; Canadian native, 113; white, 9, 85, 87. *See also* Males

Merton, Robert K., 66-67, 140-41

Mexican-Americans, 10-13, 88, 95-96,

100-102, 152. *See also* Chicanos; Hispanics

Mexican mafia, 123

Middle class, 67-68, 73, 139-41, 143, 189. *See also* Social class

Middle passage, 7

Miller, Walter B., 138, 140, 143-44

Milton, Catherine H., 153

Ming Dynasty, 124

Minnis, Mhyra S., 116

Minorities, 3, 10, 15, 17, 21-35, 39-54, 62, 169, 172; arrests of, 39-51, 131-36, 163; and crime, 3, 39-54, 57, 62, 65, 69, 72, 75-76, 119-28, 131-44, 149, 165; and the death penalty, 157-59, 169-70; delinquents, 39, 131-44; discrimination against, 7-10, 12, 14, 17, 72, 75-76, 86-87, 113-14, 149-59, 180-81, 183-85; employment of, criminal justice, 183-85; ethnic, 3, 15, 25, 34, 39, 41, 46, 48, 50-51, 53, 74-76, 95, 99, 108, 131, 137-38, 165-66, 172, 181, 185; historically, 3-17; incarceration of, 163-74; lower class, 90; and organized crime, 119-28; racial, 3, 25, 40, 46, 48, 50, 57, 72, 75-76, 89, 99, 102, 120, 137-38, 152-53, 159, 163, 165-66, 172, 181, 185; theories of crime, 57-76; victimization rate for, 22-23, 25, 27, 30, 33; as victims, 3-17, 21-35, 75-76, 151; violence against, 4, 9, 14-15, 33-35, 75; women, 172. *See also specific race or nationality;* Crime; Criminal justice system; Discrimination; Victimization

Minority Correctional Officer Association (MCOA), 184

Money laundering, 124-25

Motor vehicle theft, 22, 25, 27, 40, 100

Murder, 4, 8, 15, 33, 39, 41, 46, 48, 74, 85, 124, 127, 134, 139, 157-58, 172. *See also* Manslaughter

Muslims, black, 166

Nagasawa, Richard, 137

Narcotics, 120, 124-26. *See also* Drugs

National Association for the Advancement of Colored People (NAACP), 153
National Black Police Association (NBPA), 184
National Council of La Raza, 14
National Crime Survey (NCS), 22-33, 35, 51-54, 84, 99-100; household crime victimization, 22, 25-27, 30, 32, 35, 100; limitations of, 32-33, 35, 53-54; personal crime victimization, 22-25; trends in violent crime victimization, 27, 31
National Opinion Research Center (NORC), 21-22, 100-101
Native Americans, 3-7, 10-11, 14, 22-23, 33, 35, 39-41, 48-49, 57, 92, 105-17, 131, 134-36, 144, 149, 190-91; and alcohol-related offenses, 7, 46, 105-6, 108, 113-14, 116-17, 165; American Indians, 3, 10, 50, 92, 112-13; arrest rate of, 39, 41, 46, 49, 105-11, 113-14, 117, 134, 149; arrests of, 40-41, 48, 54, 106, 108, 113; assimilation of, 5-6, 114; and criminality, 105-17, 165, 190-91; Dawes Act of 1887, 5; on death row, 157-58; and delinquency, 131-35, 144; discrimination against, 152-53; and drunkenness, 46, 106; explanation of crime, 113-17; imprisonment of, 111-12, 163-66, 172-73; incarceration rate of, 105, 112, 163-65; rate of crime, 92, 105, 113, 116, 135; on reservations, 6-7, 105, 114; Seminole War, 4; treaties and, 5; and unemployment, 6, 116; victimization of, 3-7, 23, 25, 33, 35, 53. *See also specific tribe*; Canadian Indians; Discrimination; Minoritiés; Racial discrimination
Navahos, 115
Neas, Ralph, 180
Neto, Virginia V., 171
New York Police Department, 154
Nonnegligent manslaughter, 39, 41, 48, 134. *See also* Murder
Nye, F. Ivan, 74

Offenders, 51, 53-54, 69, 83, 100, 137, 157, 172, 179, 186; black, 51, 83, 157; juvenile, 137; minority, 53; women, 172. *See also* Crime; Criminals
Official statistics, 22, 34, 39-51, 72-73, 106, 131-37, 140, 152, 186, 188; inadequacies of, 49-51; limitations of, 136; prison, 169. *See also Uniform Crime Reports* (UCR)
Ohlin, Lloyd E., 67, 141-43
Organized crime, 119-28, 138; Asians in, 119-21, 123-28, 138; blacks in, 119-23, 128; Chinese in, 123-25, 126, 139; Colombians and, 122; Commission on, 122, 124, 126-28; Cubans in, 122; defining, 119-21; "ethnic succession" in, 121; fighting, 127-28; Hispanics in, 119-23, 128; Irish and, 119, 121; Italians in, 119, 121-23, 126; Japanese in, 125-26; Jews and, 119, 121; Mexicans and, 122-23; Puerto Ricans in, 121-22; Vietnamese and, 126-27; violence and, 121, 123
Organized Crime, President's Commission on, 122, 124, 126-28
Organized Crime Control Act of 1970, 127
Oriental Exclusion Act, 16

Pacific Islanders, 23, 41, 111. *See also* Asians
Parental supervision thesis, 75
Park, George, 167
Parole, 155
Part II offenses, 40-41, 46, 48, 50, 54, 134, 136. *See also* Crime; Crime Index
Patterns in Forcible Rape (Amir), 87
Pearl Harbor, 16, 125
Penitentiaries, 113, 123, 163-74. *See also* Jails; Prisons
Personal crimes, 22, 31, 100. *See also* Crime; Violent crimes
Personality disorder theories, 63-64, 91
Pierce, G. L., 157

Police, 39-40, 100-101, 121, 126, 149-
54, 158, 167, 182-83; and deadly
force, 153-54; discretion, 149-52;
discrimination, 151-52, 154; and
minority employment, 183; New
York, 154; practices, 149-54, 182;
violence, 152-54. *See also* Criminal
justice system; Law enforcement
Pornography, 120
Poussaint, Alvin, 83
Poverty, 14, 73, 75, 86, 116, 155, 182
Prejudice, 7, 17, 34, 86, 151, 156, 159,
165
Principles of Criminology (Sutherland),
67
Principles of Criminology (Sutherland
and Cressey), 106
Prisoners, 58-60, 86, 97-98, 111-13,
163-74; and capital punishment,
157-59, 169-70; and crime theories,
58-60; federal, 86, 98, 111-13, 163,
171-72; female, 86, 98, 111, 163,
165; gangs, 96, 121, 123, 166-68;
jailed, 86, 97-98, 111-14, 163, 166,
170-71; juvenile, 86-87, 98-99, 172-
73; male, 86, 97-98, 111, 163, 165;
minority, 163-74; race relations between, 166-69; and racial discrimination, 163, 165; recidivism rate of,
113, 165; state, 86, 98, 111-12, 163,
171-72; statistics, 111; white, 86, 97,
163, 165, 167, 169, 173; women,
172. *See also specific minority group*;
Crime; Criminal justice system; Delinquency, juvenile
Prison gangs, 96, 121, 123, 166-68.
See also Organized criminals
Prisons, 86, 97-98, 111-14, 121, 123,
163-74, 181, 189; administrators,
166, 168; Canadian, 112-13; gangs
in, 96, 121, 123, 166-68; juvenile,
86-87, 98-99, 111, 172-73; minorities
in, 163-74; rape in, 168; statistics,
169; subculture in, 166-69; wom-
en's, 171-72. *See also* Crime; Criminals; Prisoners
Probation, 155
Prohibition, 122

Property crimes, 22, 40-41, 74, 108,
135, 142, 157. *See also* Crime Index;
Larceny-theft
Prostitution, 33, 46, 120-21, 124, 126-
27, 135, 142
Psychoanalytic theories, 62-63
Psychological theories, 62-65
Psychopaths, 64
Puerto Ricans, 10, 12-13, 95-96, 102,
121-22. *See also* Hispanics

Quinney, Richard, 90

Race, 7, 16, 27, 32, 40, 46, 51, 62, 64,
114, 120, 136-37, 151-53, 156-57,
159, 169-70, 172, 180; bias, 151-53,
156, 158; and jury prejudice, 155-
56; relations, 166-69, 181-82; riots,
9, 84, 153, 168, 172, 181; and sentencing, 156-59. *See also* Discrimination; Ethnic minorities; Minorities;
Racial minorities
Racial discrimination, 8, 87, 113, 151-
53, 157-59, 180, 182. *See also* Discrimination
Racial minorities, 3, 25, 40, 46, 53,
57, 75-76, 89, 96, 152-53, 155, 159,
165-66, 172, 181, 185. *See also* Ethnic minorities
Racism, 8-9, 14, 16, 33-35, 71, 75-76,
92, 149-50, 153, 155-56, 158; and jurors, 155-56; and minority crime,
75-76. *See also* Prejudice; Racial dis-
crimination; Victimization
Racketeer Influenced and Corrupt
Organizations Act (RICO), 127
Racketeers, 19, 121-22. *See also* Orga-
nized crime
Radical criminology, 71-72
Rape, 4, 8, 21-22, 25, 40-41, 46, 51,
74, 87, 152, 157-58, 168-70. *See also*
Violent crimes
Rapists, 157, 170. *See also* Rape
Rasch, C. E., 157
Reaction-formation theory, 140-41
Reagan, Ronald, 124
Reagan administration, 34, 180-81
Reason, Charles E., 106

Rebellion, 66
Reconstruction, 9
Reiss, Albert J., 152, 154
Retreatism, 66-67
Reuter, Peter, 121
Riedel, Marc, 157
Riffenburgh, Arthur, 115-16
Riots, 9, 15, 84, 153, 168, 172, 181
Ritualism, 66
Robbery, 22-23, 27, 40-41, 51, 67, 73,
    124, 126, 139, 142, 152, 172
Robin Hoods, 124-25
Robinson, William, 159
Ruchhoft, Robert, 138-39
Ruling class, 71
Runaways, 135-36

Scarr, Sandra, 64
Schur, Edwin, 70
Seidman, Robert, 90
Self-report surveys, 39, 73, 131, 136-
    37, 157; shortcomings of, 137. See
    also Official statistics; Victimization
    surveys
Sellin, Thorsten, 114
Seminoles, 4. See also Native Ameri-
    cans
Seminole War, 4
Sex crimes, 108, 169. See also Rape
Sexism, 172
Sexual assault, 73. See also Delin-
    quency, juvenile; Sex crimes
Sexual slavery, 125. See also Orga-
    nized crime
Sheldon, William H., 59
Shoplifting, 137
Siberman, Charles, 87-89
Slavery, 7-8, 88, 92. See also Blacks;
    Victimization
Smallwood-Murchison, Catherine,
    85-86
Smuggling, 126
Social class, 61, 64, 67, 72-74, 87, 99,
    137, 151. See also Lower class;
    Middle class; Upper class
Social structure theory, 65-67, 140
Social theories, 90-91
Socioeconomic theories, 72-76, 90-92

Sociological theories, 65-72, 76
Southern Commission on the Study
    of Lynchings, 9
Spalla, Louis, 127
Spaniards, 10. See also Hispanics
Staples, Robert, 89
Stateville Penitentiary, 167
Status offenses, 136-37. See also De-
    linquency, juvenile
Stewart, Omer, 106, 116
Street crime, 62, 71-72, 165. See also
    Crime; Violent crimes
Subculture of violence theory, 90-91
Subjugation, 4, 6, 10, 17, 75, 166. See
    also Victimization
Substance abuse, 33, 48, 67, 97, 108,
    113, 117, 136, 139, 142, 172, 182.
    See also Alcohol-related offenses;
    Drug abuse
Sundance, Robert, 7
Superego, 63
Suspicion, 48
Sutherland, Edwin H., 67-68, 106,
    141
Swain v. Alabama, 156
Symbolic interactionist theory, 70

Termination, 6
Theft, 67
Theories of crime, 57-76, 88-92, 99,
    113-17, 140-44
Thomas, William J., 70
Tittle, Charles, 73
Toch, Hans, 166
Tongs, Chinese, 123-25, 139. See also
    Asians; Gangs, Chinese
Transportation in Aid of Racketeering
    Enterprises Act (Travel Act), 127
Treaty of Guadalupe-Hidalgo, 10
Triads, Chinese, 123-26. See also Or-
    ganized crime
Truancy, 137
Twin studies, 60

Underclass, 182-83
Under Class, The (Auletta), 182
Unemployment, 6, 9, 71, 73-74, 99,
    100, 102, 113, 116, 139

Uniform Crime Reports (UCR), 21, 39-51, 96, 106, 108, 131-36; and delinquency, 131-36; inadequacies of, 49-51; limitations of, 136
"Unorganized" crime, 119
Unwelcome Immigrant, The (Miller), 14
Upper class, 139, 141. *See also* Social class
U.S. General Accounting Office, 171
U.S. Penitentiary (Atlanta), 97
U.S. Supreme Court, 154, 156, 158-59, 166, 170, 184. *See also* Courts

Vagrancy, 108
Vandalism, 34, 73, 136
Vander Zanden, James V., 8
Victimization, 3-17, 21-35, 51-54, 67, 71, 99-102; of Asians, 14-17, 25, 33-35; of blacks, 7-10, 22-23, 25, 31, 35, 53, 83-85, 158; burglary, 30; colonialism, 17, 99; criminal, 13, 21-35; discrimination, 7-10, 14, 17, 72, 87, 92, 113-14, 149-53, 155-59, 165-66, 183-85; exploitation, 4, 10-12, 14, 72, 102; of Hispanics, 10-14, 23, 25, 31, 33, 53, 96, 99-102, 123; household crime, 25, 27, 30; imperialism, 17, 99; minority, 14, 22-23, 25, 27, 30-31, 33-35; multiple offender, 51, 53; personal larceny, 25; prejudice, 7, 17, 34, 86, 151, 156, 165; and race, 22, 31, 35, 51, 158; racism, 8, 14, 33-35, 75-76, 92, 149-50, 155-56, 165-66, 172, 179-81, 183, 185; rape, 8, 25; rates, 22-23, 25, 27, 33, 35, 84, 92, 99-100; robbery, 23; single offender, 51-52; slavery, 7-8, 10, 88, 92; subjugation, 3-4, 6, 8, 10, 17, 75; surveys, 21-33, 35, 39-40, 51-54, 99-100; trends, 27, 30; and violence, 4, 8-9, 14; violent crime, 27, 31, 35, 100; of whites, 22-23; of women, 31, 96. *See also* Discrimination; Minorities; Official statistics; Violent crimes
Victimless crimes, 33
"Victim Risk Supplement," 84

Vietnamese, 34, 126-27, 138; and organized crime, 126-27
Violence, 4, 9, 14, 33-35, 75, 84, 88, 91, 121, 123, 139, 152-54, 167, 181-82; arrests for, 34; toward Asians, 14-15; and blacks, 8-9, 84-86, 88-89, 91-92, 134; crimes of, 41, 51, 84, 100, 134; against Hispanics, 12, 96, 100; of juvenile gangs, 139, 142; toward minorities, 4, 8-9, 12, 14-15; against Native Americans, 4-5; physical, 154; police, 150, 152-54; prison, 167-68; racial, 9, 34, 167, 181; teen, 134; theories of, 90-91. *See also* Crime; Police; Racism; Delinquency; Victimization; Violent crimes
Violent crimes, 4, 9, 14-15, 21-22, 25, 27, 30-31, 33-35, 39-41, 49, 51-52, 72, 75, 83-84, 92, 108, 116, 134; arrests for, 34, 40-41, 49, 54, 108; toward blacks, 22, 25, 31, 84, 134; Crime Index, 39-41, 46, 48-50, 54, 83, 108; toward Hispanics, 23, 25, 31; minorities and, 22-23, 25, 39; by race of offender, 51-52; rate of, 22-23, 41, 46, 84, 108; theories of, 60-62, 72, 74, 90-91; trends in, 27, 31; victimization, 22-23, 27, 33-35, 100. *See also* Assault; Crime; Criminal justice system; Murder; Property crimes; Rape; Robbery; Violence
Voir dire, 155-56. *See also* Courts
Von Hentig, Hans, 105, 114, 116
Voting Rights Act of 1965, 180

Warren-McCarran Act of 1952, 16
Wax, Murray, L., 116
Weapons possession, 108
Weinberg, Richard, 64
Weis, Joseph G., 73, 137
What the Negro Can Do About Crime (Parker and Brownfeld), 84
White-collar crime, 50, 91, 186
White Patriot Party, 34
Whites: arrests of, 40-41, 46, 49, 83, 106, 108, 134; crime rate of, 87-88, 91; delinquency and, 134, 137; in-

Whites (*continued*)
  carceration rate of, 112; institutionalized, 163, 165; as offenders, 3-17,
  33-35, 50, 156-59, 170; as victims,
  22-23, 25, 27, 30, 35, 51, 84, 151,
  158-59, 168, 170; and white-collar
  crime, 50, 91, 186. *See also* Crime;
  Criminal justice system; Discrimination; Prisoners
White slavery, 127
Wickersham Commission, 88
Wilson, James Q., 90
Wire fraud, 127
Witkin, Herman A., 60
Wolfgang, Marvin E., 87, 90, 157, 169
Women, 9, 31, 85, 96, 113, 123, 171-
72, 180; Asian, 172; black, 31, 85,
157, 170-72; Canadian native, 113;
Hispanic, 31, 96, 123, 171-72; incarcerated, 171-72; Native American,
172; white, 9, 85, 157, 170, 172. *See
also* Sexism; Victimization; Violent
crimes
Working classes, 71. *See also* Lower
class; Social class
Wretched of the Earth, The (Fanon), 89

XYY Chromosome, 60

Yablonsky, Lewis, 66
Yakuza (Kaplan and Dubro), 125
Yakuza, Japanese, 125-26

About the Author

RONALD BARRI FLOWERS, criminologist, scholar, professional writer, and research analyst in the study of crime and criminal justice and human and social issues, is the author of *Criminal Jurisdiction Allocation in Indian Country*, *Children and Criminality: The Child as Victim and Perpetrator*, and *Women and Criminality: The Woman as Victim, Offender, and Practitioner* (Greenwood Press, 1986, 1987).